PANOS / SO:

— AT THE —
DESERT'S EDGE

ORAL HISTORIES FROM THE SAHEL

EDITORS: NIGEL CROSS AND RHIANNON BARKER

Published by Panos Publications Ltd
9 White Lion Street
London N1 9PD, UK

British Library Cataloguing in Publication Data
At the Desert's Edge: Oral Histories from the Sahel
I. Cross, Nigel, 1953- II. Barker, Rhiannon
966
ISBN 1-870670-26-4

The Sahel Oral History Project was substantially funded by NORAD. Other funding was provided by the European Commission, HelpAge, International Institute for Environment and Development Drylands Programme, the Linnean Society and Womankind. Funding for publishing *At the Desert's Edge* was provided by NOVIB, HelpAge, Christian Aid, Ernest Kleinwort Charitable Trust, Thomas Sivewright Catto Charitable Settlement and UN Trust Fund for Aging.

Any judgements expressed in this document should not be taken to represent the views of any funding agency. Signed articles do not necessarily reflect the views of Panos or any of its funding agencies.

The Panos Institute is an information and policy studies institute, dedicated to working in partnership with others towards greater public understanding of sustainable development. Panos has offices in Budapest, London, Paris and Washington DC.
For more information about Panos contact:
Juliet Heller, The Panos Institute

Production: Sally O'Leary
Cover design: The Graphic Partnership
Cover illustration: Abdias Thera, Mali
Maps: Philip Davies
Printed in Great Britain by Ebenezer Baylis, Worcester

Contents

Acknowledgements

Many people have assisted in this project. We owe everything to the interviewees who freely gave their time and shared their histories, and to the cooperating agencies, interviewers and coordinators who are separately listed at the beginning of each country section.

Other contributors include:
Translators: Rosie Bartlett, Alan Bradley, Tim Burford, Joy Cherkaoui, Mary Creagh, Daphne Day, Kyar De Conich, Chris Follett, Mandy Garner, Michèle Hagard, Libby Hare, Stephanie Irvine, Anne Marie Knighton, Pierre Labrousse, Deirdre Leask, Nikki Mandou, Tamara Pollard, Anthony Ross Price, Jack Shulman, Ruth Valentine
Photographers: Adrian Adams-Sow, Rhiannon Barker, Nigel Cross, Patrick Darling, Rosalind David, Alex Mavro (Mali), Gill Vogt
Indexers: Mary Coburn, Jo White
Country profiles and glossaries: Justin McKenzie Smith
Sub-editors: Wendy Davies, Patrick Darling

Finally we owe particular thanks to all our colleagues at Panos and at SOS Sahel in Africa and London, who have been an immense support and made the whole venture possible; and especially to SOS Sahel board members Dr Gerald Wickens, who undertook the considerable task of sifting through the botanical and agricultural information, and Olivia Bennett for supervising the complex publication process and editing the final version.

Nigel Cross and Rhiannon Barker

PREFACE

Obo Koné died in 1991. He was one of the most outspoken and entertaining contributors to *At the Desert's Edge*. Born in 1912 in 'An'oro'ui, Mali, he had seen foreigners come and go and come back again to run development projects, most of which were "an absolute mess". He had, by his own account, been well off. He owned over 100 cattle and for most of the first 60 or so years of his life had enough to feed his family, with grain to spare for his less fortunate neighbours.

He lived in the heart of the Sahel where, although the land is hard to farm and the climate is dry, there was just enough rainfall (350 mm a year or more) to grow rainfed crops and graze animals. He coped with earlier droughts and food shortages, but after the drought of 1984, following a decade of poor rains, he was ruined. "Suddenly the rain lost respect for the old cycle....Today the environment is sick, the soils are poor and hard, and the trees are dead....I believe these changes can be attributed to the fact that we have lost respect for our customs. We have violated old prohibitions to allow room for modernisation and in so doing we have disregarded God's laws."

Everywhere in the world the elderly hold trenchant views about decline and fall. But in the Sahel, where climate change, population growth, and political and economic mismanagement have combined to create one of the toughest inhabited environments in the world, Obo Koné is not exaggerating.

In his youth, there was perhaps just one shirt to share among all the men of the village—borrowed for special occasions including deputations to the colonial authority. There were traditional medicines, but no clinics. It took days to walk to the capital, Bamako; now those with money can arrive in hours. But not all change has been for the best. Today, women take 10 hours to gather fuelwood where it previously took 10 minutes; there are few trees and almost no wild animals. Children go to school, but young people leave the village. The wells are running dry.

Over the last two decades, the annual rains have reached less far north than before. Now, a 150-km swathe of previously fertile land is often too dry to farm. As people leave the drier areas and crowd south on to wetter if still marginal land, new patches of degraded land spread like blight, caused by overgrazing and the expansion of agriculture on to poor soils. This in turn adds to the "albedo" effect—the land, stripped of vegetation, reflects heat and can inhibit cloud formation; less rain and less soil moisture lead to more loss of vegetative cover and an increase in desertification.

There are plenty of theories about desertification, none of them indisputable. People and animals combine, in ever increasing numbers, to degrade their own environment. But there are larger forces at work. While the causes of climate change are imperfectly understood, it seems possible that the discharge of CO_2 and other pollutants by the industrialised world has contributed to global warming—and the drying of the Sahel. While Obo Koné and his neighbours may cut down too many trees (out of necessity), or graze too many cattle for their own good, they are not responsible for the incremental pollution of the planet—the violation of "God's laws".

At the Desert's Edge

The Sahel Oral History Project, which this book summarises, was conceived as a way of enabling Obo Koné, and hundreds of others across Sahelian Africa who had lived through the twentieth century, to inform and enlighten development "experts". Few in the rural Sahel are literate. What little of their history that exists in print has been recorded by outsiders: priests, colonial officers, anthropologists, and development planners from the ministries or donor agencies.

In 1988, the UK voluntary agency SOS Sahel reviewed its policy towards the elderly. Environmental projects, designed to increase food production through investment in natural resource management, are long-term. Obo Koné would be dead before he could sit under the shade of a newly planted neem tree, or see his children increase their millet production thanks to agroforestry and soil conservation.

Because many of the elderly are frail, they are rarely able to share in the physical activities that underpin conservation and development projects. They are considered marginal to the future; they do not, and apparently cannot, contribute to sustainable development. After systematically interviewing 500 older Sahelians, we can assert with confidence that to be old, in the Sahel, is an achievement, and an achievement well worth recording.

Only the elderly can cast sufficient light to answer the most difficult questions: what was the way of life; what was the land like; how and why has it come to its present pitiful state? And how and why do Sahelian farmers and nomads keep going, in the face of such odds?

Nigel Cross
Rhiannon Barker

THE SAHEL
ORAL HISTORY PROJECT

Oral history is both a methodology and an academic discipline. It has not yet been widely used in a development context. One aim of the Sahel Oral History Project was to explore how the application of oral history techniques can assist the development process. By talking at length with farmers, pastoralists, refugees and other groups, we hoped to gain a better understanding of traditional land-use practice, land tenure, farming and pastoral systems, the causes of desertification, and many other aspects of Sahelian life. Our aim was not only to record indigenous knowledge and improve rapport with those with whom SOS Sahel and its partner agencies work, but also to develop a practical methodology which could then be incorporated into development planning, project implementation and evaluation.

We do not claim that *At the Desert's Edge* and its supplementary material will become a seminal text for historians of Africa. In most of the places where we worked, there was no written record to support or contradict the oral testimony. In some instances it was possible to record the first tentative outlines of village histories, but this, though fascinating, was peripheral. The principal aim was to record the perceptions of Sahelian men and women—which are neither right nor wrong—about their changing environment and way of life. All history is informed by someone's testimony—his or her story. We did not set out to accumulate facts, but rather to find the stories, to improve the techniques for their collection and, most important of all, to demonstrate their value and utility.

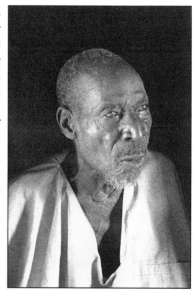

The pace of change
Social change in the Sahel has been rapid. Many children now have access to formal education. While this may increase their own economic prospects, it also leads to a loss of cultural continuity. Traditional knowledge is considered "out-of-date" by young villagers as well as outsiders. Recording traditional

"In some ways we have remained passive in the face of all the change that has gone on around us—we have felt out of our depth," was Obo Koné's comment on the rapidity of change in the Sahel.

knowledge both rescues it from oblivion and demonstrates its value to a younger generation. Environmental and economic pressures in the Sahel have combined to create a period of unprecedented social dislocation. Academic analysis of economic, social and physical change, while it may be objective, lacks the authenticity of first-hand testimony and fails to capture the important subjective aspects of these upheavals.

Not the least of our concerns has been to offer alternatives to the received image of Sahelians as passive, grateful beneficiaries who have been helped to fish or farm (the aid agency cover photo), by giving some 500 men and women—classic development "targets"—the chance to talk back and to broadcast their experiences, priorities and perspectives.

We have not edited out the tragedies or the disasters as these are graphically described by those who have lived through them, but the same witnesses demonstrate their ingenuity and tenacity, and reflect on the "good life". The interviews reveal the complexity of everyday Sahelian life: people's relationship to and care of the environment; the position of men and women on the land and in the household; and changes in family relationships and social customs. As the interviews make clear, these individuals are neither emaciated victims nor happy peasants. They are themselves.

THE PROCESS

The preliminary research, identification of sites, liaison with   other agencies and development of a questionnaire were carried out between January and May 1989. The interviewing began that June and continued until October 1990. Over 500 interviews were completed, of which just under half were with women. A small proportion were group interviews, bringing the total number of respondents to more than 650. The project worked in eight countries—Senegal, Mauritania, Mali, Burkina Faso, Niger, Chad, Sudan and Ethiopia—at 19 sites, in 17 languages.

From the outset, interview sites were linked to ongoing development projects. This strategy provided participating agencies with new, village-authored extension and evaluation materials and the Sahel Oral History Project with a ready-made base. Although it is never easy for development agencies to provide such support, there was a high level of cooperation. As a control, interviews were also conducted in non-project areas. In general, project sites were easier to work in—the relationship that had already been established between the project and the people proved an enormous asset.

A major consideration in the selection of interview sites was that they should cover a range of tribal, economic and social groups. These were divided into five main categories:

- refugees (political and economic): Eritreans and Tigreans in Sudan, ex-pastoralists in Nouakchott, Mauritania
- pastoralists and agro-pastoralists in Mali, Niger, Chad and Ethiopia
- farmers in rainfed areas in Mali, Burkina Faso, Niger, Sudan and Ethiopia
- farmers in irrigated riverine areas in Senegal and Sudan
- fishermen in Mauritania and Chad

We chose interviewers from extension workers, research students and local journalists; inevitably a mixture of luck, judgment and availability circumscribed our choice. The most successful interviewers were good communicators who had a natural curiosity and interest in the respondents. In terms of grasping the complexity of some of the questions and to ensure effective transcription and translation, a relatively high level of education and literacy was essential. Given the nature of the fieldwork—with the inevitable frustrations created by limited transport, inaccessibility of interviewees and difficult living conditions—the energy and enthusiasm of the interviewer was as important as previous interviewing experience. Undoubtedly the most successful interviewers were those who had a thorough knowledge of the area and, in most cases, had been born and brought up within it. They could, in the fullest sense of the phrase, "speak the same language".

Finding the right questions
The first task of the project was to prepare a guide for interviewers outlining a standard methodology, together with a draft questionnaire. Initial research for the guidelines involved consultation with development agencies and academics. An interview outline was tested in Sudan. Further consultation, and feedback from interviewers, led to a number of changes. In addition, discussions were held with development workers on each interviewing site prior to the work, in order to establish their own priorities.

To draw up a questionnaire which can be used effectively in many different countries, even though they share common problems and conditions, is a near impossible task. Questions which would strike a European as being neutral and rather mundane, such as "How many children do you have?", may prove offensive. To divulge such facts to a stranger may tempt fate—an open invitation to God to take a child away.

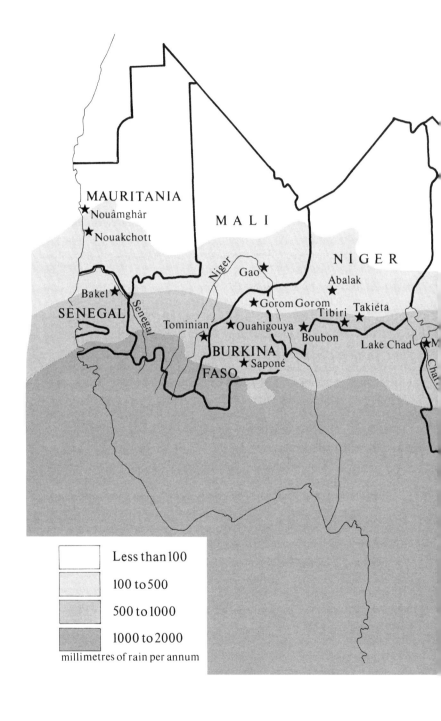

MAURITANIA
★Nouâmghâr
★Nouakchott

MALI

NIGER

Gao★
Abalak
★

Bakel★
SENEGAL
★GoromGorom
Takiéta
★
Tominian
★Ouahigouya
Tibiri
★
Boubon
Lake Chad

BURKINA
FASO
★Saponé

Less than 100

100 to 500

500 to 1000

1000 to 2000

millimetres of rain per annum

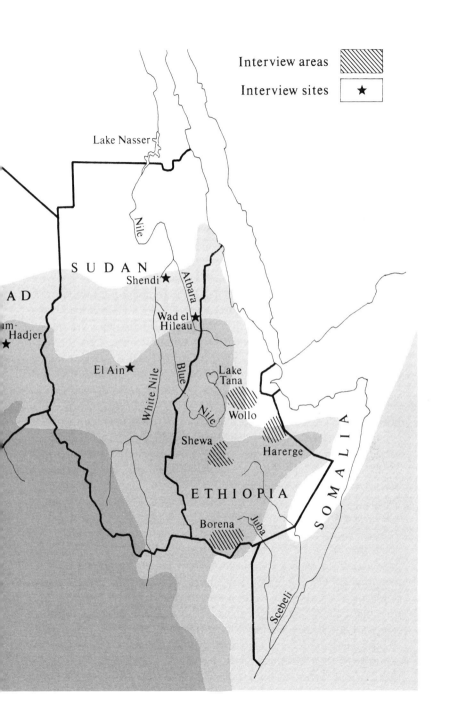

Interview areas

Interview sites ★

Lake Nasser

Nile

SUDAN

Shendi ★

Atbara

Wad el
Hileau ★

ım-
Hadjer ★

A D

El Ain ★

White Nile

Blue

Nile

Lake
Tana

Wollo

Shewa

Harerge

ETHIOPIA

SOMALIA

Borena

Juba

Scebeli

A cultural bias in the interview outline was inevitable—we saw the project as having a development education role and so were seeking to inform a Northern public as well as an "expert" audience. We found ourselves seeking answers to questions which members of the community concerned might never have thought to ask. To balance our concerns, interviewers were given scope to exclude anything they felt unsuitable, and encouraged to include questions of their own design. Similarly, questions were added or subtracted depending on the specific country or site and according to the prevailing political, social and environmental conditions.

Working with women

Most of the Sahelian countries in which we were working have strong cultural and religious influences which tend to restrict the movement of women and inhibit easy communication between the sexes. To avoid marginalising women, one male and one female interviewer were sought for each site. But employing women proved much more difficult than men, largely because of cultural constraints restricting their freedom to travel. Women interviewers had less work experience than men and generally needed more training and confidence building.

Despite the extra work involved, the policy of employing women proved critical to the success of the project. On a number of occasions, as an experiment, men were asked to interview women and women to interview men. Their comments on this experience were enlightening. Women generally found the interviews ran smoothly. The men, on the other hand, appeared at a loss to know what to ask women and their questions quickly dried up. Some said that they found talking to women boring and unenlightening, but it is also possible that male respondents found women interviewers less intimidating than the other way round.

As interviewees, women again required a higher investment of both time and energy. In the first place, they were harder to involve since their domestic chores could rarely be postponed—there was always grain to grind, wood to collect or a meal to prepare, and they preferred to be interviewed while continuing their chores. Men were more inclined to lay down the task at hand, benefiting from a male culture which sets aside time and space for communal debate. They generally talked with greater ease for long periods of time without faltering, whereas women usually needed much more encouragement. Women also tended to reflect less critically on their life situation, attributing their hardships to fate rather than external factors, making it more difficult for the interviewer to follow up further lines of questioning.

Problems sometimes arose from men wanting to take over or disrupt interviews with women. Men would decide that they should act as mediators between their wives (or other female relatives) and the interviewer. In some cases it appeared that the woman was reassured by male encouragement; at other times the consequences were disastrous, with the woman feeling unable to talk about certain issues and the man asserting that he knew the woman's mind better than she. It was also noticeable that men often laughed at the questions to women and the women's responses, whereas they took their own contributions much more seriously.

Training

The time allocated to interviewing in each country was about one month. In this period interviewers were recruited by the project coordinator and the actual interview process was completed on two to three different sites. Within this tight schedule, a short three-day training programme was devised which proved an invaluable component of the work.

The first day of training was spent on a thorough review of the questionnaire outline and guidelines, together with some role play where the new interviewer would test interviewing methods and also play the part of respondent. On the second day the coordinator carried out the first one or two interviews, using the interviewer as an interpreter. The flexibility of the interview structure was stressed, with the coordinator demonstrating the value of follow-up questions. On the third day a sample interview was conducted, transcribed and analysed.

Selection

On each site we sought to interview roughly equal numbers of men and women. Initially, interviews were exclusively with the elderly, but as the project progressed it became clear that it would be useful to include younger people in each sample to allow comparisons between the differing perceptions of two generations.

Before interviewing began, those helping to facilitate the work were asked to identify the different economic, social and ethnic groups in the community, to ensure the interviewers covered as wide a spectrum as possible and were not simply choosing to talk to close friends, neighbours or relatives. While the majority of the interviewees were farmers or pastoralists, we also sought specialist occupations such as midwife, hunter, traditional healer, blacksmith and village chief. In most instances people were contacted through the village chief or head of the women's committee. Although this was often time-consuming, once the interviews were endorsed by respected members of the community, the respondents had greater confidence and were more willing to cooperate. We always took care to stress that there was no material advantage to be gained by participating in the interviews, beyond the intrinsic value of sharing knowledge and experience.

Our method of selection was not statistically random since our sample, averaging perhaps 12 men and 12 women in each community, was too small and the logistics too difficult. Some people were selected by the chief, others by village groups, and some were self-selected. On occasion, people were too busy to talk or were simply suspicious of the questions and unwilling to participate.

In refugee camps, and other situations where a well-established social structure was absent, selection methods were more haphazard. Where a community leader could be identified, the channel of communication was relatively easy. More often the camps, lacking ethnic and social homogeneity, had no elected representatives, obliging us to wander from house to house making our own introductions. Interviewees, however, seemed prepared to accept this rather intrusive approach.

The interviews

The majority of interviews were conducted with individuals, although there were also a small number of group interviews of up to 15 people. While our main interest was specialised material on the environment and work practices linked to personal histories and anecdotes from individuals, group interviews were useful as they provided a consensus account. Individuals in a group situation are often animated by the discussion to follow through certain lines of inquiry in greater detail. Also, in many Sahelian societies the group is the familiar and preferred forum for discussion, especially with strangers.

Most interviews were conducted in private homes or in the shade of a lone but convenient tree. In some instances the village chief would call people to the village square or to his house. We encountered several problems in interviewing in the open: the heat of the sun rapidly wilts the interviewer and respondent; strong winds interfere with the microphone, affecting the quality of the recording; and droves of curious, often disruptive, onlookers are attracted to the site. Wherever possible we sought shelter and quiet.

Interviews lasted between 40 minutes and two hours, although initial introductions, rapport-building, tea ceremonies and other hospitalities often extended the time. Two hours is about the maximum sensible period for such intense dialogue. The interviewer has to be constantly alert, planning the next question, encouraging the respondent to talk and looking for interesting areas of knowledge and experience to examine in detail. Since the "fatigue factor" is high, no more than three thorough interviews were conducted in one day, with an obligatory break after five days of interviewing.

All interviews were recorded on cassette and interviewers were encouraged to take notes to supplement the recordings. A number of people found the note-taking difficult, complaining that it slowed down the dialogue, distracted them from the questions and meant that they lost valuable eye contact with the respondent. Despite this, we stressed the value of brief notes as a useful means of cross-checking, providing back-up for a bad or faulty recording, and for recording non-verbal expressions and descriptions.

Translation

Following the interviews, the interviewer translated and transcribed the tapes into French or English. Transcription is a tedious and time-consuming process and fraught with problems, to which there are no easy answers. An extension worker from Mali poignantly described the type of problem she faced translating the interviews from Bobo into French. Bobo, she explained, is rich with subtly worded proverbs which cannot easily be translated. She cited the following example: "If you want to stop the mouse, you must first get rid of the smell from the soumbala spice."

Apparently the proverb refers to the value of a good upbringing. In the past children were brought up to be polite and obedient and therefore could be relied upon to behave well. Today children fail to receive proper instruction from their parents, and for this reason cannot be blamed for behaving badly, just as the mouse is not to blame for taking the soumbala spice when it smells so enticing. Given the complexity of the proverb, the extension worker finally opted for a gloss which omitted the proverb itself. Indeed, so much of Sahelian expression is laced with proverbs which are often exclusive to a particular group that only members of the group can fully understand the meanings and implications. The outsider is left bemused—for example: "Les termites sont loin de la lune."

THE RESPONSE

An analysis of the material collected reveals that the project did not recover as much indigenous knowledge, in its specifics, as originally intended. For instance, recipes for medicines, meals and organic fertilisers, and accurate descriptions of plant uses, changing vegetation, animal numbers and herd composition, are often mentioned only in vague terms. The fact that many rural populations have been made to feel that their traditional techniques for agriculture, veterinary and medical care, are in some way "backward" and unscientific was undoubtedly a constraint. They are aware that the educated élites, who come on sporadic visits, tend to promote the adoption of new technologies and encourage a more scientific approach to development and conservation. For this reason many are reluctant to divulge methods of animal treatment, land conservation practices, or herbal remedies, which may label them as ignorant or out of touch with the "modern" world.

Our questions about traditional veterinary practices in a camp for sedentarised pastoralists in eastern Chad met with blank faces, shoulder shrugs, and a denial of the existence of any such systems. It was only after the interviewers began to talk in positive terms about techniques they were acquainted with from other areas that the respondents were persuaded to share their own extensive knowledge.

No time for numbers
Then there is the problem of trying to search for common ground across the different modes of cultural expression. The desire for quantification and specificity that preoccupies research in the North is not an easy notion to convey to a Sahelian farmer. Efforts to find out the number of cattle in his herd will more often than not provoke raised eyebrows, derisive laughter and evasive responses. "God is generous, I have enough animals to fertilise my fields!" ... "We have to make do with whatever God gives us." The question is comparable to asking a European or North American for their bank balance or an inventory of their assets. Similarly, the question "How many hours does it take you to grind your corn?" may be answered, "I begin when I return from collecting the water and finish when my husband returns from the field."

Responses which involve reference to figures, dates, weights and times are often spoken in French or English. Because such numerical accuracy is not perceived as relevant, it is not usually contained in the local language. For this reason the accuracy of ages, dates of specific droughts and famines is questionable. Indeed, throughout the interviews phrases such as "in the past" are always preferred to something more precise such as "in 1919" or "in 1940".

It is difficult to know how such constraints on the collection of indigenous knowledge can be effectively overcome. It may be that the problem lies not so much in the method of collection as in the setting of inappropriate targets. Is there simply too romantic a notion of indigenous knowledge? Such knowledge, after all, is not static but evolves to suit a changing environment. It must be open to the acceptance of new equipment and technologies. Farmers and pastoralists will adapt to whatever method serves them best, be it traditional or modern, old or new; archaic practices are usually retained not from nostalgia but because they still serve some purpose. But, as the interviews make clear, some traditions are retained through inertia or prejudice. There are reactionaries in every culture, but in the Sahel today such conservatism can lead to a cruel lack of development—particularly for women, as evidenced by the widespread resistance to education for girls.

One obvious drawback in employing non-specialist local interviewers is their lack of academic training in the detailed environmental or agricultural field. They could run through the checklist of questions but did not have the specialist knowledge to follow up on detailed points of concern and interest. On one site, in Kordofan, western Sudan, we tried a different approach. The coordinator, herself an agriculturalist working in the region, was briefed by an authority on Sudanese ecology who had worked in the area 30 years earlier, producing the first published botanical and environmental surveys. The questions were more informed, and the ability to cross-check details of change against the written and remembered record led to the interviews being much more specific than at other sites.

However, although a tight interview conducted by a specialist can get closer to accurately recording traditional knowledge, it also moves further away from the respondent's priorities and views. These may sometimes be incoherent or even factually wrong, but they have an integrity of their own. There is, then, a tension between the interview that seeks to focus on indigenous knowledge, and the interviewer who solicits opinion and impressions. For the former the "facts" are primary and the respondent is secondary—a cipher; for the latter it is the other way round.

Perceptions of change

Despite these reservations, the interviews as a whole, although "unscientific", describe a wide range of environmental knowledge and traditional farming and pastoral systems. Farmers talk about tried and tested methods of improving soil fertility; pastoralists explain how they control animal reproduction, the pastures preferred by each of their animals and the ideal ratio of males to females. Healing methods and herbal remedies are mentioned in varying degrees of detail. There is a great deal of repetition (some of which has been edited out of this book) which we have taken as evidence of a consensus about environmental and

Alkhayna Walet Ibrahim, a pastoralist in Mali, commented on changes experienced by nomadic women like herself: "Our work has changed. Before women only looked after children and did housework, but now we gather produce that we can sell, trade in tea, and make cushions out of wool and leather to bring in some money."

social change. Some of these "findings" are new, some confirm hunches and others restate the obvious.

Change is everywhere recorded—no one can be left in any doubt that Sahelians have a thorough understanding of their own predicament, and of the causes of desertification. Whereas 30 years ago farmers were able to grow sufficient crops for subsistence plus a surplus for sale, they are now often cultivating from three to five times as much land in the uncertain hope of a yield that will provide enough for their subsistence. Many of the men are seeking employment in the towns so that their families, left behind in the villages, have enough to eat.

Plant breeders have succeeded in developing new varieties of sorghum and millet requiring a shorter growing season, which are able to take better advantage of the meagre rainfall when it occurs. But the extension services are still woefully inadequate and the costs of introducing new technologies often prohibitive.

Those who had led a nomadic life and lost their livestock through lack of pasture have been forced to settle and attempt to make ends meet by cultivation or by seeking employment in the towns. Many long to return to their nomadic way of life and attempt to rebuild their stocks, preferring sheep and goats (especially the latter), since they reproduce more rapidly and are better able to survive on the scanty pasture than cattle and camels.

The shift from pure pastoralism to agro-pastoralism and herding for wages (from absentee owners) is visible across the Sahel. When—and if—more "normal" rainfall returns, the pasture will be slow to recover, passing through various stages of rehabilitation before approaching the levels of former years. A prerequisite for any recovery, which is well understood, is for livestock numbers to be kept well below the actual carrying capacity of the existing pasture.

There is clear agreement among those interviewed about the main reason for environmental degradation: inadequate and sporadic rainfall. Man-made factors are also cited: pressure on land due to rising population and the fact that more and more pastoralists, whose herds have been decimated by the droughts, are turning from pastoralism to farming. Bush land is being cleared with increasing rapidity to make land available for cultivation. The increased pressure on land and natural resources has disrupted what was a "previously amicable relationship between farmers and pastoralists": conflicts between the two are frequently reported.

Although the majority of the interviewees felt that degradation was attributable to climatic change, many were confident that steps can be, and are being, taken to counter the damage. Trees are being planted; the fertility of the soil has been improved by adaptations to traditional farming methods, such as compost holes and bunds to reduce soil erosion and improve infiltration of water.

Patterns of life
It was also our aim to record social and cultural change. In this, the Sahel Oral History Project exceeded its expectations and has established a fuller

picture of community history and social evolution than originally anticipated. It has revealed the extent of the breakdown of traditional relationships between groups: adults and children, sedentary farmers, pastoralists and agro-pastoralists, men and women.

Much of the information contradicts received development wisdom and provides ample evidence that many standard generalisations simply do not stand up, or are so general as to be seriously misleading. For instance, the interviews highlight the dangers of generalising about women's position in rural communities. According to Fatchima Beine, president of the women's committee of Abalak village, Niger: "Before, when natural resources were abundant, women did not have to work so hard. Now, however, women do the same work as the men and during the day they work in the field." But in Tibiri, another village in the same district, local farmer Sayanna Hatta commented: "New technologies have helped to lighten a woman's load, she no longer has to spend several hours a day grinding grain due to the presence of diesel-powered mills; there are wells and pumps from which she can collect water. The men plough the fields and if the family don't have enough food then it is the men who have to go in search of supplements."

As always, there are marked differences in circumstances within villages and between communities that are lost in generalisations. "Years ago all the wood we needed was near. It used to take us only five minutes to collect. Now it's a 10-hour trip, so those who can afford it buy it from the men who sell it in the market." (Rékia, woman farmer, Takiéta, Niger.) As far as fuelwood collection is concerned, the gap between women with some money and women without has widened.

In the Nile province of Sudan, married women whose husbands have remained in the area as farmers welcome their improved quality of life: "Now we don't have to pound the dura, or pull water from the deep well; also our participation in agricultural work has decreased." (Um Gazaz el Awad, Shendi); "When I was young I used to do some work on my husband's farm. But now women are just sitting at home waiting for the men to bring money to them." (Hajeya Juma Ahmed.) But in the same area the widow of a pastoralist has had to work as a paid seasonal labourer and is the sole breadwinner for a family of eight.

The value to projects
Development projects are often caught up in an almost obsessive drive to produce quantifiable results which can be presented to donors as proof of the project's success. In this quest for measurable achievements, other more subjective parameters are either forgotten or ignored. We believe

this study, in creating a dialogue between development workers and local communities, has demonstrated the value of improved communication at all levels of project activity.

Each development project associated with the interviews was at a different stage, so it was possible to assess the value of participation throughout the project cycle. In Niger we conducted interviews before the project started; the woman interviewer was subsequently employed by the project to manage the women's programme. In Mali the project was at an early stage, in Sudan about half-way through. It became clear that it is never too late to use oral history as a project evaluation tool, but it is most useful if implemented at the planning stage. In Niger, for example, the interviews were used in the project design and followed through thereafter, and extension workers now set up oral history interviews each time they enter a new village.

Feedback from project sites shows that interviewing work conducted by extension workers has had a number of spin-offs—it is an effective method for creating links with new communities, and also a valuable training tool. The coordinator of the interviewing work in Mali notes in her report that the work provided her with a new training area, from which both she and extension workers have benefited. She concludes: "The general utility of this research to the project is that it does something to counteract the idea that farmers are ignorant, conservative and fatalistic. Such preconceptions persist amongst our staff, although they are more subliminal than explicit. Little attempt is made to link the techniques we are trying to popularise with the farmers' own experiments. Thus the extensionist appears as a giver of solutions and the farmers' own capacities are undervalued. And, seeing themselves as surpassed, the farmers are less likely to volunteer suggestions, further aggravating the imbalance....The more details we have of farmers' knowledge and ingenuity, the more we can hope to counteract these problems of attitude."

In the same vein, a Senegalese non-governmental organisation (NGO), Fédération des Paysans Organisés du Département de Bakel, noted: "We wanted to participate in this project from the start because we realised that it would be of benefit to our own work....We felt that it would be particularly useful to our literacy trainers. In this respect the results have gone beyond our expectations. What might have seemed like a lot of extra work from the outside in fact worked to our advantage. We put our trust in young inexperienced workers and were delighted to discover that they were able to carry out the work well....In addition they discovered a rich well of knowledge. We have decided that we cannot leave it here; we will continue the oral history work in our own project."

Thus not the least of the benefits of employing oral history methods in a development context is the impact on project workers, nearly all of whom have acquired valuable new insights, often into their own communities. If oral history techniques are institutionalised in project work, they can increase understanding and sensitivity towards the participating community.

A two-way process

A major obligation of the oral historian is to "return the compliment". When "outsiders" initiate a programme of research, there should be a commitment to seeking new ways of ensuring that the resulting material is of value to the people who provided it. The NGO Fédération des Paysans at Bakel, for instance, published the interviews in Soninke, the local language, for use both as a local resource and as a tool in their literacy programme (see p72).

Perhaps the most immediate and practical value of the Sahel Oral History Project has been in identifying the benefits to projects and project workers of taking the time to learn, through interviews, as much as possible from individual life histories and reflections. Secondly, when such work is collected together, important "under-researched" areas become apparent and can be followed up to ensure that objectives of the developers take into account the many variations in attitudes and priorities of the individuals who make up the community.

To end with a story from Mali: There was once a village so wealthy that the young people decided to make it a youth village of eternal joy, by killing all the old people. On the chosen day there was a single youth who had pity and hid his father so as not to have to kill him. In the new, joyful village of youth, all were strong and worked for themselves, and there were no old people to feed. One day the village was visited by a delegation from the local government, who suspected that something was wrong. They asked the young villagers if they could make a rope out of sand. Impossible. Wild attempts were made to gather up the soil, to no avail. The youth whose father was alive crept off to consult him. The father advised the boy to ask to see the old sand rope first. Thus the delegation realised that this boy's father at least was still alive, and while the others were punished, he was spared.

Editorial Note

The material in *At the Desert's Edge* has been selected from over 500 interviews conducted in 1989 and 1990, and represents perhaps 10% of the Sahel Oral History Project. (This is reflected by the "missing" numbers between interviews.) The editorial principle has been to select on the basis of narrative interest as well as representative views, and to tamper as little as possible. Some interviews have been condensed where they repeat a well-established point, although we have not touched contradictions, confusions or errors of fact. Because all the interviews have been transcribed from the original languages into English, or French and again into English, some misinterpretations and mistranscriptions have undoubtedly crept in. Ideally, we would have cross-checked the edited interviews with the interviewers and, indeed, the respondents themselves, but unfortunately we found this to be hugely impractical.

Within the text, plant names are italicised and there is a full **Botanical Glossary** on p233. Words in bold are defined in a separate **Glossary** on p227. It is a tribute to the richness of the languages spoken in the Sahel that it has not always proved possible to find a helpful English equivalent for certain words: for example, for different kinds of fishing net, some foods and livestock illnesses, or for the many species of fish and wild animals described. Such words are left unglossed. For conveniance, the plural form of Arabic and local words has been denoted by simply adding an "s".

All unedited interviews have been translated into English and are stored on disk, together with a full published index available from SOS Sahel, 1 Tolpuddle Street, London N1 0XT. A complete botanical index to all interviews is in preparation.

———————

Sources for country profiles:
Human Development Report, UNDP 1991. The Human Development Index combines national income with two social indicators, adult literacy and life expectancy, to give a better measure of human progress than GNP alone, since economic growth is not always translated into improvements in people's lives.
Country Reports, Economist Intelligence Unit, 1990-91, Business International Limited.
Sub-Saharan Africa, From Crisis to Sustainable Growth, The World Bank, 1989.

The brief histories have been provided to give a framework to the interviewees' recollections, and hence go back no further than the colonial period.

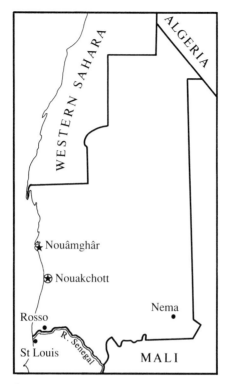

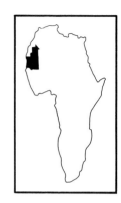

Country Profile: MAURITANIA
Human Development Index (UNDP): 148th out of 160 nations
Population (1990): 2 mn. **Growth rate (1990-2000):** 2.9%
Life expectancy at birth (1990): 47 years
Population per doctor (1984): 12,120
Adult literacy (1985): male 40%; female 16%
Labour force employed in agriculture (1985-1988): 69.4%
GDP from agriculture and livestock (1988): 38%
Principal exports: fish and fish products, iron ore, animals

1904 France establishes Mauritania as a colony, although full authority over the territory not achieved until mid-1930s. **1960** Independence, Islamic Republic declared. **1975** War with Polisario movement over claims of Mauritania and Morocco to Western Sahara. **1978** After military coup, new regime withdraws troops and renounces all claims to Western Sahara. **1984** Col. Maaouya Sid'Ahmed **Ould** Taya takes power. **1989** Conflict with Senegal. Up to 200,000 Mauritanians return from Senegal. **1991** Plans outlined for a new constitution.

MAURITANIA

Interviews took place at two sites in Mauritania and were all conducted in Hasaniya. The first set of interviews were gathered from former pastoralists and other migrants from rural areas, living in shanty settlements on the outskirts of the capital city, Nouakchott. The interviewers were **Mohamed Lemine Ahmed Bakar**, a journalist, and three students from the University of Nouakchott: **Safiya Mint Hamody**, **Waranka Bâ** and **Cherif Ahmed el Med Moussa**. The second interview site was with Imraguen fishermen at Nouâmghâr, a coastal district to the north of Nouakchott. There were no ongoing development projects in this area. The interviewers were **Mohamed Lemine Ahmed Bakar** and **Ali Ould Mohamed Ould Thayor**. Work in Mauritania was coordinated by **Rhiannon Barker** and **Nigel Cross** and supported by **Aliou Bâ**, **Boud Bouda** and **Mohamed Mahmoud**.

Treinicha Mint Beidi (F, 40-45 years), Nouakchott　　　　　　　*MR2*

Beidi was sitting in the open window of her front room, guarding her small table of merchandise—the packages of biscuits, sweets, tobacco and cigarettes all covered in a thick layer of fine red dust. During our visit, Beidi had no clients and answered our questions enthusiastically. Her sister busily prepared **couscous** *next to her. Children milled around, some absorbed in play, others crying for attention. One young boy perched himself on the corrugated iron roof, dislodging odd lumps of caked sand on to us.*

I come from El Handiiya village, one day's walk from Mbour. My mother had borne many children before me, but they'd all died during birth or shortly after. When my mother saw that I was so small, she called me "treinicha", meaning "little amount of money", because she hoped I would last as long as the picture of the man drawn on the newly introduced 20 **CFA** note. In fact, I've outlasted both that picture and the currency!

My mother was a midwife and I used to accompany her when she went to see her patients. Gradually I learned her skills and, by the time she died, I knew a lot. That's why people chose me to take her place, both as a

Everyone, midwife and to help cure many different kinds of disease. If a child is born
even the with hypo-glycaemia, we give it hot water mixed with salt and sugar. For
blind and fever or headache, I tend to use modern medicine, such as aspirin. The
handicapped, number of capsules I give depends on the age of the patient. Before aspirin
had a role was available, patients drank an infusion of *jujubier*. For other children's
diseases, we give pounded *taychêt* and sugar.

One complaint suffered by babies is tyah el jaye, recognised by a fever
and the low position of the uvula. To treat this, we hold the baby tightly
by its hands and feet, while the woman expresses breastmilk into the
baby's mouth until it can hardly breathe. Although the procedure is painful
for the baby, we continue until the uvula returns to the right place. To treat
severe diarrhoea and stomach complaints, we make a medicine of dried,
ground and boiled *tichifitt* leaves.

Even though modern medicine is available, many of us prefer
traditional methods. The medical man for this area has a suitcase, which
we call our hospital! Recently, a young literate girl was employed to
record everything dispensed.

Working the land

Our people really knew how to farm during the rainy season. Both men
and women worked the land. Men went first, breaking the soil with their
awasills; women followed, planting wheat with their **debayës**. We toiled
endlessly under the hot sun—our picks turning the soil, so that it would
absorb rain when it fell. Everyone, even the blind and handicapped, had
a role. Children are still important in the fields; this little four-year-old
girl is in charge of carrying bowls of earth dug by me and my husband.
When seeds begin to sprout, she noisily scares animals away from the
fields. After harvesting, those of us with enough crops stayed in the
village, whilst those with poor harvests were forced to leave Mbour to
earn enough money to buy food and other essentials.

Locusts used to be a big problem, mercilessly eating everything. At
such times, we consulted the **marabout**, who gave us four little
books—each costing 100 **UM**—to place at each corner of the field as a
charm to keep locusts away. Sometimes this worked; sometimes it didn't.

We grew two types of wheat, *takalite* and *nounaa*. *Takalite* was
preferred: it grew well, was good for our health and tasted delicious.
Nounaa grew quicker; its black, moist seeds were used for fodder and its
stems were made into mats. Any surplus wheat was sold in the market or
to the government. We used to sell a kilo of wheat for 5 **CFA**—now we
buy it for 50 **UM**. After harvesting the wheat, we cultivated corn and beans
before clearing the field ready for next year's rains. Farming was risky:

in some years, a farmer's crop failed completely. In such cases, neighbours each contributed a few kilos of grain to the unfortunate family. When I was young, we pounded our own wheat to make **couscous**, cooked it and served it to the family. Anything left over was covered until the next morning, when we mixed it with milk and gave it to the children. At midday, we made butter and used up any flour left from the day before to make **el aich**—made by cooking butter, flour and milk for a long time over a hot fire. Our food was simple: we never had snacks or bread. Meat was saved for special occasions, when we had guests or on holidays, such as the last day of Ramadan or the holy day of meat—Id el Laham. Sometimes, a group of people pooled their money to buy a goat, so that they could eat it together with a big **couscous**.

Donkeys carried water from our village well. Twice a day, we tied our **kerbas** on to the donkey and filled them with free, clean water. When camels drank, they dirtied the water. So we dug small irchwin wells, 1-1.5 metres deep, in the sand: these were only for cooking and drinking water and people weren't allowed to bathe or wash clothes anywhere near them. When I lived there, I didn't buy wood; I carried it on donkeys' backs, tied on with ropes. Even men sometimes collected wood: they carried larger pieces than women did. The wood was used to build our cabins, to support the roofs made of **banco** and to make cattle-proof fences round our fields.

Family roles

Men and women are equal in the family, but have different roles. By custom, men are in charge. We women know we should respect them but sometimes this is difficult. Some miserly men use their position to control the money; most men, however, leave household finances for the women to control. Men have power in other areas. A man can marry his daughter to a suitor of his own choice. I know a man who asked the **qadi** to divorce his daughter, claiming that she married without his consent. One woman disagreed with her husband's choice of groom for their daughter, waited until her husband went away and then married the daughter to the man she preferred. When the father returned, he explained what had happened to the judge and the courts agreed that his daughter would have to divorce her husband. Women also have rights. According to Islam, men must do everything possible to make their wives happy. If not, then a woman is entitled to leave her husband.

I have seven children: the oldest girl is married, the rest of them are still young. I breastfed each of my children for two years—just as God told me to. I weaned them gradually. After one year I gave them extra milk and boiled wheat, until they began to eat from the family dish.

By custom, men are in charge. We women know we should respect them but sometimes this is difficult

All the education a child needs comes from its mother   Unfortunately, my married daughter can't help me financially because she's a farmer and has little herself. Farming is unpredictable—one day you have plenty and the next you have nothing. Only my eldest daughter went to school. She went for five years until she married, then her husband wanted her to stop going. She was a good student, but many things are more important than being able to study. We do not attach much importance to education: that's why we do not send our children to school. All the education a child needs comes from its mother.

Traditional ceremonies

Then, when a child was born, the father killed one or two goats, as the Prophet tells us to do. The meat was shared by the whole community, who joined in the festivities. Marriage contracts were agreed by the old people, and then the groom sent the required dowry. The next day a feast was prepared by the girl's family and everyone was given food and drink. The bride had her hair specially plaited and her hands painted with henna. The next day, the man's family celebrated by providing more music, food and drink [milk] in festivities lasting up to three days.

When somebody dies, we bury them in the earth. Often a goat is sacrificed. An old **marabout** then reads the Qur'an from start to finish—we call this selk. It is necessary to cleanse the soul of the dead. The women read the section called **el fatiha** from the Qur'an in the **etejhtan** ceremony, during which a goat's skin is ceremonially filled with date pips until it weighs 36 kilos. The material possessions of the deceased, such as his bowl, rope and **boubou**, have to be given to charity.

The move to the city

We have been in Nouakchott for two months now. We had never seen the city before. We'd never had any need to come here, so why bother? We had animals and crops to give us milk and food. We stored enough food from each harvest to last us through the year to the next planting season. With all this, why should we want to know Nouakchott? Only after two successive years of drought, when there was no rain or water for our crops and our animals, when the grass grew less than 10 centimetres and our animals died, only then were we forced from our home by the famine.

The government tried to help us when they saw that our cattle had died and we were hungry. They brought a tremendous amount of goods —wheat, oil and powdered milk—but we had to pay for them. The only way we could raise the money was to sell all our cattle. At that time, one cow fetched only 500 **UM**, whilst a 50-kilo bag of wheat cost 1,200 **UM**. So the government provided us with food, but failed to help us find the

money to pay for it. Consequently, the government never prevented   *In the city,*
people dying of hunger. Some families were totally wiped out when the   *we struggle*
famine was at its height. My father was one of the famine victims.   *to find ways*
During the famine, we had to change our diet completely. Our usual   *of making*
milk or cereals were not available, so we made do with eking out what   *money*
little wheat was around. You could tell from a glance that most of us were
hungry. Our climate changed during the drought: there was no difference
between the seasons. Normally, the weather turns cold after the rains but,
with no rain, the weather stays hot all year round.

The government brought mechanical equipment to dig wells. Where
these were dry, they installed pumps, which proved a great help to us
during years of poor rainfall. Now the rains are improving and we find
these pumps difficult to maintain. We can't repair them when they break
down so we have gone back to using our wells. They contain less water
than before but at least there is some.

Famine
During the famine, our cows' ribs stood out, the land cracked and people
became hungry. We decided to come to this city in order to stay alive until
the rains returned. It was the first time I'd left home. Before that, only my
husband had migrated for work. During the famine, all the men left—only
women and children were left behind under the protection of Allah, who
wanted us to stay alive. Some women had one or two animals: a camel or
a goat. Occasionally they sold one to buy food or clothes. Those with no
animals had no security. They couldn't stand life, so they also left.

Our cows and goats died because there was no hay to eat. Our cattle
used to be beautiful—big and fat...now they have gone. Even after our
animals died, we did not give up. We continued to farm the land since,
although milk was important, our crops always took priority. Then we
were forced to give up farming. We came to Nouakchott by car and paid
4,000 **UM**—an exorbitant price. My eldest daughter, who came later, paid
half this. At least the journey was comfortable: we drove through a night
and a day, stopping only to say our prayers.

Here in the city, we struggle to find ways of making money. My
husband found some work loading and unloading trucks at the Nouakchott
garages: it was the only way he could earn anything. When I came here,
I knew no one. I was happy to find work as a servant, earning 3,000 **UM**
a month. I did this for a few weeks but realised I was neglecting my
children, which didn't suit them or me. I gave up that job and started a
small restaurant, cooking from home. But some days I spent 500-700 **UM**
on food and made a profit of only 60-80 **UM**. So, with the money I had

"Sand dunes have become a huge problem....Some are as big as buildings and move around with the wind. As they move they destroy our crops."

left, I bought matches, tea, sweets and biscuits, which I sell from this little table. I don't earn much but it helps me to keep alive. Also, my 16-year-old daughter takes a bucketful of zrikh —the national drink made from milk, water and sugar—to sell to people in front of the hospital.

Last year, some people who left Mbour during the drought began to return. Pasture has improved slightly, although it's nothing compared to what it was before. Life hasn't returned to normal there. Although the area is filling up again, many people realised that they wouldn't find enough to eat if they were to return. The situation remains very difficult, for the rainfall is only "better" when compared to the drought. Many people left for Senegal during the drought. Some were repatriated and returned last year, but we have no news of many others: we don't know if they're dead or alive. Old people were particularly sad when the young began to leave

the area. Many still pine for the return of their relatives. I understand how
they feel. If you are blind or paralysed, it is unbearable to have sons who
leave. I think that even if their children had nothing to give them, they
would prefer them to stay put. For if a young person goes away to earn
money but fails to do so, they often never come back. *If a young person goes away to earn money but fails, they often never come back*

We do not need much to be happy. I don't think much of modern life,
with its lighting, television and cinema. The only things I would like to
take back with me from Nouakchott are wheat, sugar, tea and a small
cassette-player. All we really want is our people, our land, our milk, our
beautiful harvest of wheat and our **shekwas**. We made our **shekwas**
carefully from the scraped skin of a small lamb or kid. The mouth hole
was closed by a piece of leather and the skin sewn up to make it watertight,
as women shake milk in it very fast when making butter.

People at home are requesting help with dam building. Some have built
their own dams of **banco**—a difficult task, because they have no
equipment and work with their hands. If only they had a tractor, then no
one else would need to migrate to this city. Dams would help store
rainwater and enable us to grow maize, beans and wheat. Men, women
and children, now working hard to build these dams, need a little help
from the government.

Shifting sands

Sand dunes have become a huge problem for us. Some are as big as
buildings and move around with the wind. As they move they destroy our
crops and cover fertile areas. The dunes have buried houses built on
low-lying land. We tried to dig these houses clear of sand with our own
hands: it would have been wonderful if we had machines to help us. Some
people tried to stop dune movement by planting trees, but found that the
trees simply got covered in sand and died. With a few improvements, we
might turn our countryside green again. At present, it's a sad sight. The
land is flat and barren, with scattered tree trunks left by wood-cutters. The
government have adopted strict policies concerning trees. They stress
their importance, so we've begun to grow them from seed. Anyone cutting
live trees risks incurring a fine of 6,000 **UM**.

Some of us have tried to rebuild our livestock. My family now has
about 10 goats. In the past, we favoured cows but now we find them too
difficult to look after. Goats are so much easier because they eat almost
anything, they are not as fussy as cows. Cows have to be brought grass
and hay. Even though camels are useful for transport, we have never kept
them, because they are so expensive, difficult to keep and tend to get lost.
We have more female goats than males. With a small herd, one male

suffices—even none, because all animals in the area are kept together and nature usually runs its course! Surplus males are sold in the market and the money used to buy clothes, tea, sugar and rice. We tether our livestock at night to stop them eating crops.

If I had the choice, I would go straight back to my land and take up my **awasill** and **debayë**. We were born to grind and pound our own grain, to eat the food we grow in our fields. This is what we love. The land belonged to us. We inherited it from our parents and they from theirs—all our ancestors were farmers.

MR3   *Fatimetou Mint Mohamed el Mokhtar (F, 70 years), Nouakchott*

The wind and sand blew wildly outside. A fine red dust filled the air, filtering through windows and doors into the small hut, where we sat with Fatimetou. Her two daughters-in-law and her niece often tried to answer the questions for her.

I was born at Mederedra, in Trarza. My parents' only wealth was their cattle, camels, goats and donkeys. We spent our time travelling in search of new pasture. We knew where the wells were, and we usually separated those for animals and those for us to keep our water supply reasonably clean. Goats were more manageable than camels: they stayed put, even when in labour, and only took six months to reproduce whereas camels took a year and ate too much during that time. Once my son climbed a tree to cut some branches to feed his camel, slipped and cut himself badly on an axe, causing such heavy bleeding that it was difficult to staunch. After that, I vowed never again to buy camels.

While we lived as nomads, I never worked. We didn't farm and I didn't even sew, because I was lazy and had many slaves to do all the menial work. Urigs—nomad women—always work together on any task, whether making a tent or weaving a mat. We needed no money: our animals gave us food, we made tents from wood and our men brought us anything else we needed. Our slaves tended the livestock during the day, and I was responsible for cooking rice with meat, peanuts, butter and milk. If lucky, we drank good, nourishing camels' milk in the evening. Our staple food was **el aich**, milk and rice.

My major area of study was the Qur'an. I knew it by heart and even taught it to children but later I found the work too tiring and forgot verses. So I gave it up, apart from the odd pupil. Today, children are difficult to teach—not listening to what's said—and their parents get upset if you chide them. In short, I've little time for them.

It was a race between us and the locusts to reach the vegetation

Famine

A famine, called El Howua, caused considerable suffering about 50 years ago. All our animals died and we had little or nothing to eat or wear. Nomadic pastoralists had to dress in animal skins. I was still just a young girl, recently married and sharing a tent with my husband, but with no children. When things were at their worst, we heard there had been good rains at Essahwa. It was a long, difficult journey but many came with us. When we arrived, we were happy because the land was very green...then the locusts came and ate all the vegetation! They even began to eat our tents and we had to start moving again. The only way we kept alive was by killing and eating our camels, one at a time.

On our travels we found fish to eat, at Nouâmghâr, but all the time it was a race between us and the locusts to reach the vegetation first. We pinned all our hopes on finding food and water in Nouakchott. In Trarza, we exchanged gum arabic from the trees for sugar, tea and rice. My veil wore out, so I divided my **varou**, using one half as a veil and giving the other to a man wearing only a rag around his waist. As we travelled, some people died of hunger and thirst.

In spite of our desperate plight, people never stole from each other: those with food gave generously to those without. We killed our last goat, hoping to quench our thirst from its meat juices. Some young people went searching for water but got lost for a whole day and were lucky to return alive. Then, thankfully, we arrived at Benichab, a freshwater well in Inchiri [central Mauritania]. We left most of our luggage there: we were too weak to carry more than the bare minimum. Children and old people rode on the remaining camels. My father was too feeble to walk, so he sat on a camel led by my brother. I walked along with a bowl of water, making him drink from time to time. Suddenly, as we were travelling, he collapsed and died. We went on for another day with his body, until we found a cemetery in which to bury him. During this delay, our companions had moved on; nobody could afford to hang back if they were to survive.

After that terrible year, things settled down until the famine which followed independence, when we faced the same suffering. That drought destroyed our environment; bare sand began to replace our thorn forest. Once we used spears to fight our way through the thick scrub, where wild animals lurked. Now both have been destroyed by hunters and by drought. Over the years, more and more men migrated, leaving their families to find jobs as merchants, shopkeepers or small traders. It did not matter what they sold, as long as they made money. If a man found a steady job in another area, he sent for his family.

We came to Nouakchott because, after months without rain, we realised we had nothing left to keep us going. So we found pasture for our camels and goats in Gouta, where we dug a well and stayed until the rains began. This was the sign for us to return to our own land at Mederedra but we found very little rain had fallen there. Vegetation was poor and many people were already searching for pasture. Realising that we would not find enough grazing, we moved on to Ndar. By then, the animals were growing weak and camels had begun to die. When we saw that there was no hope for the rest of the herd, we began to kill them ourselves—at least we could eat the meat. We stayed in Ndar, watching our cattle die around us. We sold a few of the strongest animals, though prices were very low: 10,000 **UM** for an adult camel and 1,300 **UM** for a calf.

Making a life in the city

Using the money from selling our animals, we came to Nouakchott. We had just battled with six years of wind and sand. Look! These lines on my face are not simply from old age. They have been caused by screwing up my eyes against the blowing sand for weeks and months on end. On arrival here, my husband—always resourceful—set up a small shop on a loan system. He got traders to lend him goods. We sold them, then he paid the traders. In this way, he did not need much capital. One of our sons helped him in the shop. As business thrived and steadily increased, he finally moved premises to the market.

Before coming here, I had never farmed: all I knew about was animals. Nevertheless, my husband put my name on the **SONADER** list and told me that I would be allocated agricultural land. He assured me that they would teach me about farming, as they specifically wanted women. As promised, in 1976 **SONADER** gave us land, did everything possible to teach us about vegetable gardening and even provided us with free water and seed for three years.

Some women advisers helped us tackle our problems, particularly fending off those who tried to take our land. Men were our main problem: many could not understand why they had not been allocated land. One man set up a tent and started cultivating. We had to tell him that without valid authorisation there was no water for him. While **SONADER** were here, this man could not argue with us.

Once **SONADER** left, in 1979, life became much harder. When I arrived here, I was still fairly young and strong. Now I had back problems and sometimes felt too weak to work. We had no control over men's

Men were our main problem: they knew that we were all women with little power

MR24b Lehbat Ould Sidi Brahim Ould Bouzeid (M, 56 years), Nouakchott
I come from a pastoralist family, became a soldier and now I have retired. I came to Nouakchott to get hold of a plot of land....My feeling is that people want change but there's been a brake on it—the means are so limited. The position of women has developed to a certain extent but there are some tasks that aren't seen as right for women. They aren't meant to go out too much. In the past a woman could have a slave working for her. The slave wasn't paid, but the master would buy him clothes and carry out all the duties that are set down by our religion for him. They didn't send them to school, but then some parents don't even send their own children.

activities and so they began to transfer water from our wells into theirs in the middle of the night. One night they even made a hole in our water tank and drained water through a pipe directly into their tank! The men had the boldness to do this because they knew that we were all women with little power. Those days were hard. Our only job became trying to find enough food for our children. Never before had we known the humiliation of searching for food—we used to be wealthy people. On top of this, we were harassed by these men stealing our water and challenging our ownership of it by asserting that "water is the right of every citizen".

Yet our gardens were productive. We grew cucumbers, carrots, tomatoes, turnips, potatoes, beetroot, salad, aubergines and mint. Then SONELEC, the national electricity and water board, threatened to cut off our water supply unless we paid 1,000,000 **UM**—an impossible sum. They backed down a little and reduced it by 50%, but it was still impossible for us. Water ran for 20 more months, then they cut us off. We have only kept going for the last month by buying barrels of water and by our friends bringing us water tanks. We feel SONELEC was unfair, since we were not warned of charges. Our water bills had always been paid for us and we never realised this service had been stopped. Moreover, why should we meet the bill for water used by the whole community? We have asked SONELEC to wipe the slate clean. If they give us a second chance, we will regularly fill a money box for the water bills.

All we ask for now is a water supply. Since it was cut off, we have used up all our savings. If we had water, we could be entirely self-sufficient from the sale of vegetables.

MR8 Ghwaya Mint Ayed (F, 42 years), Nouakchott
Red crickets were a delicacy. We say that since crickets eat from all kinds of trees, they must be the cure for all diseases, since there is a tree to cure every ailment.
MR9 Salma Mint Mbeirik (F, 75 years), Nouakchott
You cannot greet a guest warmly unless you are able to kill a goat and share the meat....
As the night fell, the relatives and friends of the bride and groom would "fight" against each other. This fight was performed so that when the groom won, he could take the bride as his prize.
MR16 Mamadou Samba (M), Nouakchott
The key to success when you have more than one wife living under the same roof is to make sure that whatever you do for one wife, you also do for the others. There is no favouritism. We prefer to marry our cousins, because we say that if you have something good you should keep it within the family!

Children
Here in Nouakchott, our children go to school and so cannot work with us. **SONADER** said that children should not help us in the gardens, since this work tires them. Now **SONADER** have gone, children help us with light work during the holidays.

We are luckier than some, because we farm our own land. The government gave it to us, with all the legal papers. When we die, our children can inherit it. I have four children. The only one educated is in his third year at school but I am worried he will drop out. My other children helped me work, especially growing vegetables. One daughter is married, but I rarely see her, as she is busy looking after her sick mother-in-law. Occasionally, she sends me money, but my sons cannot. They are struggling to look after their own families.

It is against our religion and the will of Allah to use contraceptives. I think it would be wrong to use something to stop me having a child. I do not understand why modern women want to do this. More often, one hears of women who want children but who, for various reasons, cannot have them. Some even consult a **marabout** for lucky charms to bring about fertility.

A naming ceremony occurs seven days after a baby's birth. If he can afford it, the father kills and cooks two or three goats and sends the meat on dishes to the women in their tent. Only women are present at the actual baptism, but all friends and relatives join in the feast. Families have changed; in the old days, adults united to look after the young. How they were related to the children did not matter—they still cared for them. Today, times are more selfish. The young no longer respect their parents. They are losing their religion and turning into hypocrites. Traditions, which once cemented our society, have disintegrated.

Women used to breastfeed their babies until they stopped by themselves, or until the woman no longer had any milk. After about one year, I supplemented my milk with cows' milk, small pieces of minced meat and dates. Today, breastfeeding has been reduced to about 40 days and mothers turn to artificial milk and other unhealthy products. I believe the best way to raise a healthy baby is to breastfeed it for two years, just as our Prophet (peace be with him) said we should.

Health
Leprosy and cancer are the two main diseases here. Very few people ever recover from leprosy. In one happy case, someone with leprosy went and lived in a tent by the sea shore: miraculously, he began to get better. He came home physically weak, but the leprosy had gone and he was able to

Traditions live a normal life. Other major diseases are measles and smallpox, which
which once once killed many people, but today most people can be cured in hospital.
cemented In my youth, those with fever were given gum arabic, mixed with milk
our society and sugar. The patient would be given barbecued lamb's liver and lots of
have fluids to aid recovery. This treatment normally worked. Our methods used
disintegrated natural products. Today, some incredible modern medicines are used.
Ultimately, the success of any treatment depends on the will of Allah. He
has the power to cure all dangerous diseases. Even so, it is good that
hospitals care for the sick.

I only ask Allah to grant all Muslim people happiness on earth. For
myself, I always want to have enough to allow me to give something to
charity. I never want to have to rely on others. If you always ask Allah
what He wants of you, then you can be sure He will help you achieve this.

MR14   *Ahmedou Bâ (M, 60 years), Nouakchott*

I am a diplomat and so have spent much time travelling. I went on my first
trip in 1962 and, since then, I have lived in France, the Soviet Union and
the Arab states, as well as visiting many other European and African
countries. In 1984, I retired to Nouakchott.

My first name is Arabic. My family name comes from one of the four
main Peulh clans: Ka, Bâ, Branky and Sow. I think that these groups were
of Egypto-Nubian origin, around the eighth or ninth century. Peulh people
are very prolific in the Sahel, to be found from Cameroon to Ethiopia. In
this country Peulh people speak a different language to our Peulh
neighbours. At the end of the sixteenth century, the Peulh tribe were led
by a big chief called Koli, who helped spread Peulh culture and traditions.
There was a division between the nomadic pastoralists and the
Pulaar-speaking Haal-Pulaar'en, who were sedentary agro-pastoralists.

My father was a doctor in an infirmary. We were a rich urban family
but also had cows and sheep on land by the Senegal River in the old Fonta
kingdom area—and here I spent all my holidays. During the winter, from
July to October, we farmed the high ground. After the rains, when the
river level fell, we cultivated the fertile floodplain. The second harvest
usually occurred at the end of March. Those with land next to the river
needed no irrigation: the seasonal rise and fall of the river provided them
with enough water.

The river was valued both for its fertile silt and for its fish. We were
some distance from the river and only fished when it flooded, which it did

for several months each year, creating other small tributaries rich with fish. To prevent the tributaries disappearing, we used to block any openings and line the banks with stones.

Land by the river is precious: it is very fertile and in short supply. It has been owned by families for many centuries, each landholding clearly delineated and passed down from generation to generation according to strict inheritance patterns. Farming methods on these plots have changed little over the years, apart from the introduction of diesel pumps to make irrigation more efficient. The higher land, with its rainfed agriculture, is not in short supply and is easily claimed. There's no opposition, because no one owns this free land.

Development

Even on the fertile floodplains, the drought has caused problems. Water levels have fallen. We pinned all our hopes on the dams built along the river by the Organisation de la Mise en Valeur du Fleuve Sénégal (OMVS). For local people, however, the scheme has caused more problems than solutions, since the government now wants to control land along the river. They tried to take the land from us and manage it themselves, but faced opposition—the land is too much a part of the people themselves and they will not give it up easily. Anyone with traditionally inherited land will not let it go to strangers. The state has now passed a law invalidating people's right to manage their own land!

Along the river, pastoralists and farmers live together and their inevitable arguments are always amicably resolved. Pastoralists are honest and acknowledge the problems caused by their animals. Local people help assess any damage done and payment is usually in animals. Such problems are always resolved by the community's own traditional justice system; even the French administration was never involved in such issues.

Colonialism

French colonial policies forced us to assimilate their own culture and beliefs and ignored our own. In the baccalauréat exam, for example, French and European history took precedence over our own African history. What's more, when I took my exams, I had to wear a suit and tie! While the French occupied our country, military service was compulsory. I only did eight months of the expected three years of service, because my mother died. I had to sort out her affairs, so was fortunate to get an exemption certificate. Others were less lucky and had to fight for the French during the First and Second World Wars.

French colonial policies forced us to assimilate their culture and beliefs and ignored our own

For this generation who your father is doesn't count much....The time when it was all "he's so-and-so's son" is over
Lehbat Ould Sidi Brahim Ould Bouzeid

In our black African society, slaves have been a traditional part of the social structure of the Pulaar, Soninke and Wolof groups since ancient times. Rich noble families kept many slaves, who performed tedious or unpleasant tasks. Some people even sent their slaves to fight wars, instead of their own sons. And when colonial schools were at the height of their unpopularity, chiefs being pestered by the authorities to send their sons—as an example to others—sent their slaves, leaving their own children at the traditional Qur'anic schools.

Social caste

Our slaves were victims of neglect. Today, slavery is outlawed. Stopping slavery is a step forward, but it is harder to eradicate the notion of slaves as a class of people. The Haratine, the largest class of freed slaves, exist in all four major ethnic groups in Mauritania: Moors of Arab and Berber descent, Wolof, Haal-Pulaar'en and Soninke. Many Moor slaves are really negroid, having been enslaved centuries ago by Arab Moors, whose culture and language [Hasaniya] they assimilated. Even though now free, they still suffer from being perceived as part of a class of slaves. If a man descended from slaves wants to marry a girl from a noble family, her father will forbid it. The whole social caste system is so deep in our mentality that it will take a long time to disappear. Only 3-4% of slaves have been educated but now, with schools being more accessible, education may help change this oppressive mentality.

When I returned to Mauritania in 1984 after a long absence, I was struck by the huge changes. I could not get over the dryness of the country, the desertification, the advance of the sand—these were the first things that I noted. After that, I thought about little else. Also the population was redistributed. Because of the drought, most people were concentrated in a small area around Nouakchott despite the huge size of Mauritania. When I went to my home along the river, I noticed that the water level was much lower than it was when I was a boy. Where before I had known greenery and vegetation, today there was only sand. The deer which once stalked the thorn forests were nowhere to be seen. When I was young, we spent many happy hours chasing game around the trees, using dogs to sniff them out from their hiding places. Today, how can the children have fun when the bush has disappeared? There are no trees or grass. People were worrying that all the water would soon evaporate from the Senegal River.

Thankfully, our condition has begun to improve. Over the last two to three years, more rain has fallen. Farmers who had abandoned their land in desperation have begun to go back to their fields. Even pastoralists are trying to return to their old lifestyle: they are never happier than when watching their cattle reproduce! Despite all this, winds still blow strongly and mobile sand dunes constantly threaten newly planted crops.

Sand is one of our biggest problems. If you look at any Mauritanian town or village, you will often see that sand has begun to creep up the house walls. If we do not immediately halt the desert spreading, then it will not be long before the fertile southern part of our country becomes enveloped by dunes. I don't think that you can blame the large Mauritanian herds for the degradation. After all, in the north of the country the vegetation has not suffered such a dramatic change—rivers still flow and there is vegetation in abundance.

Everyone corresponds to a plant and when somebody dies, a plant dies
Aminéton Mint Meki

Desertification

In the Senegal River region, I believe man has been the major destructive force on the environment: we are to blame for desertification. Too much wood has been used for construction and cooking. That's why some NGOs have recommended energy efficient stoves. We hope these will help preserve our environment. NGOs can help us confront and improve our situation but if they are to do this successfully, they must work directly with the people involved—otherwise their efforts will be in vain. As regards the serious problems facing agriculture, pastoralism and fishing, I would advise NGOs to put their energies into peasant education and into the introduction of new, appropriate technologies to improve efficiency.

Education must be the first stage of any NGO programme. Although farmers know the problems of their land better than anyone, and how to get the best immediate results from one harvest to the next, they do not have long-term management skills: how to plan more for the future, how to save their money and resources, how to adopt a more sustainable approach. Also, they need clear guidance in the use of new technology to maximise its benefits. Most farmers are receptive to new ideas, as long as they can clearly see their potential benefits. They have already seen some benefits of development work, especially welcoming the new fast-growing seed varieties. They're calling out for new technology to increase production.

Other changes have occurred in our social structure, particularly in the relationship between young and old. In marriage, for example, I had less control over choosing a partner for my children than my parents did. My daughter can marry whom she wants. When I was young, women were protected by men; today, they have to live life on their own. As far as I am concerned, it's best to let the young lead their own lives. There are so many taboos, cultural constraints and strong religious values in this country that it's best they find their own way of dealing with them.

It makes me sad when I think of the many customs we have lost. It is hard for us to look on, as our old patterns of behaviour are shunned by the younger generation. In the past, a young man couldn't go into his relatives' house with his shoes on, nor could he look an adult directly in the eye. Even today, I never look directly at my mother. It is not the same with my own children: as you can see, they look directly at me. Our whole way of thinking is rapidly changing. When I returned here after my travels, I was happy to be home—I did not find it hard to readapt. I think it was worse for my children, because the young are not as robust as the old!

MR18   *Group of pastoralists, Bouhdida, Nouakchott*

We sat and talked on a small dune, overlooking the goat and camel market. This group had been pastoralists all their lives and were in the city to earn money from trading cattle.

Once, we knew a Mauritania rich in camels, cows, sheep and goats. In our home region of Brakua, we kept mainly goats. We were nomads, moving east in winter to find fresh pasture. We wandered from place to place, living in tents which women wove from wool. Our diet was based on milk during the rains when the cattle were well fed, and on millet in the dry season. We bought most of our grain in the market; only those with small herds also grew crops. Those concentrating on farming used their children or paid herdsmen to tend their livestock. Our cattle caught many diseases, one of the worst caused streaming eyes and chronic diarrhoea. We'd make a broth to try and cure them but few recovered.

As a boy, one favourite game was cora: we use a wooden bat to hit a ball made from a stone wrapped in a piece of cloth. We also had horse and camel races and played hide-and-seek. Young people today have less time for such amusements—they have their studies.

Men and women's work was clearly divided. The women cooked, educated the children and were very creative in making mats from dried plant stems and pieces of leather. Men looked after the animals or worked in the fields; those with guns hunted gazelles for their families to eat.

If good rains fed our fields and filled our dams, we celebrated by firing shots in the air. After a good harvest, we'd organise a feast with **tam tam** music and dancing. In those days, we were fit and healthy—able to endure hunger, thirst and tiredness easily. Sometimes I stayed up all night digging wells, so that my animals had something to drink. Once, after three nights without sleep, I caught myself dozing right on the brink of the well I'd

A life without animals is not fulfilling
Mohamed Ould Beya

Milking a camel. "Despite the tragic loss of our herds, most Mauritanians still feel passionately about them...we live in the hope that the vegetation will recover enough for us all to resume our nomadic life. Only those earning a fortune in trade or commerce would stay in town."

We believe just dug! The best time for cattle to drink is in the evening, because this
many of our is when the water level rises. Our wells were often shared between
traditional different camps and this frequently gave rise to disputes.
cures are more   I specialised in taming oxen and camels. Often, I had really ferocious
effective than animals to train. Once I took a violent, non-castrated camel, I chased after
those of vets the beast, grabbed him by the tail, tied his back legs together, moved in
front and, singlehanded, brought him to the ground. After muzzling him
to stop any biting, I climbed on top and made him run. Sometimes camels
have to be broken in gradually. Others are agitated if you climb on
carefully so you have to take them by surprise and jump on their backs:
after a few days they're quite docile. Some lazy camels need to be goaded
into going faster. Camels are the most difficult animals to train, taking up
to a year, whereas oxen take just a few days.

Camel birth

Oh yes, I know a lot about animals. If they're lost, I can track them. If a
she-camel is in trouble with her labour I can help her give birth. If she's
in pain, I can feel the position of her calf in the womb and, if it's wrong,
I can move it round with my hand. Before I put my arm in, I brush it with
oil and cut my fingernails to avoid causing unnecessary harm. I've saved
many baby camels' lives this way, though some are stillborn. If we know
an undeveloped calf has died in the womb and has not been miscarried,
we cut out the baby, removing it piece by piece. When we've removed all
we can, we wash the womb with oil. We believe many of our traditional
cures are more effective that those of the vets.

     We used to see many wild animals. I knew two brothers who shot a
wild cat during their breakfast one morning: it had suddenly pounced on
and seriously wounded their camel. When I heard this story it made me
weep, because it struck me that Mauritania used to be full of many more
such surprising incidents than it is today.

     It's difficult to forecast drought. This last one suddenly descended on
us; before that, "drought" was a word we never used. We didn't fight it
or protect ourselves, because we thought it would only last a few months.
When our cows, camels and sheep began to die from hunger—not
disease—we realised our mistake. Many of us fled to Senegal and Mali,
looking for pasture. We've always relied on Senegal for pasture, because
they have fewer animals than we have.

     When our animals died, we had to rely on state food provisions for the
needy. Some people salvaged a little money by selling a few cattle before
they all died. They hardly made a profit—prices were about a hundred
times less than those today. A cow then sold for just 150-200 **UM**; today

they cost 20,000-30,000 **UM**. Sheep then went for 60 **UM**, but now fetch 6,000-7,000 **UM**.

Attitudes towards education have changed enormously. Only a very few nomads still refuse to let their children have a modern education. Today's parents see that it can benefit their children. Some even move near a school, although nowadays there are schools in most places so education is more accessible.

Everyone in Nouakchott comes from different areas. There's no pasture for our animals, so they're penned in and brought food. As this poses problems, most animals are kept further away, to the east, and only brought to the city for sale. Most of us now stay in Nouakchott permanently, while a few "transporters" shuttle to and fro with the animals we buy and sell. Our profits fluctuate with the seasonal supply of animals. Before any sales, veterinary approval of fitness for consumption has to be obtained.

The importance of animals

Despite the tragic loss of our herds, most Mauritanians still feel passionately about them. We love our animals, even though we've just had to watch them die. We're encouraged by this year's better rains and many have returned to the bush to rebuild their herds. The bush is our home, we feel lost in the city. As we sit here, we live in the hope that the vegetation will recover enough for us all to resume our nomadic life. Only those earning a fortune in trade or commerce would stay in town.

Town women differ from those we left in the bush: they have more freedom and participate in more activities. Rural women are more reserved, though even they are changing. Once they made clothes to last five to six months, now they make excuses to visit the city to keep pace with the new fashions of the scantily dressed town women. In the past women were modest. They never shouted—just clicked their fingers for attention. They never met or walked alongside men as now, but sat down until any men had passed by. Once, women only married within their tribe, usually to a cousin. Now they're freer to make their own choice; some even marry ex-slaves! We don't have slaves any more, at least, not in name: people should be paid for their work. Slavery is history now.

As we've now engaged in more direct trading of our animals, it's likely that we'll continue this when we return to the bush—as we will, because we can't spend our time worrying about another drought! Pastoralists are not alone in realising that animal sales bring in cash for other essential goods; merchants and government officials have built up large herds of their own, employing herdsmen to tend them.

In the past women were modest. They never shouted— just clicked their fingers for attention

Young people brought up in towns don't know the first thing about animals, whereas those who grew up alongside them understand perfectly the way of life. Yet urbanisation is still only skin-deep; most people in this town still use their holidays and spare time to return to their camps, where more solid dwellings are now replacing scattered tents. Transport has improved between Nouakchott, Nema and Rosso so men travel more, leaving their women and families at home, as they look for pasture or employment. Some of us like travelling so much that we become ill if we stay in town too long. Usually it's only those without animals who like town life.

Last year, I went to Aïoun with my family. I filled my lungs with the fresh air of the countryside and was so impressed with the greenery there that I went and bought some cows. Every holiday, I return to look at them.

MR31   Dah Ould Mohamed Leabeïd (M), Sebkha, Nouakchott

The market gardens of Sebkha shanty town stretch as far as the eye can see. Dah sits on the ground tending his plants. His dozen or so vegetable beds are all carefully weeded and young vegetables are already pushing up through the soil.

My interest in agriculture began about 15 years ago, when I lived in Male, in the region of Brakua— a land of plentiful water. We had several wells and only had to dig down 2 metres to find water. I grew millet, maize and haricot beans.

My family is now with me here, five girls and four boys. My eldest child is over 30 and works as a housekeeper. She isn't married. Another daughter has one girl but no boys. One of my sons must be about 20 and is an apprentice mason. His brother wants to be a soldier. They went to school, but all failed and gave it up. I still live with their mother—I have never divorced her, as other men would. I never worry about the size of my family. It is beyond my control; destiny is in the hands of Allah. All good Muslims believe this—if one hasn't eaten today, one will receive food tomorrow. If I have 20, or even 40 children, I must have faith that Allah will provide for them.

A changed environment

I haven't been home for over 20 years, but cousins often visit and tell me about my father (who still farms) and about the changed environment. Before I left to work in the city, the area consisted of a mixture of sand dunes and rich clay soil, giving a balance of fertile and barren land. Now sand dunes cover the whole area. If I went home, I would lose my way. The *zabiu* tree landmark has disappeared beneath the sand like everything else. Even steep gullies have turned into dunes. Just a few strips of fresh land have been created by dunes shifting away from some areas.

In my youth, the vegetation was rich. The edible fruit of the *usder* was sold in town as a cure for rheumatism or stored (broken open) in gourds as a reserve food supply for the rainy season. In winter, after the September growing season, we collected gum arabic and sold it in Kaëdi and Boghé. We children were always on the look- out for gum trees, just as children nowadays seek sweets and other goodies. *Adress* trees provided dry season fodder for goats and camels. *Ignine* trees restored strength to sick animals and we liked to eat its grape-like fruit. The wood of the *imigige* tree was made into traditional household furnishings, such as screens. We didn't have to manufacture charcoal, because there was plenty of wood nearby.

Most villages there had no livestock, but we owned goats and a few cows, so women could make butter. Millet was the main crop, harvested once during the rainy season and once during the dry. My father taught me about agriculture from when I was about eight; I used to go to the fields with him. I did not learn about vegetable growing until I came to Nouakchott.

Farming was really profitable then, with mild weather, blue skies, fertile soils and plenty of water and everything else. When a cow had grazed for just two minutes, milk began to ooze from its udder—a good cow produced over 10 litres a day. After clearing the crop, we burnt everything left and felled any trees. We sowed the day after it rained. One person turned the soil over with a **duba**; another followed scattering seed. We relied on the rainy season to water the crops and on our hands to till the land. In good harvests, I filled hundreds of millet sacks; sometimes I had to store it in underground holes. Pests were a problem but we never used pesticides or fertiliser. Rainwater killed worms and washed away other things damaging our crops. I used to weed the millet to prevent it from being smothered. We drove locusts off with noise and fire, and birds with stones and banging. There was plenty of good land available so, if the ground became rain-sodden and lost its fertility, we could move on or we could leave fields fallow for a year. We grew *bichure* and the faster-ripening *takalite*, which we harvested unripe, sun-dried and then ground to make **couscous**.

Once, when I was quite young, some **phacochères** destroyed all of a local family's millet and as their father was away, I volunteered to kill the animals—though I had never seen one in my life. At nightfall, I hid in the field, ready for action. I heard strange squeals in the dark. Suddenly, the beasts appeared. I was terrified, forgot I had a gun and began to scream for help! Another dark night, I was stalked by a fierce-looking animal. Finally, I turned and said: "You there, listen to me! You've been following me all night. If you want to eat me, let's have an honest confrontation, otherwise leave me alone!" That was the last I saw of it. Later, people told me that it might have been a lion!

I was happy in my early years, carefree and easily satisfied. Life is still good nowadays because I have my family to live and work for, but survival has become more of a struggle. Worries were not so pressing, as we could live well on millet and, when that ran out, we had plenty of other food—tree fruits and other plants.

City life
Our village did not really suffer during droughts until 1967. Then I left home for city life and arrived in Rosso, where I was nearly eaten to death by mosquitoes. The only jobs were as dockers. After two months, I came here. I stayed with friends, who looked after me for a while but soon became tired. I doubt if anyone can live indefinitely in someone else's house without becoming a burden. After all, this was city life and city values. For half a month I had nothing to eat. I was famished! I can't tell you how I survived those 15 hungry days. Finally, I found a job again—still in the tough docks earning 50 **UM** per day. A friend then found me a company job as an unskilled builder's labourer earning 1,400 **UM** a month, rising to 3,000 **UM**. On my time off, I sometimes returned home.

MR16a Fatimata Diallo (F, 60 years), Nouakchott
In the old days our people knew so much -their knowledge was vast. But it seems as if the drought is drying up the skills and knowledge that we had....
If a woman decides to marry someone who is not from her own tribe, she plunges herself into the unknown. She puts her blood into the multiplication of strangers. It is not a good thing.

MR33b Ahmedou Ould Behi (M, 65 years), Mheijratt
I don't know anything about the dates you people speak of. For us, time is marked by important events, such as the death of somebody important, a fall of rain or an invasion.

MR40 M'Bareck Ould H'Meyid (M), Nouakchott
We used to say that in Mauritania there were three things to prevent you feeling sad: the water, the grasses and the beautiful views. Today, if we want to lift up our hearts, we have to search hard for these things.

I stayed in Rosso nine years, until we were made redundant. *I don't need*
Shortly before this, I was married. We lived with our children in a tent, *better land.*
until the state gave us a plot of land for a house. I was unemployed or *Water is my*
working only for short periods, until an international humanitarian *priority*
organisation enrolled all us poor people and offered us plots to cultivate,
12 by 15 metres. They gave us water and seed—sometimes even clothes,
rice or butter. Shanty-town dwellers like myself were visited by their
representatives and given land, completely free! Their main aim was to
help us set up market gardens. After 18 years, when they saw that we could
look after ourselves, they left. Only once did we feel let down by
them—when food handouts were stopped. It was explained to us,
however, that others needed help more than ourselves and we could now
live independently.

The need for water
In my early days, it was difficult to get enough millet from the two annual
harvests. Even though the rains lasted three months, large areas still never
got enough. Lack of rainfall remains my prime concern. More profitable
horticulture has taken over and the state is now taking an interest in market
gardening, because it is essential to our country's economy. I don't need
better land. Water is my priority and, when I have it, I can guarantee a
good yield from my garden and make a decent living. Each plot can sustain
40 vegetable beds—I have 35. We can cultivate all kinds of vegetables
and, if we had enough water, you would see a mass of young plants here.
We don't need gifts of money, food or clothes, only for the state to provide
water again.

The water and electricity board, SONELEC, used to provide water
from a purification plant, but it broke down three years ago. Since then,
we've dug reserve wells and irrigation channels to bring water from the
town but there is never enough. Apart from water brought by the
humanitarian organisation, we have paid for all our water: I remember
paying bills for 10,000 and 12,000 **UM**. The water plant didn't collapse
for want of money!

Anybody who works with water expects to pay for it from his profits.
When we were supported in our work here, we had good results. Since
then, we make the most of what we have: the water problem is the only
thing that holds us back. Land is plentiful and the few insects which
survived the drought can be controlled with powder that we buy.

We demarcate our land with posts or tree trunks: it is too big to cultivate
all of it, so we have no problems in dividing it up. We could cultivate this
land repeatedly without reducing soil fertility, as it is good clay soil,

Men and women no longer treat each other with respect. It's as if a protective barrier between them has broken down

washed clean and replenished by the rain. I work alone in my garden, just as I have always done. Sometimes animals come in here at night and damage my vegetables, forcing me to search for their owners and demand compensation. Farming and livestock are kept apart, especially during the dry season, when herds move less and are more likely to damage crops.

We sell our surplus vegetables to camel caravans from far and wide or take them on donkeyback for sale in town. Then we can buy tea, clothes and other things we need. Sometimes our vegetables fetch good prices but, in recent years, the market has become rather glutted, because nearly everybody has started growing vegetables. People from the interior have to ask low prices, or watch their vegetables rot. Those living near markets and trade routes, like us, find it much easier: we can keep our produce until we get a decent price for it. When there are no vegetables on the market, women customers buy a whole patch of land for 600 **UM**, then collect the produce daily until the bed is empty.

For breakfast, we eat a biscuit made with millet flour and milk. We have **couscous** for lunch, and millet biscuits again in the evening. In the old days, children ate what we did and were not particularly interested in food, unlike young people today. We men would work in the fields and our womenfolk would bring us breakfast, drinks and lunch. We never let women lift a hand in the fields; they worked at home, in the kitchen, fetching water and looking after young animals. They also gathered maize in the forest to offer visitors. All this has changed. We are now in a different age. Yet I don't think that times change—only people.

Social change

Rural children used to tend livestock or help their fathers in the fields from the age of five. Today, in theory they go to school. Really, they miss lessons and roam around the city streets. Young people used to respect their elders in the old days. They didn't eat in front of them but kept themselves to themselves. If a young person had done something wrong, he would be counselled by his elders and wouldn't dare to speak or look them in the eye. Today's youth has no respect—they do as they please.

You would never see women showing their teeth when they laughed. They did not appear at gatherings of older people. Girls might attend a special ceremony but would be confined to a particular area. Today, young girls talk back when they are spoken to. My own daughter stares at me when I scold her. Women used to wear thick garments but, today, they are so transparent, you can see their whole body through the cloth.

My wife works hard selling vegetables, getting them from me or someone else if my supply has run out. My sons help me when I call them, though young people prefer the pleasures in life—going out with their friends—rather than working. This is a bad age: men and women no longer treat each other with respect. It's as if a protective barrier between them has broken down. Divorce rates have risen because women have many more needs. Women used to be content with clothing and food; now they ask for more. Some leave their husbands for wealthier men—they are fickle. Mind you, some men desert their wives after years of marriage for a younger woman.

My heart fills with joy when I think of my marriage. I like to remember the night when I prayed that Allah wouldn't kill me before I'd experienced married life! When my prayers were answered, I was happy. The birth of my eldest daughter was a good day. My mother died just before I married, leaving my father all alone. I remember telling him my good news and he congratulated me. In my life, I have no cause for regret. I have never harmed or fought anyone. I have always shown respect to my family and relatives. My mind is at peace and I have a clear conscience.

Mariem Mana Mint Ahmed (F, 80 years), Tiwilit   MR34

I must have been born in Bellaatt before 1910, for I was very young when I first saw **Emir** Ahmed Salem **Ould** Brahim Salem. My parents kept many cows and I spent a lot of time

taking them from well to well. They often fell ill with lahrach, a common intestinal complaint. We could do nothing to help them: they died or they recovered. Gorgi was another ailment—a type of paralysis. We didn't have any herbal remedies for our cattle, though we had plants for healing ourselves. The dried, ground roots of the *kbeibtadab* tree were a cure for diarrhoea and we took *tedba* for coughs.

When I married, I came to live in Tiwilit by the sea. It was at the time of Mohamed el Mauron, just when a group of healers had left and a young local **emir**, Ahmed Salem,

People caught fish by swimming or wading in the shallows with nets made from local plants

replaced them. I have no sons but have four good, married daughters, who come to see me regularly. They never disobeyed me, but if they had, I would have forgiven them.

I have known difficult periods, such as El Irya "the time of cloth shortage", though I was lucky and managed to buy some veils made of **katikan** from a northern merchant. My parents were rich, so I normally managed to get what I wanted—but famine affected everyone. Neither crops nor animals were to be found. Our milk supply was drastically reduced. We had to get used to the sea and learn to fish, and so we suffered less than those in the interior.

When I first arrived I knew nothing about fishing. There were many different kinds of fish, mainly coming from the north. There were **ivr** and **bazdoul** and our main catch was mullet, but motor boats seem to have scared off many types of fish, and **courbine** is now more plentiful. Before the use of motor boats, people caught fish by swimming or wading in the shallows with nets made from local plants—unlike any seen today—and just waited for the fish to come.

The power of marabouts

Marabouts played an important role in fishing by hitting the surface of the water with wooden batons to attract dolphins: they drove other fish into the shallows. Once I helped a **marabout** call the fish. He threw sand into the sea and assured us that dolphins were coming: he didn't know when but he was certain they would. To repay the **marabouts**, each fisherman gave them a share of his catch. They depended on such gifts. When the **marabouts** were angry, the sea grew rough, though today they seem to have lost some of their ancestors' power...perhaps it's because we fish in a different way, and don't rely on their powers so much.

When girls reach puberty, they stop bathing in the sea, because a woman's odour makes the sea angry, with tall, rough waves which scare the fish away.

In the past, a woman would never sit down with her husband with another man present, nor would a young person smoke in front of an old person. We women used to be busier, making grass or leather mats, finding wood to build our houses, and preparing fish. The mats were an important supplement to our income. If we had a tent to make, we would make it together. We would complete it in about five months; on our own it would have taken up to a year to finish. Now women are redundant. The grass used to make mats is no longer available; all our animals have gone, so we can't make tents from their skins or wool; and there's no more wood to collect for housing or fuel.

When the fishing nets were full, men brought them to the shore where *A woman's* women extracted the oil from the fish, cut off their heads, and dried them *odour* quickly before they rotted in the heat. People come here to obtain our fish *makes the* butter, which heals all sorts of stomach complaints and is good for infertile *sea angry* women. Mullet is the fish most commonly used for its healing properties, perhaps because it's the one that has always been caught here.

The height of the pile of fish bones outside one's house was a status symbol; a sign of one's success as a fisherman. Dried fish were sold to passing nomads or to the occasional European in a car. When we were young, we never dreamed we would see a car or a plane in our lifetime. I remember when the first plane passed over our heads, we all hid in the bushes because we were so scared. Not so today: I've even heard about the railway line....

Only men fish here and women are responsible for everything else. We used to cook with wood from the surrounding countryside. When there was not enough, we used fish head bones. They burnt well and smelt less than bones from other parts of the fish! Today, many fish are sent directly to town, so there are fewer fish heads and instead we use charcoal or calor gas. Gas is quick and easy but, as you can see from the burn on my daughter's arm, it can be dangerous. She covered the burn in toothpaste, because she was told this would help. Before we used to apply wet earth or henna to cool burns. Another treatment uses a red crumbly mineral, called khindinderaya, which falls from the sky; we grind it into a powder, mix it with water and put it on the wound. The dried and ground *sallaha* plant also heals burns. After treatment, the area is hit with cotton until blood begins to flow. This is to ensure that the burn heals without leaving a white patch on the skin and must be repeated several times until the mark disappears.

Before the famine, few people lived in Tiwilit. Then many of those repatriated from Senegal arrived to learn fishing from us, the Imraguen, who were born and grew up by the ocean.

Life was better in the old days. We had meat, milk and sometimes even rice from St Louis. We all had donkeys to collect water from the wells. Today, water is only found in Nouakchott—too far away even for our donkeys—and water-sellers charge very high prices.

Bad memories
We do also have some bad memories. Sometimes, when the nets had been drawn in and the share-out had begun, fights would break out—usually if it was felt that a fisherman was choosing out of turn or without permission. Much worse, though, was the fact that our villages were always being

Old people persecuted by neighbouring tribes. As we had no guns, we couldn't protect
know how ourselves. Invaders often struck in the early morning, when everyone was
to cope with asleep. As soon as people realised what was happening, they headed for
questions the sea—but usually the strength of the invaders meant they overcame
better than and captured us Imraguen. The lucky ones escaped to neighbouring
the young villages, returning only after danger had passed.

Our only hope was that our **emir** would hear of these atrocities and
bring justice. Once we were invaded by Mohamed el Mauron and
Mohamed **Ould** Lejrab. They ransacked Imraguen camps, took black
people as their slaves and looted our goods, cattle, grain—everything.
Emir Ould Brahim Salem was so angry that he pursued them. My brother
and I went with him and found them at Sebkhii el Ghazi, distributing all
our goods amongst their people. **Ould** Lejrab fired at **Ould** Brahim Salem
but, thankfully, didn't kill him. **Ould** Lejrab told us we'd better flee, since
it was clear we weren't going to win the battle. **Ould** Brahim, however,
refused. "We've only just come," he said. "How can we leave before we
have fought the battle? I will fight until one of us is dead." Happily, the
dispute was resolved before anyone was killed. We found one of my
sisters there, she'd been captured as a slave some time before.

Community responsibilities

Our chief is elected by the villagers and we trust him. A good chief must
be able to speak well, so he can tell people from other areas what we want;
and he must be old, because we find that old people know how to cope
with questions better than the young. Women cannot be chiefs, although
one small village near here has a woman chief. Her father, a very famous
marabout, had no male relatives to take over when he died, so his
daughter was elected. I can't see why a woman shouldn't be put in charge,
as long as she is strong and intelligent—the problem is that our culture
doesn't accept it. When our chief holds a meeting, only men attend;
women hold their own meetings to discuss issues important to them, and
elect a representative to speak to the men. The women's group organises
collective activities: they make mats and cushions from dyed leather, and
show visitors how to dry fish. The state gave them some knives and tables
for gutting fish, stands for drying them, and big cooking pots.

MR37   Hadi Ould Saleck (M, 50 years), Nouakchott

I was born in Wilaya du Trarza in the R'Kiz region which has grown into
a prefecture now. In those days R'Kiz was rich with big herds of cows,

Drying fish in the sun, Tiwilit village.

camels and goats. Our whole way of life was based on caring for these
animals. We stayed in our village for two months but spent the rest of the
year travelling. As soon as the rains came, we left R'Kiz and moved east.
We covered long distances, from pasture to pasture and well to well,
before finally returning home. If we needed anything, relatives or other
families in our group would help us. We never thought of getting help
from the state—we just helped each other.

Our groups were composed of 10 or 15 or more people. Women and
children rode on the back of donkeys, oxen or camels. Men were stronger
and more solid, so they usually walked to build up their muscles. The
relationship between different groups of pastoralists broke down when
resources were low; often arguments over access to well water escalated
into bloody gun battles. Our blacksmiths have made good quality guns
since before colonial times. Other guns have been bought in Senegal or
elsewhere. The main reason we have guns is not to make war, but to
protect our cattle from wild animals—lions, panthers and foxes—and to
a lesser extent, from animal thieves.

Pastoralists keep moving to find lush vegetation for their herds, so that
many young will be produced. They are aware of each animal's preference

I don't like to see water wasted—today's generation washes too many things
Treinicha Mint Beidi

for different food and water: sheep and goats are more domesticated and can eat the same things as human beings, and camels can last up to a month without water. Sheep and cows are fairly easy to look after because they wander about together—herds of 200-300 sheep and 300-400 cows are possible. Camel herds are more difficult to supervise, as they tend to go off in different directions—herds are limited to 50-100.

Building wells

We often arrived at wells with insufficient water to quench our animals' thirst and the only thing to do was build a new well. As a rule of thumb, we assumed a metre a day could be dug—though the deeper wells took longer. Before digging, the area was examined to decide upon the spot most likely to have a high water level. Lowland was normally better than highland. We dug with wood and iron tools, then the walls were lined with thin flexible strips of vegetation to prevent sand falling into the well.

My father and his ancestors were pastoralists, so I consider myself one too. To be a pastoralist, one needs animals. To travel with these animals, donkeys are necessary—they carry women and luggage. To provide drinking water, one has always to carry outres. These are goatskins filled with water, which keep the water cool. To sleep, one must have a **khayma**, made from bits of fabric or from sheep's wool woven by women. To wander without courting unnecessary danger, one needs a thorough knowledge of the countryside, because many get lost in the bush. If a shepherd is lost, he shouts, hoping that somebody will hear him. If his people know he's lost, they light a big camp fire and wave large burning torches but it's rare for an experienced nomad to get lost—he uses trees and other landmarks to find his way.

Environmental degradation is all around but we don't know how to fight it, which is why we have sounded alarm bells to summon governments and NGOs to our aid. We ask all good men to give a voluntary helping hand to all the Sahelian countries facing problems, especially Mauritania. If they do not respond, then I hold out little hope for human survival in this region.

Winds blow persistently throughout the year, forming dunes and sand hills. Our villages are surrounded by dunes, constantly threatening to close in on us. Sand blows across roads and tracks and accidents are caused —despite constant government efforts to clear the paths and start planting shelter belts to halt the sand's movement. The major reason for this desertification is the drought, which has killed much of our vegetation. There is also a human factor, particularly the cutting of trees for fuel and charcoal. It is encouraging to see government introduction of improved cooking stoves, which burn less wood.

All my animals were killed by the terrible drought. I became so poor that I had to leave my home to find food for myself and my family. I decided to move to Nouakchott. I was a pastoralist, a man of the desert, so was used to walking long distances: 210 kilometres did not seem such a long way. When I came here, I had no money. I did some daily labouring but found it so unreliable and unprofitable that I abandoned it and became a city farmer, tending this small vegetable garden.

Let my stomach burn from hunger but let me never leave my country
Mauritanian saying

Until I came here, I knew nothing about vegetable gardening, so a friend showed me how to use insecticide and fertiliser. These are of great value to us and improve production. Until recently, we spread fertiliser before planting new seeds. Now we have a severe water problem; it is pointless using fertiliser without enough water. We obtained water from the city's sewage treatment plant but they have recently cut off our supply because of money problems. This lack of water makes things worse—we already have enough to fight against each day. Prices are rising; we have no transport; moral values are being eroded; the young have no respect for the old and have begun dealing in drugs; delinquency is increasing.

Urban benefits

More positively, city living confers certain benefits, notably better access to a good education for our children. We never had this chance in my day. The Structure d'Education des Masses (SEM) organises many schools: it was set up by the government some years ago to implement social and community projects, including some for old people who have access to literacy and other classes. Also, we can go to clinics and dispensaries if we are ill. Most of the time, they just give out prescriptions to buy medicines but at least people are there to advise us. Here, we no longer use wild plants and herbal remedies.

I have six children. Four of them go to Qur'anic school: the others are too young. This is important, since the Qur'an is at the root of everything that we do. When we had animals a **marabout** accompanied us wherever we went. He gave us wisdom and taught the divine word to our children.

Women traditionally looked after the children and did all the cooking but today they play a bigger part in this country's development. Many women work alongside men in the vegetable garden and others are responsible for selling the vegetables in the market. In this garden, I mainly grow carrots, which my wife sells for between 40 and 50 **UM** a kilo. On an average day, she sells 4 to 5 kilos, thus my monthly salary must be between 4,800 and 7,500 **UM**.

Circumcision

In our tribe, we circumcised both girls and boys. A girl was circumcised by a skilled woman on the first Tuesday after she was one week old. Sand was mixed with charcoal and put around the clitoris, which was cut off by twisting a fine string around it: then the sand and charcoal were rubbed over the wound to stop the bleeding. Boys are circumcised when around ten years old. In the past, someone in the village traditionally performed this operation but today this is more commonly done in a dispensary.

Our group moved together and was mutually supportive. If other families were ill or in trouble, we helped them. If they suffered a particularly bad loss of animals, we made a collection to help them rebuild their herd. When someone dies, we are sad, but we never implore Allah to give us back the person's life. Allah gave us that person and Allah decides when the time has come to take them away. We bury the dead in the cemetery and spend a day reading through the Qur'an in their memory.

MR39   *Ladiba Mint Med Billal (F), Nouakchott*

> *Ladiba and her husband had recently been moved to a camp 8 kilometres from Nouakchott—an area designated by the government to rehouse the old people of Kebba (a shanty town outside Nouakchott). Their room was full of mementos. The wall was lined with bits of newspaper and colourful posters issued by the tourist office during a period of greater prosperity and before* **Sharia** *law was introduced. Outside, a goat sniffed the ground for food, tempted by Ladiba's wares on a small table. Ladiba had just ground some grain and was sifting out the husks into a bowl to feed her goats. She asked her husband's permission to talk and he encouraged her.*

My name, Ladiba, means serious or timid. I was born in Bousdeika village: it had a huge *sabraya* tree, under which we used to play as children. The thorn forest there stretched for kilometre after kilometre. I was a farmer's daughter and helped my parents in the fields. Our land was fertile and we grew enough millet, maize, haricot, sorghum and water-melons to be self-sufficient. We practised mixed cropping. Sorghum grew better with water-melon, and millet with groundnuts and haricot. Everything we grew, we either ate immediately or saved for the dry season. We rarely sold any produce, unless there was a large surplus.

Sometimes we supplemented our diet with wild animals killed by hunters in the forest. There were hares, antelopes, does, bustards and ostriches, as well as more dangerous lions, panthers and hyenas. Oh, I wish I could bring back those days, when nature was so kind to us! Now the soils are unproductive and the animals have gone. The reason for this must surely be the drought, which has impoverished the environment. I can no longer find the *talh* and *tijit* plants that I used to treat colic. We farmed a large area of land, needing many pairs of hands to reap its full benefit—which is why we like to have such big families. We prefer boys to girls because, in the long run, they turn out to be more profitable.

We prefer boys to girls because, in the long run, they turn out to be more profitable

I married my cousin, a common practice in Mauritania. Sadly, this marriage failed, so I left my village and moved to town. The first time I travelled, I went to live in Senegal. My village was scandalised by this because, traditionally, women do not migrate. Only men move to find work, some trading in foreign countries, returning but rarely to their villages, though often remitting money to support their family.

Women and men share labour between them, each one taking different jobs. Men work as hard as women: in the dry season, they transport millet, sugar, tea and cloth in camel caravans. But most important of all, they look after their animals, finding them water and pasture.

Women assert themselves more than when I was young. They were subservient, resigned to all traditional practices. They cooked and cleaned, cared for the children and helped in the fields. We have a saying: "Women go from house to grave." Today, with women elected into important public positions and government posts, people see them in a different light. Women here do all kinds of work: university professors, school and college teachers, traders and shopworkers. Even I do a bit of trading—you can see my tobacco, Omo, sweets and biscuits on that table.

Modern times

We have adapted to modern times, no longer cooking with wood and charcoal on open fires but using canister gas or improved wood-burning stoves. Also, instead of just millet and haricot, we now have rice, vermicelli, fish, macaroni and a wide choice of vegetables. Babies used to be breastfed for the first two years but now, particularly in the city, many women use feeding bottles. Personally, I have little experience of breastfeeding: I had one girl but she died when still a very small baby.

It used to be assumed that women should always look after their children. Now that more women think a change is in the air, it is a thorny problem. Increasingly, women leave home to go to the office and have to find a nanny or a creche to look after their children.

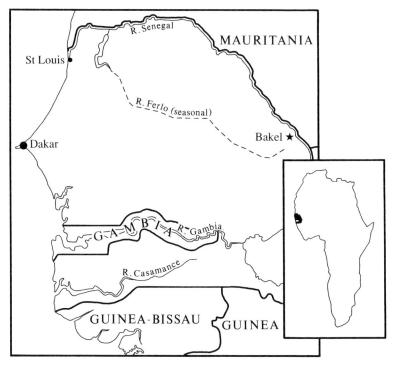

Country Profile: SENEGAL

Human Development Index (UNDP): 135th out of 160 nations
Population (1990): 7.3 mn. **Growth rate (1990-2000):** 2.9%
Life expectancy at birth (1990): 48.3 years
Population per doctor (1984): 13,060
Adult literacy (1985): male 45%; female 19%
Labour force employed in agriculture (1985-1988): 81%
GDP from agriculture and livestock (1989): 22%
Principal exports: fish and fish products, groundnut products, phosphates, chemicals, petroleum products

1960 June: after 300 years as a French colony, Senegal achieves independence in federation with Mali. September: Republic of Senegal proclaimed under President Léopold Senghor. **1966** Senghor creates a one-party state after outlawing other political parties. **1976** Constitutional changes allow formation of political parties. **1980** Senghor stands down, Abdou Diouf succeeds. **1988** Six parties contest general election: Diouf's socialist party wins 103 of 120 seats. **1989** Conflict with Mauritania. Up to 70,000 Mauritanians deported to Senegal.

SENEGAL

Interviews in Senegal were conducted in cooperation with the Fédération des Paysans Organisés du Département de Bakel along the Senegal River. **Oumar Dramé** and **Almamy Sy**, extension workers from this organisation, interviewed groups of farmers, pastoralists and fishermen, and work was coordinated by **Adrian Adams-Sow**.

Touré Timéra (F, 72 years), Yaféra   SE2

I was born in 1918 in Yaféra where I grew up. My father is a **marabout** who once had a lot of followers. Now there are no more **xarannimbe** left. To me, that's almost the end of the world. It was with my father that I studied the Qur'an.

My husband's name is Issa Hayidza. We had seven children, three of whom are dead. Three daughters and one son are left. All my children are married.

In the past, the bush was full of trees and the harvest was good. There were many trees, such as *gese, kuñe, tefe* and *xaame. Gaafe* and *fa* grew on the banks of the river. Grasses such as *baava* and *saaraxotte* flourished.

There were a lot of wild animals in the bush, such as lions, panthers, hyenas, hares and deer. I have seen them with my own eyes. In the river there were crocodiles and hippopotami. There used to be hunters in our village, but now there is no more game and the young today are not good hunters. There are too many machines, and all the animals have fled because of the noise.

There was no sand in the river before. The river has been getting shallower and shallower for some time now because it doesn't rain any more. When I was young, boats from St Louis passed by on their way to Kayes [Mali]. People came by canoe, bringing salt, pepper and other spices which we used to buy.

In the past, the wind was strong but there wasn't any dust. During the cold weather, you had to light a fire to warm yourself up, and the rain fell in bucketloads. During the floods, the water used to come right into our houses. It no longer pours as hard during the rainy season. I have lived through seven years of drought.

Peasants and pastoralists have always quarrelled but not as much as today

We used to reap a good groundnut harvest, about 10 or 12 sacks, and were even able to sell some of the crop. My husband also grew *ñobugu* and maize. Now you can pay out 5,000 **CFA** for a field without even reaping two **muudes**.

The peasants and pastoralists have always quarrelled but not as much as they do today. The pastoralists don't look after their animals, which damage the peasants' fields, and they don't want anyone to take their animals away. When I was young, it was the cows, goats and sheep which damaged the land. We built fences round our fields to stop this. Now the fields are no longer fenced in. Everyone has become too lazy.

In the past we bought our cooking pots, plates and other goods in Bakel. We walked 25 kilometres in a day. Now the traders bring us everything.

Men and women had different tasks in the home. Men made the roofs of the houses. Women wove and dyed the yarn, which they then sold. Women were also responsible for preparing the meals. In the past we used to make **couscous**, leru and *gombo* sauce, sangume or xaralle, and dried fish with groundnuts and *ñecce*.

For wedding or funeral ceremonies we made **couscous** with meat sauce. There was no coffee then. Instead of oil there was animal fat, and honey instead of sugar. While our children were being weaned we gave them milk and **pain de singe**.

We women suffered a lot in the past because of a constant chain of pregnancies. Some of our children died as a result. We had no way of avoiding these pregnancies.

I get ill every year. I suffer from asthma. I took modern medicine to fight it and God helped me. But I also use traditional medicines and they work very well.

When you are given a child to educate, you have to look after him, help him understand life without beating him and make sure he knows how to work and how to respect people so that when he is grown up he won't get into trouble. I was well educated and carried on the tradition. It's the adults who have changed. No adult nowadays wants his son to be scolded. That's why a child is rarely given away to be educated.

I will tell you a proverb: "I knock your head and you knock mine: all that happens is that we both get a headache." And now I will tell you a story. Once upon a time, there were two close friends who were together night and day but both of them were after the same married woman. Neither of them knew this for certain, but they each suspected it. The husband of the woman concerned decided to travel to Kayes, but he changed his mind because it was raining hard that day. One of the friends went to the woman's house. He listened to see if the woman and her husband were in the bedroom. He wasn't sure and climbed on to the roof. He was naked, and clutching his wet clothes which he then dropped. His friend, who was leaning against the door also wondering if the woman was alone, was hit on the backside by the wet clothes and ran into the woman's bedroom.

The woman's husband asked what was going on. The man replied: "I was asleep and a hyena came and licked my backside." Then the woman's husband chased him from the bedroom. He left quietly and went to find his friend. Telling him the story, he explained that when he had leant against the door a snake had fallen on to him. The friend told him he was wrong: "It was me who dropped my wet clothes on your backside. You told me that you didn't hang around there." Then the friend felt ashamed. That is why betrayal is a wicked sin.

Siga Gassama (F, 63 years), Bakel   *SE5*

I was born in Gandé where I grew up. I went to the Qur'anic school where I learnt just a few prayers. Otherwise, I learnt to farm the land, to dye cloth and to spin thread from cotton. My husband, too, was born in Gandé and we have had seven children: four boys and three girls.

In days gone by, you could find every sort of thing in the bush. The trees that grew by the river were *fa*, *turo*, *jebe* and *xiile*. At Jeri there were *kiide*, *saasingull*, *deye*, *tefe*, *sexenne*, *samba* and *xoofe*. Plants on the banks of the river were *bage*, *garaaje* and *binne*, while at Jeri you could find *soole*, *barra* and *dambare*. For dyeing cloth we used *tumbe*, *gese* and *yaafe*. *Xaame* and *deefe* were used in the treatment of illness. In the years of drought we lived on *jaaje* and other grasses, and cut *jongoone* or *dere* to survive.

Wild animals that lived along the riverside and at Jeri were lions, hyenas, wart-hogs, monkeys, **boyinaajos** and panthers. The village was full of hunters—Soninke and Peulh.

Before, when there was plenty of rain, the waters came up to the village and we could live off fish. Now the waters don't rise any more and the river has become shallower.

All the villagers went fishing together with the permission of the village chief and the **marabouts**, and when the catch was a good one we would offer fish to all the important people in the village. There were so many fish that we would dry some to eat during the winter.

In our fields we plant *yufa*, *xaarigille* and *niwa*. We inherited our fields from our ancestors. When I was young I worked in the fields with my mother and we grew groundnuts and *gombo*. When I married I grew groundnuts, millet, *gombo* and indigo. We cleared the fields and burnt the scrub. When it rained, I worked the soil. Our groundnut crop sometimes filled 5...10...even 20 sacks. We would go to Bakel to sell them in order to meet some of our needs. The millet grown by the head of the family was enough to feed everyone in the family—even if they were a thousand people!

There were no more worries once the food was stored away, except that from time to time the mice would gnaw away at it. We caught them with a boli, whereas today we use modern traps.

We used to work in groups. For example, we would get together to work for a rich man who would pay us after the work was done. This money was put aside for the whole village, ready to spend when the need arose.

The men from our house grew millet and maize. They harvested the grain and the chaff together and kept it in grainstores. Some harvested enough for up to 10 donkey loads, others four or six. That does not mean that the young men today are not prepared to work. It is only the lack of rain that makes them idle.

We let some fields rest for two years and we can tell when a field needs to be left if the crops that grow there look weak. In the past we didn't put manure on the fields but with the lack of rain people are forced to use fertiliser. It used to be that the rains always came and some fields were completely waterlogged.

Some people inherited their fields. Others held on to them by looking after them well for a neighbour, or they were given them by relatives. *Our farming practices of yesterday can no longer be of any use to the young* When you are lent a field, after the harvest you give the **jakka** to the field's owner.

Nowadays, we cannot grow food all year round. There is nobody left in the village. Since the rains have stopped the young can no longer produce good harvests. That is why they have emigrated. Our village started irrigating the fields in 1974 but it did not last long. We used to reap good harvests but nowadays, with all the problems that we have with the irrigated fields, we can't do much. But it's better than just staying still with our arms crossed. Our farming practices of yesterday can no longer be of any use to the young.

People from Mali used to come looking for work during the cold weather and during the hot season. The men from our village often went to Dakar or to France. They sent us money to buy rice, groundnuts, oil, dry fish and sugar for the family. Before, there was no real shortage of food but now there is never enough. We depend more and more on what our people who have gone away send us. It is the head of the family who distributes and buys the food.

I used to keep goats, sheep and cows but the illness called soono killed them all. Other people in my family also had plenty of animals. I look after the animals with my husband and we hire a shepherd whom we pay every month. The other illnesses that attack them are daaso and biriga.

We have quarrels every time we work our fields. There was a time when the Peulh knew how to respect us and when we found them in our fields they would offer us an animal by way of apology, whereas now the pastoralists are ready to quarrel with us and let their animals graze in our fields. This is all the more true since the harvests are no longer as good as they were.

Sometimes grasshoppers attacked the fields and the whole village organised itself to fight them by beating them with branches from the *xaame* tree or by burning dry grasses.

We use implements invented by different people. The sieves were the invention of **les blancs**, while the boxes for sowing the grain were made by the Peulh. We use gourds which grow in our fields as well as cooking pans made by **les blancs**. We make our beds by weaving *tabar* grass. In days gone by, we made our own cloth. Nowadays there is ready-made fabric for those who can afford it.

Social customs

If a new wife comes to the house she comes with clothes or cows, or goats or gold, if her mother has sufficient. Other wives join the household without all of that. The women prepare the food in turn, according to their position—the first wife, the second wife, and so on. That is still the way with the Soninke. Some new wives do not take their turn preparing meals on their own for two months, but during this time they help the other wives prepare. If she has enough, the new wife kills an animal for the first meal she makes.

At marriage ceremonies or funerals we eat meat or fish with ñecce. When a fattened cow is killed we cook it in its fat. We cook big fish in

All the young want today is to leave for France the same way. We used to eat honey collected by the young boys in the bush. We bought salt brought by ship and peppers brought by the Malians. Before, when we weaned our children, we gave them nothing but flour cooked in water and **fanco**.

During festivals, the young organised drumming sessions. They asked for the help of a **shaman** to drum the **tam tam**. It is the same for the marriage ceremonies. It creates a good feeling. We eat and dance and enjoy ourselves. Before, when a man saw a girl he liked, he would seek her parents' permission to marry her and they would ask him if there was enough to eat in his home, or whether you could hear the sound of grain being pounded there. He would reply: "Even in the hot season there is food to eat." Not much money was asked in those days, but now they ask for too much.

It is easier to bring up a child now than it was in my days. There is enough to eat and there are clothes to wear. If the arrival of **les blancs** brought bad things to the country, it also brought good. Our independence has not brought us respect, yet the colonials knew how to respect us. All the young want today is to leave for France. If they were brave enough to stay they could get out of their bad situation, because God has not created us only for pleasures.

SE9   *Wakary Gassama (M, 70 years), Bakel*

I was born in Gandé. In my youth I took a course in the Qur'an, but now I have forgotten everything that I learnt.

My wife was born in Moudery. We have had eight children: four girls and four boys. Nearly all of them are now adults. The village has changed since I was young. In those days if we went walking in the bush we had to take precautions against the wildlife.

Today nature is not as generous as it used to be. In my youth we used to be able to make beautiful mats using the grasses which grew around. From the *fak turu* we used to make **boubous** which men wore in winter.

Our livelihood was never a worry to us. It was the man who was responsible for buying the food. He gave it to the head wife who shared it with the other wives when it was their turn to prepare the food. During the hot weather the women prepared porridge for breakfast and **couscous** for lunch. There was also meat and fish available if we wanted it. For an evening meal we had *ñecce* and fish.

Our food supply for the year has to be well planned. After each harvest

we have to store a certain amount of grain, which we try to look after until the following year.

When a man asks to marry a young girl, her mother has to arm her with courage. Everything the mother can gather is given to the daughter to prepare her for her marriage. Even the father may help in collecting the cooking utensils, such as **calabashes** and ladles, that she will need for the house. Before permission is given for the wedding the man has to go and see the parents of the bride. On each visit the family repeat a number of questions. Have you got enough to eat? A hoe? A sickle? When they are satisfied with the answers they begin to discuss the sum of money involved: 25,000 **CFA** might be fixed upon as the **kola** for the father. The first instalment is given, and "eaten" by the parents, and then the rest of the money is given.

Marriage

People's attitude towards marriage has completely changed. In my day you could offer your daughter in marriage to anyone you liked. It was your choice, not hers. Today if you were to offer your daughter to someone she did not like, without her consent, you can rest assured that sooner or later she will cause you problems.

A new bride does not have to do any food preparation until she leaves her husband's bedroom. Women find nowadays that since the animals are not so well nourished and have so little fat on them, they have to cook the meat in oil. Children being weaned were given gruel and **fanco** to eat, seasoned with salt, pepper and milk if these items were available. Older children used to go to the river to catch little bakata, which they would eat for breakfast and lunch.

Young people used to be industrious. After working in their parents' field, they would go and look for their own work. But today all the young people have watches, and at midday they return to their houses to sleep. In the evening they go and play ball.

Certain households have beehives which supply them with a lot of honey. When sugar was difficult to get, we used honey instead. If visitors came we used to give them a bowl of honey to take away as a present.

A number of important items were supplied by traders. The Bambara came with pepper, onions and giiri. **Les blancs** came in boats, bringing salt which we bought with cash or exchanged for other items.

When somebody dies among the Soninke people, we kill three goats, one on each of the three consecutive days following their death. Those who do not have enough money to buy the goats get into debt, although people who come to offer their condolences, and relatives who have moved away from the area, should make contributions to help the bereaved pay off their debts.

When the rains were heavy the banks of the river would flood, covering our land in water. Sometimes we would have to bail the water away from the front of our house. If things were really bad we would be forced to move house completely. The young people would fish in the lakes created by these floods for our midday meal; the rest of us would wait for the water level to drop so that we could farm our land.

During the winter we only plant maize. On the lands which have been flooded by the river we grow a variety of sorghum. On the land where the water level has fallen we grow millet. Before planting the crops we have to clear the land and burn the weeds. Often the whole village would work together in one field, and in return for their labour the owner would

Nature is not as generous as it used to be prepare a big meal. After the harvest we give a small part of what we produce to the poor. All the white millet which remains we put in a grainstore.

Some years ago the women used to grow their own crops of wild rice, maize and indigo. Certain women sold a small part of their produce and put the rest in grainstores. Some would also help their husbands in the field, a practice which is not continued today.

When my father was alive he had nine cows which lived on the rich grasses. The animals used to suffer from a number of illnesses such as daaso and jofe. They were given injections which healed them. In those days one cow would be enough to supply milk for the whole family.

There have always been quarrels over land rights between farmers and pastoralists. The Peulh people leave their animals to destroy the crops in the fields planted by the Soninke. If a Soninke finds an animal causing damage he asks the village chief to resolve the dispute. If the chief does not settle the problem it is taken to the judge, who is the next level up in the hierarchy.

Today people do not pray or fast, or give a share of their harvest to the neighbour who helps them in their field. When the **imam** asks what sort of a man you are, the people will be forced to tell him that you do not pray. The day will come when you die and you will not have prayed. You must pray so that you will be saved in this world and in the next. Did you not know that we can only build with soil which is wet?

Today people do not pray or fast, or give a share of the harvest to the neighbour who helps them

Mbaré Ndiaye (M), Bakel   *SE10*

I was born and brought up in Gandé. I never attended any lessons at the Qur'anic school. My parents both came from Moudery. My mother grew cotton from which she used to make **pagnes** and **boubous**, since in those days there was no ready-made cloth to be bought in the market.

When I was young there were a great many trees and plants in this area. *Xiile* was used to make the framework for the roofs of our houses, on top of which we put layers of tightly woven *bili* grass. *Jebe* was used for the lintels of certain buildings before the **banco**

Young people was plastered on. Ground *xaame* was used for treating sick animals. It
don't seem to was added to their food. Nowadays, young people don't seem to know
know the the many uses to which trees and plants can be put. Besides, certain plants
many uses to that we used to gather, such as *saake* which grew in the flood waters, have
which trees now disappeared.
and plants   We were not the only ones living in the bush—we shared it with wild
can be put animals such as lions, hyenas and antelopes. They might not have been
immediately visible but they were all hiding somewhere. There were four
hunters in our village who used to hunt game, but since there are no more
animals they have had to find other activities.

The fish we used to catch in the rivers, lakes and tributaries included
balde, **anjobe**, accaare, **silanye**, **bappoore**, and **alluxunne**. The
community used to decide on a suitable day for going fishing together in
the lake, and those appointed in charge of fishing rights would oversee
things to ensure that all went well. Nowadays there is not so much water,
nor so many fish. Since 1971 the river has been drying up. Every year it
is a little shallower.

I remember thinking when I was young that the east was very black,
since the wind and the rain came from that direction. When winter began,
the temperature dropped as the hot earth soaked up the water. Today the
sky turns red from the colour of dust and sand—there is no rain.

Money had no value
People farmed land lent to them by friends or neighbours or given to them
by the village chief. In my family six of us used to farm together: my elder
and younger brothers and me. We planted maize and prayed that the rain
would not be too heavy and ruin our crop. The last thing we planted in the
agricultural year was *ñobugu*. Even the smallest of fields would produce
a large harvest. Now that there is no water we have to work much harder
to reap the same benefits. Once the harvest was gathered we put it directly
into grainstores; we had no need for sacks. In those days we didn't sell
our grain. Money had no value—the only time that we ever needed it was
to pay our taxes. Anyway, it was not a good idea to sell the grain since
everyone depended on it and families were large; men often had more
than one wife. Some years there was so much grain that there was no room
to store it. Women sometimes exchanged some surplus grain for cotton
to make into cloth. It was only in 1972 that for the first time we needed
money to buy food.

Since the drought began there has been no real improvement. It is only
thanks to the irrigated shore of the river that people have been able to grow
enough to stay alive.

Women used to have their own fields to cultivate, near the river banks. *Today the sky turns red from the colour of dust and sand—there is no rain* They grew millet, groundnuts and indigo. Although they plant the same crops, an important change has been that they no longer have to give most of their produce to the head of the family, but can keep it for themselves, sharing the profits with their daughters who help them in the field.

My father used to own a number of animals: cows and donkeys. Women owned their own animals—some had up to 15 goats—and quite often acted as shepherds for their own herds.

Rows between peasants and pastoralists were frequent since the animal herds used to do a lot of damage in the fields. During the colonial period there were rules of compensation about how much the pastoralists should pay to cover a farmer's losses. Now there is no formal system: all we do is row and fight with each other. I think the government should impose stricter sanctions against the badly behaved pastoralists so that we all begin to treat each other with more respect.

Land ownership

Not owning your land is a problem, since you have to move off if the owner wants it back. During my youth if you were lent land you had to pay the owner a **niinan kande** after the harvest—about 30 kilos of grain for each field. You also had to make a contribution to the **marabout**, who had no land himself. In return he provided us with verses from the Qur'an and magic charms. Although there were no rules about collective labour, we used to work on each other's fields and build houses together, as and when it pleased us.

In those early days grasshoppers were one of our biggest problems. We had various ways of fighting them. Some would lose their wings and fall into holes that we dug for them, and then we buried them. Or we would build fires under the trees where they settled, the smoke causing them to choke and fall to the ground. Nowadays science has advanced so much that we can get rid of them quickly and easily.

There has been a big rise in the number of people who travel around looking for seasonal labour on people's land. Some members of my own family move to the west of the country for the groundnut harvest. Others run to Europe or to other African countries where they hope to earn more money.

We used to make most of our tools and clothes. We carved **calabashes** and drinking vessels from wood. We even made our own beds. But for many years now, people have brought with them ready-made fabric from Europe, so the art of making our own cloth began to die out. There is a great range of goods that we can buy close to home, from markets and

Today, if shops, but everything is expensive.
you want to   I have two wives. My first wife gave me five boys and two girls but
get married only one of my boys has reached adulthood. The first wife used to be
you walk responsible for preparing the meals, although she was assisted by the other
around with wife in grinding the millet and gathering other ingredients. Nowadays the
a head full work is more evenly divided, each wife taking her turn at preparation.
of problems They make a number of different dishes: broth, and **couscous** served with
a sauce of haricot bean leaves or groundnuts.

     I was married in the traditional Soninke fashion, with young girls singing, and **griots** beating on the **tam tam**. At that time getting married was not such an expensive business. You simply had to prove to your wife's parents that you had enough money to feed her. Today, if you want to get married you walk around with a head full of problems.

Birth control

I have heard that the women used to have ways of avoiding unwanted pregnancies. Specialists in this area of knowledge, who were sometimes **marabouts**, would make charms which the women wore close to their kidneys. It is important that women should be well prepared before they bring up children since it is a task to be taken seriously. There was a time when mothers used to guard their children so closely that they would react if you so much as touched them—you would never consider hitting a child if it was not your own. Personally I don't think it's good to be over-protective. If you love your child too much there is a risk that it will not turn out well.

     Medical science has made huge progress and is beginning to be more important than traditional medicine. We suffer a lot from eye diseases. For common complaints such as stomach ache we drink a broth made from the ground leaves of the *sambe* tree. *Xiile* makes another popular traditional remedy. The branches of the tree are cut, put into water and boiled. When the resulting solution has cooled down, we bathe in it and drink it in the hope that we will soon feel better. For malaria we use the branches of the *jomba* tree. Again we boil the mixture and use the solution for drinking, bathing and massaging our bodies.

     When **les blancs** left and we gained independence, many people believed we would enter a time of total freedom, but we have found that even today we have to obey certain laws, regardless of whether or not we agree with them. I believe that young people should work in their own country, preferably in their home town or village, so that we can move forward in peace and goodwill. As long as we can recognise the correct paths to follow, we should be able to find a way out of our problems.

Kissima Binta Timéra (M, 69 years), Bakel   *SE13*

I was born in Yaféra, where I grew up. I followed Qur'anic courses for nine years. I learnt about traditional medicine, which I used to practise during the dry season, and I would also spin cotton into cloth. My wife was born in Tamba. From our union we had six children, four of whom are now married.

. In the old days people used herbs from the *deefe* and *yaafe* trees to heal themselves. The bush was full of wild animals such as lions, hyenas, panthers, monkeys and wart-hogs. In the water there were crocodiles and hippos. There were many hunters in the village but now there is nothing left for them to hunt. Before, when the wells filled up, the water would overflow and run into our houses. We had to use canoes to go in or out of the village.

In the past, we grew maize and sweet potatoes along the riverside but this was nearly 10 years ago. Now things are more difficult since the rains no longer fall. The women used to cultivate groundnuts and indigo on their land. They could harvest 10 to 15 bags. Today they can never gather more than three bags.

There used to be a clear demarcation between the seasons. The climate was a kind one. It enabled us to reap large rewards from small areas of cultivation. Nowadays, we can sow our seeds over the entire bush and still not reap any harvest. In my youth we used to harvest between three and four bags of grain, which proved enough for four of us to live on, and even after we had taken what we needed some grain was left to sell. But even in those days there were times that were not easy.

The land we cultivate is far from the village. During my youth I worked on the land with my older brothers. We cultivated millet, maize and sorghum. The land we farm belongs to us but not everyone owns his own field. Those whose ancestors were amongst the first to settle in the village have inherited land. Those who came later had no land of their own, so they were lent fields. After the harvest the tenants would give the owners a **jakka**.

We clear the field in preparation for the crops a few months before the rains. As a rule we can cultivate a patch of land for two or three years

Historically, before productivity begins to fall and *worowolle* and *taxaleeme* grasses
farmers and begin to grow. Today, we have tried to compensate for declining fertility
pastoralists by using lots of fertiliser. This practice is entirely new to us. We never
do not get on used to apply anything to our land.
well since   In addition to farming I used to breed cows, goats, sheep and poultry,
they are in until my animals were decimated by ill health. In the past cows might fall
competition sick once a year but nowadays they face a number of different illnesses
in one year. There are as many illnesses as animals.

Conflict

Historically, peasant farmers and Peulh pastoralists do not get on well
since they are in competition for the same land. After the farmers have
cultivated their plots it is not unusual for their land to be invaded by herds
of animals looking for pasture. The animals destroy everything and the
Peulh refuse to give compensation. Once, it was only cows that caused
damage. Now the sheep and goats are just as destructive.

It's not only against domestic animals that we have to guard our crops.
We have a particular problem when our grain in the store is attacked by
rats and insects. Today this difficulty is eased since we know how to fight
such troublesome pests. We lay traps for the rats, and we suffocate the
insects with smoke.

Since there is never enough work to last all the villagers throughout
the year, there are a lot of seasonal labourers. I myself went to a foreign
country to look for a job. I found life quite easy as I only had myself to
look after. If I earned extra money I sent it home to my family. It is the
head of the family who receives such gifts and distributes them among
the women of the house.

When we're not working in the fields we work on our houses, repairing
roofs and doing other odd jobs. We do not have the same sort of huts as
we did in the past and fences like the ones we used to build are hard to
find, as vegetation is more scarce.

Colonial times were better than post-independence days. Today, if you
beat your child he or she will lodge a complaint against you at the police
station. The present regime encourages children to rebel against us in this
way. When I was young we knew that if we were to be given food to eat
we had to plough the land night and day, asking all the time for God's
help—whereas today young people talk rubbish. The behaviour of a child
depends on the way in which he is brought up. If you are given a child to
raise, the most important thing you must show them is how to work. These
days it seems that the children bring up the adults, rather than the adults
bringing up the children.

The world is constantly evolving. Yesterday there was no cloth *Today, if you* whereas today even the very young and very old cover themselves in cloth. *beat your* In the past if you had a sweet you would have a few sucks and then pass *child he or* it on to someone else. Everything was shared in this way. *she will lodge*

For the future, I would ask young people to make sure that they educate *a complaint* themselves either in French or Arabic. One should always be searching *at the police* for knowledge. *station*

El Haji Mahamet Timéra (M, 84 years), Bakel SE17

I was born in Yaféra where I grew up. I never attended the Qur'anic school. Since reaching adulthood I have taken three wives. I only have four children, a boy and three daughters. Two of the girls are married.

In the days of my youth there were many trees and wild animals. If you happened to have a firearm in those days and went hunting, you couldn't come back empty-handed. There were plenty of hunters in the village.

The trees had great importance for us. For example, traditionally we used *tefe* to treat certain illnesses, and we used the dry wood of this tree as firewood. Medicine was also derived from the *ketebene* tree. The white herb, *sokkin gulle*, provided animal forage. The trees and wild plants could be very useful to the young people of today, if they bothered with them like their ancestors did. The other problem is that now it doesn't rain, and so the bushes don't grow any more. In my youth, when it rained it flooded. There was water everywhere. When you went into the fields you had to use canoes.

People fished together in the ponds. Those entrusted with the care of the ponds used to send messages round the surrounding villages. When everyone had taken his place the fishing would start. Nowadays there are far fewer fish.

In my youth maize and beans were grown beside the river and the yields were good. Nowadays the land doesn't produce and the river has begun to lose depth. That started nearly 16 years ago, and since then it's only got worse. The cause is the lack of rain.

The fields we farm are inherited. In my youth I worked with my father and my younger brothers: nine of us in all. We grew sorghum and maize. The fields were first cleared, then sowed. When the crop started to come up, you worked the soil: once, twice, then a third time. As soon as the first fields were ready, all the family and friends came to help with the harvest, and to carry it to the granaries. And so on to the next field, until all of them

In my were finished. At that time of the year everybody worked together. The
youth, bonds between family and neighbours were stronger than they are now
when it and even the weakest were respected.
rained it   We didn't put the harvested grain in bags. It was the custom to take the
flooded whole ear of millet to the granary. Normally there would be about 30
donkey loads of it. We didn't sell our harvests, except when we hadn't
enough money to pay taxes. The whole family lived on these harvests, as
well as those strangers who lived among us.

In my youth I lived through many years of drought. It was the members
of our family who had emigrated who gave us the financial help to survive
those bad years.

Fields would be cultivated for seven to eight years. You would know
the soil was losing its fertility when the weed called *worowolle* started to
come up. We didn't use any fertiliser.

Our village started irrigating crops scarcely 14 years ago. The first
years gave good rice and maize yields but with the passing of time the
yields got less. I don't know what's wrong.

I used to rear many kinds of animals, such as cows, sheep, goats, horses

Often when the rains do fall, they carve gullies out of the parched soil.

and poultry. The drought killed a lot of them. In the end there were only nine head of cattle left. The main problem was disease. There are many more diseases these days than before.

Crop damage

I have helped to mediate many times in disputes between peasants and livestock raisers, since animals will always cause damage to the peasants' fields. In the end the owner of the animals would compensate the injured parties. In the old days the bonds of this relationship were tighter. If somebody's animals damaged your field you'd forgive the offence gladly, whereas nowadays the injured party must always be compensated.

The animals which used to damage the fields when I was young were wart-hogs, monkeys, birds and locusts. We used to combat this by shooting them or hunting them with dogs. To scare the birds off, we used to beat drums or anything that makes a noise. These days there are different methods of combating these pests, such as modern firearms and even explosives.

In the past, insects used to destroy the food we kept in granaries. We used hot cinders against them.

Seasonal labour

Many people used to come to our village looking for work. A family would take in one or two. In that way they could share the week's work: three days for the one in charge, and four days for the seasonal labourer. The seasonal labourers of our youth were real workers and respected the agreements made with those in charge. Today, the seasonal workers don't

---

SE18 Sadio Dramé (M, 62 years), Gandé

At night, the women used to spin cotton threads for weaving. From one fence of the enclosure to the other was enough to make two or three **pagnes**.

Fishing yesterday and today are two different things: yesterday you went to fish in the lakes, whereas today you have to fish in your pocket. If you have anything in your pocket, then you can get a fish, but if you don't—you won't have any fish.

The **marabout** used to have a field of his own that his disciples cultivated. He had a hundred disciples. He used to go to the bush carrying a collapsible chair, while the disciples laboured.

In the past there were ways for avoiding pregnancies in too rapid succession: forms of traditional medicine, or methods known to the **marabouts**. One way was to take the veins from the neck of a black monkey, and attach them to the neck of one's child. A woman would do that even if she was already pregnant, in the belief that she would not be delivered of the second child until the first one was ready for weaning, or that even if she gave birth too soon, that the two babies might take milk together, as though they were twins.

In the old days, your child was everybody's child work honestly—they knock off early. They are shirkers! I have never been a regular seasonal worker but I have been to Dakar, where I stayed for three months, and the Congo where I stayed for three years. Some of our young people have gone away to France. When they emigrate, those who think of us send money from time to time. The rest forget us completely. Some come back when they've saved a bit of money; some stay away for good. To me, that shows a lack of feeling. If you leave your country, surely you must have it in mind to return one day, with or without savings. We don't depend on them but on the head of the family.

It's the head of the family who buys the food for the household. If he has a reliable younger brother or son, one of these will help him in the task of buying what is needed, whether rice or millet or oil.

The key to the granary is entrusted to the oldest woman, who is responsible for preparing the meals and asking for millet, rice and oil to be supplied. This requires good understanding in the family. When that exists, there is complete unity. When it doesn't, you can be just as sure of complete breakdown.

Before, when there was a marriage, we fattened some bullocks or some sheep, but our children have seen that there is too much waste in this custom as everybody wanted to do as well as his neighbour. The poorer people would get up to their ears in debt to buy a cow or two. So we have come to make do with just fattening up some smaller animals, such as a ram. At the wedding the boys used to dance the **jamba** or the lombi, and the girls had other dances.

When you chose a girl, you would give a present to each man in her family, either individually or something for all of them. Some of them asked for a lot of money. Eventually, all that was done away with. Now, everybody concerned gets together and discusses it: first the

be, o d'i ga giri soxoodi muurindi rexe, n'i misaale.
Baane yan ciro ga ni feela ke be, i q'a xilli csм
219. Ku beeni ga d'a soxo, i do soxaanon katta
me deemana na me ku soxoodi.
   ▶ Golle tana ñagi, nga daga
   bogu debin lemme yogo
   desamburu 1987. Kamo
   naxati sere yan ñi ken
   debe, xa ken debin lemme
   ya, yugu xaso karagi do
   funbe ga tagana tan-
   jikke yaxare d'i remmu
   baane yan toxo debe
   ke ya.
   Kutten cu daga
   golli muuri dingira
   tana.
Yaxaru ku beeni ga
toxo debe ke ya, yogoni
saage fexen jaagu katta dingiro
beeni yillen neyen ga ni. Xoteyen ñi maxa
baawoni m'i gan da fexe ke wutu tambo, a
jonkon ñi xotoon'i da. Yaxaru tanani ña mulla
na basallen coxo gede kurumba yogo kaara xa
xaalisi ma ñ'i maxa kuudo na soxoodin qobo.
   Yaxaru ku ñi deemanden mulla x'i ñi kanna
tambon guttu, woyiri, xaalisi be ga kinini
                              4

Oral history in Soninke. The Fédération des Paysans Organisés,which conducted the interviews in Senegal, is now drawing on the community's recollections for their literacy training programme.

men, and then the women. They decide on a sum of money which is shared between them all, men and women. The big change is that formerly everything was done in absolute secrecy, whereas now everything is in the open.

These days it seems that the children bring up the adults

Kissima Binta
Timéra

Health

It was the **marabouts** who looked after people's health, preparing holy water and **gris gris**. They used to check up with people to make sure that they weren't affected by any disease and would prevent or cure ailments. The healers didn't ask for much. In fact, it was the sick man who made the offer. Nowadays, the healers ask for a lot.

When I was 18, I was stricken with **segeremmes** and the infection made me very tired and weak. I cured myself with *xiile*. I boiled the plant in water and when it had cooled I drank some of the liquid and used some to bathe my foot. When the wound swells up you have to make a little hole to let the infection come out.

Two members of our family caught leprosy: my brother, Moyi, and my son, Mamadou. They lost their fingers and their toes. They went away to Mali to be looked after by the Bambara who gave them a special medicine to drink and completely cured them.

The **marabouts** had their own personal fields. Each **marabout**'s land was worked by his pupils, around 30 in number. Nowadays it's different. People prefer the modern Qur'anic classes for which they pay. Personally, I have never farmed for a **marabout**. I will only go to see one if I want him to do **gris gris** or to pray to God for me when I have to travel.

Today's education is different. Nowadays it is rare for a child to listen to his parents' advice. The adults' attitude has changed too. In the old days, your child and another person's were equal in your eyes and your child was everybody's child. If a child did something wrong the first person to find him would give him a sound beating, without any fear of upsetting the parents. Nowadays, you've only to scold a child and the mother gets angry. Besides, the child will not listen to you.

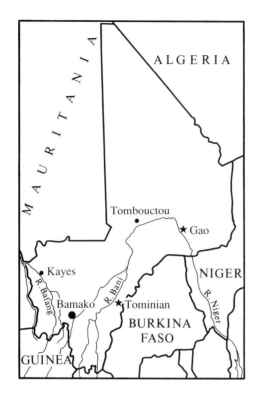
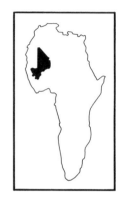

Country Profile: MALI
Human Development Index (UNDP): 156th out of 160 nations
Population (1990): 9.2 mn. **Growth rate (1990-2000):** 3.2%
Life expectancy at birth (1990): 45 years
Population per doctor (1984): 25,390
Adult literacy (1985): male 31%; female 15%
Labour force employed in agriculture (1985-1988): 86%
GDP from agriculture and livestock (1988): 49%
Principal exports: cotton and cotton products, livestock, gold

1883 Colony of French Soudan established. **1960** June: Independence in federation with Senegal. September: Republic of Mali established under civilian government of Modibo Kéita. **1968** Coup led by Moussa Traoré, head of Military Committee for National Liberation. **1985** Five-day war with Burkina Faso. **1991** Traoré overthrown, Lt.-Col. Amadou Toumani Touré sets up transitional administration, promising full elections before January 1992.

MALI

Interviews were carried out at two sites in Mali. The first set of interviews were gathered on the site of SOS Sahel's Community Environment Project in the Cercle de Tominian. **Pascal Dembélé,** senior extension worker with the project, and **Brigitte Koné**, head of the women's programme, conducted interviews in Boré with sedentary farmers. The second set of interviews took place in the Arrondissement de N'Tillit near Gao. Work was undertaken in cooperation with Association Tassaght,and two of its members, **Agali Ag Alhouda** and **Hadijatou Walet Mohamed Aly**, acted as interviewers. **Pathika Martin**, head of extension and training at SOS Sahel's project, coordinated interview work at both sites.

Zouma Coulibaly (F), Somalo   *M3*

I was born and raised here in the village of Somalo. My parents were true peasants who lived off the land, whereas I earn my living in a number of ways. I spin cotton, grow onions and gather fruit from the *karité* and *néré* trees. Together these occupations bring me a comfortable living.

I remember **les blancs** coming to look for labour for road and bridge building, but I didn't go to work for them as my parents were comfortably off. They had slaves to do all the work on our land. With only two children—me and my sister—our parents could afford to spoil us. I was particularly pampered because I was the youngest daughter.

In my youth there were no schools around here. I got married when I was very young although I don't know exactly how old I was. My parents found me a fiancé and of course I had to marry him. In those days the groom's family would give baskets of groundnuts to the

My mother told me of people so desperate that they gave their children away in return for grain parents of the bride to secure her for marriage. After my marriage I had 10 children but some of these were lost.

Long ago I remember a serious famine—there are not many of us left who can talk of this. There was so little rain that the ground dried up and men could no longer work in the fields. We had to resort to picking wild leaves from the trees. Those were hard times and many lives were lost.

We have also suffered plagues of grasshoppers. They cause enormous damage, ravaging our crops and leaving nothing but a few leaves on the trees. My mother told me stories of some people becoming so desperate that they gave their children away in return for grain to eat. When the insects appeared the second time, I was quite grown up. I knew how to look for food on trees—something that the young people of today would not dream of doing. We ate leaves from the *prunier* and the *matous* trees. We would find newly laid birds' eggs which we ate before they hatched and the birds flew away. We also managed to kill a few of the grasshoppers to eat. We would kill these little enemies by hitting them with sticks and stamping on them. I must have been about eight years old at this time—at least I remember that I was old enough to wash the dishes for my mother!

Solidarity

There were no acceptable means of earning extra money during periods of shortage. In those days you never heard of anyone turning to prostitution or theft to survive. People helped each other in the only way they knew how. There has always been a strong sense of solidarity and support in our community.

When the rains were good and trees bore fruit, we spent a lot of time making butter from the nuts of *karité* trees. Some people convert a corner of their house for this work. The *karité* butter is stored in large clay pots where it keeps well, although it will eventually decompose, especially if it is left in the sun. We sell the butter in the market, along with nuts from the *néré* tree, which people use to make **pro'h**. If we don't want to sell it straight away, *néré* can be ground into a sweet powder for use in cooking. We do the same with another popular fruit, which comes from the baobab.

These raw materials were plentiful in the days when the land was thick with trees. This area, where today the houses are standing, was once like a forest. You could barely see that village in the distance through the trees. Now they have all gone, and we can only blame God for the crisis. Of course, we do not say that we have not played a part but we are not the main factor. After all, is it man who makes rain? No! Do not point the finger at men. But I do fear for the younger generation who disregard our customs and traditions.

The uses of trees

Each tree had its own uses. The best fuel came from the *karité*, the *botouro* and the *ye'o*. We did not cut the tamarind tree for fuel because people believed this would result in someone getting hurt. Today, to find these trees you have to travel much further than in the past.

A great number of trees were used in the preparation of traditional medicines. The *karité* can be used to treat many childhood diseases whilst the *raisinier* and the *néré* are used to reduce fevers. As far as food preparation goes, we make **tô**, from a millet flour base, and **couscous**, **dégué** and a broth. Vegetables such as peas and haricot beans are cooked and eaten with oil. Each cook has her own special methods for preparing the food—although some things are quite standard, such as the way we pound the millet to make it into tiny pieces, or into the fine flour used to make **tô**. Some foods which were popular in the past, such as sweet potatoes and yam, are now very difficult to come by. We used to grow a lot of these root vegetables, but now we have to pay a high price for them in the market. But although it is difficult to acquire certain foods we are not undernourished.

Years ago I remember when the ponds were so deep that fish swam around in them. Today the water sources have dried up, and all the trees which were so useful to us have suffered from the drought.

The landscape is now so empty that it is safe to go out alone without fear of being attacked by wild animals. Paths and open spaces have replaced the trees. In my youth, if you left the house to go to the village of Somalo you had to carry arms to protect yourself. Women could not travel on their own, but had to be accompanied by a man who was armed.

Climate change

The climate has obviously changed and the periods of heat and wind are more extreme. In the past the heavy rains, lasting between six and seven months, used to cool the temperature. During the rainy season we did not leave the house until the sun had risen. Now the wind is stronger because there are no trees to block its path.

The soil in our fields is red and sandy. It is no longer as rich as it used to be and so the harvest has diminished. Today, in order to feed the many mouths, we have to cultivate larger and larger areas of land. We have always applied natural fertiliser to our soil. Animals are often left in the fields after the harvest, to enrich the soil. They are put in one field, from which the manure may be gathered and applied to other areas. Nowadays chemical fertiliser is available too but you have to be rich to afford it.

I have noticed that certain crops which we used to grow, such as

We can only blame God for the crisis....After all, is it man who makes rain?

sesame and haricot beans, are no longer so common. Those crops we still grow are troubled by weeds—the most common are *zna*, *nama*, *vi'chinmin* and *oro'dodo*. What is more, the soil is cut into by deep ravines. These have appeared since the trees died, when the land became exposed.

The use of water is not restricted. It belongs to everyone because it is a gift from God to us all. If you want to you can dig a well for yourself—but if somebody wants to take water from that well then it is their right. Our philosophy is that you must never refuse to give someone fresh supplies of water. Whoever digs the well is responsible for its maintenance, although they can ask for help from their neighbours.

Apart from the wells we have few facilities. There are no schools and no dispensaries. We are isolated, with very little to find encouragement in, but we have to manage. We have dug dykes and built stone barriers around the lake to try to protect the soil, but they have done little to improve the situation. We need help with our work. Up until now I do not recall any help from the government or from development projects. It seems clear to me that the new project planned here has not come to harm

M32 Wareifar Ag Innala (M , 70 years), N' Tillilt
People who farm and keep animals at the same time don't have the same problems as those who only practise one activity....When nomads plant trees we can look after them as long as we stay in that place, but as soon as we move on, stray animals destroy them. So long as we are not settled, we have no means of protecting the trees.

us. If it manages to do some good then all of us will gain.

Women's work has had to adapt to the changing environment. Today, women do not always seem to reap the reward they deserve from their labours. We put a lot of energy into the land but we get little from it. If you are too ambitious you will be disappointed because you gain so little. Men have freed women, and now women are always looking for something that they have not got.

Women work all through the year; men work only during the rainy season

I think it is true to say that modern women are busier than ever before. The work of men and women is divided unequally. Women work all through the year, whereas men work only during the rainy season when the crops are growing. After that, they can rest until they have to prepare the fields for next year's crops.

Batomi Dena (F), Somalo   *M5*

I do not know what my age is today. I was born in Pa'amalo and grew up in Embere'ui. My parents were farmers but I chose a different livelihood, selling tobacco. I never went to school but my youth was easy since my parents had slaves to work on the land. My parents had a fiancé for me but I never married him because he was called away to do forced labour. When he did not return, I had to marry someone else. By this husband I had 12 children but only two are alive today.

Some time after I had married and moved to Somalo there was a terrible drought. I stayed where I was but my family left the area because there was so little to eat. Another terrible memory is of the time the grasshoppers arrived and feasted upon my brother-in-law's ripe grain. All we could do was try to kill them by stamping on them and hitting them with sticks.

Many things have changed since my youth. Once there were many trees, but now they have all perished. Can anyone other than the good Lord be responsible for this? Perhaps it is because we no longer observe our customs and traditions.

Today there are so few trees around the village that counting them would not take long. We have always valued trees to use as fuel for cooking. For construction the favoured trees are *ye'o*, *an'anou* and *houanaou*, while artisans use *bor'rio* and *bro'iwe*. Because the trees are now so scarce we spend a long time collecting wood.

Reduced rainfall
I think the trees have disappeared because it no longer rains. It used to be much colder and water would stay in the ponds throughout the year. Today

we suffer from an extreme heat which we cannot relieve by bathing because we are so short of water. In the old days there was a custom, according to which you could not go to the pond carrying objects made of iron—nor were **griots** allowed to go to the water. These traditions are no longer respected.

Where the pond once was, the land is dry. I can remember when everyone—even the Peulh people—used to come and use the water. Nobody was refused access. There was only one well in the village but that too dried out and so we blocked it up. In its place other wells have been dug by local people.

When the rains were good our harvests were plentiful. The soil was so rich that even if we did not weed our land we would still reap a good harvest. With a small field a peasant could grow sufficient for his needs. We try to improve the quality of the soil by keeping animals in the fields. Some people also use chemical fertiliser which has recently been made available but it tends to dry out the millet crop when the rainfall is poor. To bring life back to the soil we may leave it to rest for a few years.

In the days when the rains were good we were happy, even though we lacked the basic equipment that we needed. We didn't have modern ploughs and we cultivated the land using **dabas**. A plough can help a peasant cultivate an area 5 to 10 times as large as that he could work by hand. But, unfortunately, intensive farming has had some damaging consequences. It has exhausted the soil. Ravines have dug deeply into the earth and many ditches have been created by ploughing. Our land has been spoilt by modern tools.

Agricultural expansion

In the past we were satisfied with small plots of land but now that ploughs are available people want to expand their farming area. If they try to tell you that they do this because there are more mouths to feed, do not believe them—they have lost their sense of reason. In the old days, farmers cultivated a small area of land, but still fed many mouths—even more than a farmer who today farms a large area with his plough.

It is the woman's job to do the cooking. Our favourite food is **tô**. When the rains were abundant we grew a range of vegetables in our gardens. Today we have fewer nourishing foods but malnutrition is not a problem. It is true, though, that our children often fall sick and we do not know why.

Of course, environmental changes have meant that our lives have altered. We no longer support each other as we did. Men and women had their own jobs, but we used to help each other, within the family and in the village. Today everyone works for him- or herself; there's no

Now that ploughs are available, people want to expand their farming

cooperation even between wife and husband.

Population numbers have risen and so has the number of cattle which each person owns. People today are full of ambition which is always driving them to want more. They expect more luxuries in the way of food and clothes. But I don't think they work harder than we used to. Whatever we wanted we always had to work hard for.

We used to live simply.... Today we buy clothes for our babies before they are even born

"The world we used to know"

We used to live simply. A young girl might reach the age of marriage before she began to wear any clothes. There were even young men who wandered around naked. Those were wise times. Today we buy clothes for our babies before they are even born. Some people even change their clothes during the day, putting on one outfit when they collect water, another when they gather wood and another when they go for a walk. In the past we were happy with what we had, including the fiancé who was chosen for us.

Children had better manners than they do today. They respected and worked for their parents, and honoured the community. Today, children think they can do without their parents. Don't they realise that their parents are not their rivals? They abandon their extended family, leaving their parents to face old age on their own. They think only of themselves. Some expect to share everything while they are here, then they migrate when they feel like it and return only when their father dies, to claim their inheritance. The way the young mistreat the old is worrying and upsetting. We are left wondering what has happened to the world that we used to know. I think it is ambition and increasing independence that make people behave this way. We are now counting on the development projects in the area because if we depend on our children they simply deceive us.

Maybe education has brought about this change between the worlds of the young and the old. Perhaps that is why children today do not bow their heads in front of their fathers. Today it seems that only parents are responsible for their children's upbringing, whereas before the whole community was concerned with a child's education and progress. As a result, some children receive no instruction. If some children are fooling around and you try to discipline them, later their parents come and complain about your interference. Since our families have become so divided, barriers have been put in the way of a good education.

Our village is run by a chief, whose power is handed down through his family. So the traditional and administrative power always remains with the same family. But it is the national government which makes more demands on us. In my youth we were never weighed down by taxes whereas today we seem to spend the whole year paying them. We have not yet experienced any development projects but I must say that anyone who is working to develop our country is welcome. We just hope that they will be able to bring us some happiness.

M8   *Kouahan Sanou (F), 'An'oro'ui*

I was born in Bè'èui. We moved to Boré'ui, and then to Ira, during a time of great drought. When the drought ended and the famine came, my father decided to return to Bè'eùi. I was only a few years old at the time. Later we came here, to 'An'oro'ui.

My parents were quite comfortably off. My father used to look after more than 80 cows a year in the bush. We had food and animals, and we children were well dressed. When I got married I brought animals for my husband and I wore the most beautiful cloth in the village. But there were also long periods of drought and famine during my childhood, when all we had to eat were leaves and roots. I was barely 10 years old at the time, but I can still remember the **Bobo revolt** when the village of Bénéna was destroyed and all the families took shelter in the bush.

After the great drought, the locusts came. It was terrible. They arrived in the year that I got married, although I don't know how old I was then. They devastated everything in their path.

I have never been to school as there were no schools where I lived as a child. After my marriage I used to help my husband with his work in the fields. I do the housework. Everything was all right when we were working. But my husband didn't live long. I have had nine children and only two of them are still alive today. This house is full of graves.

I have never thought about resorting to stealing to solve my problems—I would rather die than do that. As far as prostitution is concerned, it doesn't exist. Our culture doesn't allow it.

We used to have traditional medicines, including a powder of dried leaves that was given to working women to bring on childbirth. It was the old people who knew all the remedies. I don't know if old people today are as wise. Some animal meat is used as medicine. For example, there is a very dangerous snake whose flesh is used as a cure for **icterus**.

Certain plants and animals are particularly important in local traditions. Every clan name is associated with a particular animal or plant. For example, for the Diarra clan it is the lion; they respect the lion and do not kill or eat it. The mere sight of a **totem** animal is considered to be a warning sign.

Our vegetation used to be very dense. Trees grew right up to the borders of the village. Now they are nearly all dead. You have to go into the heart of the bush to find wood. When I was young we only ever used *dua* as firewood. In our area, Bobo, we use all the plants in our cooking.

We use *an'anou* and the *an'ansouire* trees as building materials. We were forbidden to cut the *karité* tree and use its wood for building, given its special properties. Nowadays, we use the dead *karité* tree for building. We use the *an'anou* for making pestles and mortars and *houanaou* for making pickaxes.

In the past you could hardly see the village for baobab, *figuier* and *néré* trees. The lack of rain and excessive sun have caused the change. There are worms in the roots of the trees because of lack of water. We sell sap from the trees at the market. In the past, because we knew as soon as a tree began to lose its sap it was nearing the end of its life, we did not over-exploit them. Nowadays, there are so few trees, we take sap from any we can find.

In the old days there was no migration. After the harvests, the young men stayed in the village and worked on other things such as building and mat-making. Nowadays, they hurry away as soon as harvesting time is over. The women are going to have to learn about such jobs. But even the women go. They leave to become servants and often come back pregnant.

In the past men had all the power. They were the bosses. Women had no rights at all. The village chief was a man and he had control over everything. We obeyed him and treated him with respect. We did as we were told, in a submissive way. Today, there are other chiefs, with authority from outside, and they have given women new responsibilities.

A different vision

Our children used to be well-behaved and did the work we gave them. They used to make their parents proud. Nowadays it is quite the opposite. The more children there are, the more moral codes they break. They are no longer taught how to behave. In the past the whole family from all over the village had a say in a child's education but now people don't get

In the past the whole family from all over the village had a say in a child's education

Today only together to discuss children's education. They are left to do as they please. *parents are* We older folk used to believe that the youngsters would take over from *responsible* us. It is every man's dream that his son will follow in his footsteps. Sadly, *for their* the youngsters today don't fulfil our hopes. They disappoint us, because *children's* they don't have the same vision of the world as we do. *upbringing;* The size of families has changed. We used to have large families. *before the* Father, mother, cousins, uncles, children and their husbands or wives, *whole* everybody shared the same meals. Today, everybody favours smaller *community* families. The child detaches himself from his father. The women want to *was concerned* create their own individual families. In the past, the head of the family *Batomi Dena* used to want his family to grow. Today's generation is self-centred. Nowadays when the head of a family dies, the children inherit everything. Before, his brothers would inherit his possessions.

Our lives have also been changed by government policies. The effects have been both good and bad. Government officials don't beat us any more. Before, they used to whip us frequently. But we only paid taxes once a year then. These days, after taxes, we still have to make other financial contributions. We spend the whole year thinking about how we are going to pay them. We'd rather be whipped than have to pay these endless taxes.

We prefer the development projects. They have brought us happiness and hope. Even if we old people don't see this future happiness, our children will benefit. **Les blancs** don't wish us any harm. The problems exist within the country itself and that is no good. When our village receives help it gives us hope. When the Canadian brothers built the well, it gave us enormous encouragement. They came to the village when we had no water. We will be even happier when we have schools and community clinics.

M10   Obo Koné (M, 77 years), 'An'oro'ui

It was my grandparents who founded the village of 'An'oro'ui. My parents had a lot of farmland and also used to hunt a lot. They grew large quantities of grain and also had slaves to work for them.

I was born in 1912. Like my grandparents, I am a farmer and a hunter. My farm was so profitable that I was able to purchase 100 head of cattle. Unfortunately, they died following a vaccination during a particularly hot May. I continue to live from the crops that my land produces, although I no longer grow so much because the land is poor and I have fewer animals.

In those early days our way of life was simple and natural. Today I think that life is better—for both men and women, although as time goes by the family becomes more and more dislocated. Migration from this area also disrupts our social structure. The **Bobo revolt** and major famines both led to much migration.

Today I think that life is better, although as time goes by the family becomes more dislocated

Traditionally, the old chief determined the laws and took the decisions. Women were given second place to men and had no right to make any major decisions. Each one of us knew his or her place. We lived together as a community. When we worked together as a group, perhaps helping someone to harvest their millet, at the end of the day everyone would be given a **calabash** full of grain—even the old men and women.

Marriage

When a woman becomes pregnant, her progress is carefully followed. If she gives birth to a girl, then one of the families who have watched her pregnancy may ask permission for the girl to become engaged to their son. Even at this early stage the family who have made the request begin to pay the bride-price. Every harvest they give a certain quantity of groundnuts to the family of their son's bride-to-be. All the time, they know that once she has matured they will lead her into their home—thus girls are raised knowing that this will happen to them. If the young girl should die, the family must search for another bride for their son.

Under this system, if you are to have wives you must be rich, and have support from your family. I had four wives, but now three of them are dead and I am left with just one. You can, if you wish, remove your wives from your home. I have had several children through my life—including two boys, both of whom have wives of their own. When a young couple get married, they are advised about the basic principles of marriage by the elderly people in the neighbourhood.

Young people should continue to follow the traditional customs of their ancestors. Instead, they are beginning to embrace strange religions which clash with their own, they talk about the price of everything, and have grown more and more lazy.

In the old days we would batter a thief to death if he was caught, which is why we rarely had any such disturbances. Today, however, we would no longer kill a thief, instead we leave it to others to judge their crimes. I think, though, that criminals are treated too leniently today, and as a result we suffer from more thefts. In the old days, we never even knew what prostitution was. Infidelity was always frowned upon and cursed. Even a widowed woman could not remarry before she had gone through a special ritual.

Claims for land can cause tensions between people in neighbouring villages. There was, for example, an old man, a real nuisance, who was chased from Bénéna and arrived in the village of 'An'oro'ui. He was given land here to help him survive. The old man had children, who grew up in 'An'oro'ui. These descendants went back to Bénéna, but now they feel that our land is theirs and have tried to reclaim it. So disagreements have arisen between the people of our village and those in Bénéna—even now our children are being constantly bothered by their claims. A meeting was held to discuss this problem. Unfortunately, the inhabitants of 'An'oro'ui could not state their claims as well as the people of Bénéna, who are richer and more powerful. So the inhabitants of Bénéna continue today to exploit our land.

Population growth

It is impossible to ignore the rising numbers of humans and of domestic animals, particularly at the beginning of the rainy season when the Peulh arrive to stay for the growing season. They camp near to the village and leave after the harvest when surrounding vegetation has begun to dry up.

Although we no longer have enough land, I do not believe that the population should be controlled since we also welcome as many able hands to help on the land as we can get.

Locusts, which have plagued us four times in my life, have been responsible for endless devastation. To try and control their numbers we hit them with sticks and build fires. We wear sandals with hard soles to trample on them—this together with the smoke from the fire may eventually chase them away. When they fly away, however, they leave the fields without grain and the trees without leaves—famine then closes in on us. Thankfully the state has given us a lot of help. They have shown us how to protect our fields and chase away the insects by digging trenches and using metal sheets.

When I was young, the rains were good and the vegetation was thick and green. Plants, men and animals lived together in harmony. The soils were fertile and productive. Then the rain gradually petered out. We began to cut the trees down and lose respect for our old customs.

Today the environment is sick, the soils are poor and hard, and the trees are dead

We don't really understand what happened: suddenly the rain lost respect for its old cycle—it no longer lasted as long and the hot and cold seasons have been disrupted. Today the environment is sick, the soils are poor and hard, and the trees are dead, having been scorched by the sun. To make up for poor harvests, larger areas of land have been given over to cultivation. We can only afford to leave land fallow for one or two years, compared to four or five years in the past. To make up for this we try to apply more fertiliser. Another major change in our methods of cultivation has been increased mechanisation. One person today, for example, using new equipment, can farm an area that would have needed 10 people in the past. Then we had to plough by hand using a hoe; today we have special tools to sow, weed and plough. Improvements have meant that we no longer have to bend double over the fields.

One person, using new equipment, can farm an area that would have needed 10 people in the past

Soil erosion

If there is no vegetation cover, the wind raises the dust and the top layer of the soil is blown away, leaving the ground bare. On soil which has been stripped of vegetation the water runs off quickly, digging ditches in the ground as it flows. In the rainy season, when these ravines spread fast, some people try to build barriers against them, although these are often carried away by the swiftly flowing water.

I believe these changes can be attributed to the fact that we have lost respect for our customs. We have violated old prohibitions to allow room for modernisation and in so doing we have disregarded God's laws.

The joy of water

In our village water is free and everyone is given equal access. Women supply their homes with the water that they need, while the men mend any wells in disrepair. At one time, we suffered from severe water shortages which we overcame by getting fresh supplies from neighbouring villages. We consulted numerous charlatans to try to find sources of water, but without success. Then we campaigned for a borehole to be sunk in the village. I made thousands of trips to the chief of the arrondissement in Koula. I was eventually granted a meeting. A few days after my return, without any warning, a car arrived in the village, driven by a white man who began the work. He worked through the night and by the next day water was gushing out. There was great joy in the village. When the job was finished the man made no mention of payment, he simply got in his car and left. After this fortuitous event the team who installed the pump made us pay 200,000 **CFA**. Beside our pump the young people have built another large well, so we now have water in abundance.

The government today has eased many of our problems and brought us peace. However, in addition to the benefits there have also been negative effects, such as the high taxes we have to pay.

As for development projects, I think they are an absolute mess. To begin with, everyone is keen on them. Then after some time certain people, who think they are clever, begin to distrust the project and avoid the work it does. Others, who realise the benefit that they personally can reap, attach themselves to it like leeches and suffocate it. Having said this, it is true that people still believe that development projects can strengthen us, and improve the desperate situation in which we find ourselves.

M11   Se'e Dembélé (M, 70 years), Tana

I was born and brought up in the village of Tana. My parents, who were farmers and also tamed horses, used to make hoes and ropes for their work. The religion they practised was animism. I followed in my parents' footsteps and have worked the land all my life.

When I was very young I was engaged to be married. During the engagement we gave groundnuts each year to the girl's family until she reached maturity and we could marry. I had four wives. One of them died, and another is in Bossokuy. Of my remaining wives, one has two children but the other has none.

Looking back on my life, one of the most distressing times was when the locusts swooped down on the fields. They plagued us for about five years, although we tried to frighten them off with sticks and sheets of metal. We tried to bury them alive in holes in the ground. We even trampled on them, squashing their bodies with our sandals. In those days we planted groundnuts and *pois de terre* as these were the only grains that were resistant to locusts.

Soil fertility

Just as today, the harvest was stored in the grainstore. Although we worked smaller plots, our yields were higher. We always managed to feed everyone in our family. Nowadays, people have less to eat but more money. We used fertiliser on the soil, and the thick vegetation helped protect it from erosion.

After cultivating a piece of land for six to ten years we would leave it fallow to recover its fertility. We did not use what we did not need—we only exploited the land that was necessary for our survival. Today there is not enough land. If we were to leave a field empty somebody would immediately ask if he could use it. In these last few years, since the rains have been so unreliable, farmers have begun to plant crops on the fertile land along the river banks.

Although we worked smaller plots, our yields were higher

The environment has been so degraded that the situation is now critical; the soil, the animals and the people are all suffering. The village used to be surrounded by impenetrable forest where many wild animals could be found. Some of these troubled us by killing our domestic animals. As the forest began to disappear the wild animals fled, seeking refuge elsewhere. *It was with* If you look around the village today there is hardly a tree to be seen—only *the arrival of* a few sad-looking seedlings. Certainly mismanagement has contributed *religion in the* to this deforestation. Trees have been cut down to make way for farmland *area that* or to provide timber for building, and other areas have been grazed to *people's* nothing by the animals. *respect for*

The best and strongest wood was used for building. The *karité*, *néré*, *the vegetation* *o'o*, baobab and *prunier* all bore fruit which the women would pick. To *began to* help conserve our crops we used to mix them with a small amount of ash, *diminish* obtained by burning bark. To dye material we put the bark of the *raisinier* or the *houanaou* in a large pot of water and soaked the garment in it. After a few days it would be yellow. The length of time that we left the material soaking depended on the exact style, design and colour that we wanted. In this way we could produce **boubous** which were red, white and yellow.

The vegetation was always respected and the use of plants restricted. We never cut down fruit trees. Anyone who broke this rule had to make a payment to the chief, in the form of chickens. It was with the arrival of religion in the area that people's respect for vegetation began to diminish.

Climate change

In those days, when the vegetation was dense, the climate was much more predictable. We knew that the rains would last from May to November. The cold season was between March and April. In May the trees began to sprout new leaves. The countryside looked beautiful and clouds floated through the sky. When the wind blew towards the east we knew winter was on the way and when it turned again towards the west it was a sign that winter was over. Now, when the winds blow strongly, they lift up the topsoil and expose the ground to the sun's rays. Where there are bushes and grasses this happens less. We don't really understand how or why all these changes have come about, but I suppose when you look at the disunity of the people it is not so surprising. After all, our customs and traditions have also been eroded.

In the old days, when the rains fell the people were united. In times of need we helped each other, and if we were able we would lend money to our neighbours, knowing that it would be paid back when times were easier. During the period of the loan one member of the debtor's family would stay with you until it had been repaid. Today all that has changed.

There is an old legend about our village which tells us that it was supplied with water by two old wells. They were connected to an underground tributary of the river, which was why we so often found rice stalks floating around in the water. The other water source was a pond

In the old days, when the rains fell the people were united which gave us an abundance of fish of all varieties. But now the source is silted up with sand and the water has dried up.

During the famine whole villages began to move from one site to another. The movement was provoked not only by the famine but also because some people were ambitious and wanted to take advantage of other areas by conquering and looting whatever they could. Women didn't leave for the towns, except in exceptional circumstances, such as if a tax payment was due which they could not afford.

In our society there is an age-old hierarchy which is accepted as part of our custom and tradition. The chief and the elders form a sort of ruling body, taking decisions on behalf of the village and resolving problems. The rules of the village are strict and revered.

There was a time when population numbers here were high, but since the trees began t disappear, the population has decreased too. It may be that the actual numbers are still higher than they were before, but it is certainly true that the death rate is higher—people are less resistant to disease. In contrast, the number of domestic animals in the area is rising. We never used to keep many animals ourselves, but now the Peulh people are seeking the chief's permission to move permanently into the village.

Urban drift

In these modern times our young people are not satisfied with the opportunities they are given in rural areas, so they have moved to the towns and cities. Many social conflicts have resulted from this behaviour. If there was greater unity and if the rains returned I think that more people would be encouraged to stay where they are and not leave for the cities.

With all the changes that are taking place, we feel as if all we can do now is to run along behind, trying to keep up. The changes have been both good and bad. We have benefited from new equipment and people have taught us new ways of going about our work. Although there aredevelopment projects in the area, at first we didn't understand what the projects were trying to do. Now we believe we should place our trust in them because we realise we cannot begin to redress the damage done without their help.

We older people feel disappointed in the young of today. Before, children and young people had a lot of respect for the elderly. I would like to see things return to how they were before, when the young enjoyed communal work, when they were considerate to other people and they followed the traditions of their ancestors.

Wa-Intane Ag Ahratt (M, 70 years), Marsay   *M25*

I am a member of the Kel-Agheris family tribal group. In the beginning
the Tuareg were divided into three social classes: Illalane (nobles),
Eklane (former slaves) and Ihadane (blacksmiths). Our way of life has
altered and it is the Illalane who bear the brunt of the changes. In the past
we had cattle and slaves, but all that has been lost. Our women didn't do
anything apart from having children, because everything was done by a
slave. As for us men, our only important work was looking after the
animals, checking that a cow wasn't lost, or even sold. If that happened,
then the slave suffered. Now we are discovering that life needs more and
more effort on our part: "Everyone for himself, God for everyone," as they
say in Tamashek.

We have had to adapt by starting small businesses, such as gardening,
and by managing our income more carefully. When you sell a goat you
are paid in a few kilos of tobacco which you sell among the former slaves,
who grow the cereals such as *fonio* and sorghum. Women are also
beginning to wake up from their deep sleep. They have started pounding
grain, tanning skins and making cushions and woollen tablecloths. Among
the Illalane, both men and women have become more aware.

The climate has changed because of the thoughtlessness of man, the

Men no longer have the right attitude towards God increased intolerance and lack of friendship. I have noticed the way that traders and merchants enrich themselves illegally. During the dry season, when life is hard, they increase the price of a pot of rice, and also when you look at the amount in the pot you find it's no longer as much as it used to be. Men no longer have the right attitude towards God.

Nature adapts

It's not by comparing this year with last year that you notice the change in climate. You have to observe it over several years. The rainfall is less, the winds have intensified and after each fall of rain there is a tornado which dries out the earth. The plant cover has changed and many species have been destroyed.

Around this camp in the old days you might see a lion or another ferocious beast at any moment. That shows how dense the vegetation was. Acacia is now the dominant species—it has increased while the others are gradually disappearing. *Cram cram* too has increased because, like acacia, it retains moisture more easily than other species. So nature is adapting to the climatic changes.

Abarom is used to construct the straw huts. *Akarkar*, too, is used for construction, and for tent supports, because of its resilience. *Ahirdjidjim* is used to treat stomach upsets and *adjar* to treat malaria. For firewood we prefer acacia, because it is easy to light and is good for making into charcoal. We still don't have to travel long distances to collect wood.

Everyone has the right to water, except that it varies according to need. Those who build a well are responsible for it. People build wells, usually 2 metres deep, when the ponds dry up.

M1 Bianhan Coulibaly (F),'O'a
In the past, nobody could dress themselves without first weaving the cotton for their garments.

M6 Kanou Kamalé (F), Tana
We old people thought that you would take over from us, and when we died we left a hope behind us but having seen your generation, we realise that we can't count on you.

M9 Nazoun Koné (M, 65 years), Worokouma
Fields used to be small. When someone made a big field, people said that this spoiled the property of Selo—the god of the earth.

M14 Noumoa Dembélé (M, 65 years),Tana
A man used to wear his first breeches when he had his first fiancée. The suitor would go to bed wearing his father's breeches, or an old sack that they used to put on the back of a donkey on journeys. My grandfather wore his first breeches at the age of 27, when he married for the first time.

There are two main types of soil: clayey soil for cultivating sorghum, and sandy soil for early millet. The yield varies. When we do not have enough, it is often because predators such as rats, locusts and millet worms have attacked the crops.

Whenever there were showers, men met together and followed the rain

Some land is left fallow for three years, and some not at all. Sorghum can be cultivated for many years in succession so long as there is manure and plenty of water. But millet needs a latent period, without which there is no yield. Different species do not work well together; even millet and sorghum grown together do not produce good crops.

A changing landscape

The slope between the small windbreaks around the fields and the variations in soil level on each side of the stone barriers tell us the direction of the prevailing winds and their strength. Dust storms can cause several types of erosion. On flat land they carry away all the plant cover. They also cause dust deposits in certain areas. On the whole the dunes are stable, but we have noticed that after the last years of drought there have been sand deposits in places where there weren't any before.

At Marsay Achachul there was a flat piece of land. The nomads used to play a game there when they gathered together before taking the animals to good grazing lands. They used a ball, usually made out of cowhide, filled tightly with straw. They hit it with special curved sticks which could send the ball a long way. This type of sport can only be played on flat land. But on this same piece of land there is a dune today.

The problem of the dunes started in 1973. Nothing is done to stop this scourge, this advance of the desert. Ravines began to form in 1985, after the heaviest rains that have ever fallen in the area. Ravines grow more quickly in the years of high rainfall than drought. In some places, such as Tinderewal, which used to be a good water catchment area, a lot of water is lost in winter through run-off.

Agro-pastoralism

For the Tuareg, the linking of pastoralism and farming is the result of a new awareness. Before, when there was abundant livestock, we didn't need to combine it with anything else. But today we have noticed that the combination could reduce our problems and help us have a better life.

There is no comparison between yesterday's way of life, when we moved around all the time in search of pastures, and today's seasonal migration. Before, all the conditions were right: we had plenty of livestock, and animals to carry people, tents and baggage. Whenever there were showers, men met together and followed the rain. But today we have lost everything. There's no question of moving somewhere else.

Now we belong to a world of cities—but in these years of food shortages urbanisation hasn't solved any of our problems. On the contrary, it has made matters worse because everyone thinks only about himself.

There has been a change in the size of the family, which is a result of poverty. When you have 10 or 15 children with no source of income, you wish you had fewer children because you cannot feed them all. In the past this didn't happen at all. You wanted to have more children.

We sell plant products when the family has more than it needs. **Jujubes** are made into **ahofar** and sold to the riverside people, the Sonrai, or the town-dwellers for 500 **CFA**. **Tanin** is also sold for 100 **CFA** a pot and wild dates are sold by the pile from 5 to 25 **CFA**.

Those who have the means manage their resources well. For example, when you have a bright son, you give him his share of the livestock in money, which he then uses to make a profit. All of you, according to your means, contribute to the family's wellbeing.

M42   Inawtil Ag Ichanaghe Yallah (M, 90 years), Tin-tihidjeren

My tribal group is the Ikarayrayane. By tradition we are nomads but in recent years the number of our livestock has decreased and we have begun

to settle. We thank God that volunteers have helped people become more settled. But there are many other changes which we find disturbing. Urbanisation is destroying the old way of life and people have lost the ancient ways of contentment and courage.

The years of drought have made us take greater care of our resources and encouraged us to work hard together in the fields. But nature is no longer kind to us. The winds have intensified, eroding the soil and causing widespread damage. Then with the first downpour of rain the good soil is carried away to places where it is no longer of any use —ponds and ravines, for example. To stop this, we are now building stone barriers.

Sandstorms have increased and many plants have suffered as the land turns into desert. Those that we can still grow today—gum, **jujubes**, wild dates and others—are generally sold in the towns for between 5 and 100 **CFA**, depending on the size of the pile. Drought has also brought rabbits and small rodents such as rats and squirrels, which come searching for food.

Farming methods

We farm in the traditional way, by hand. First we clear the fields and then begin to sow, and at this stage all the available members of the family take part. You make holes, putting two or three seeds in each, and then cover them with a thin layer of soil. When the seeds begin to sprout, you have to watch them and pull out the weeds, and protect them from rodents and other animals. After the harvest the grain is stored in granaries. In the past, before we began to settle, we did not use granaries and when there was a surplus we dug a pit in the dunes to store it there. But this system had several drawbacks: the grain could easily be stolen, and it was affected by the heat.

Our government encourages participation whereas once it was only the heads of the tribal group who were told about government plans. Today we are informed about government decisions, representatives live among us and our children are in charge. Everyone is responsible for their actions. We can only thank God for that.

In our society it is our nephews who inherit. According to legend, a man of the Imghad tribe wanted to know how much his daughters loved him. He pretended to be suffering from a mysterious illness, and he said: "Only the blood of a grandson can cure me." His daughters refused, but his niece immediately offered her son. From that day on he promised that only his nephews would inherit. The **marabouts** have not been able to break this custom although some people leave their goods to their children. The son receives double the amount the daughter receives.

I think that young people should be more courageous. They become too impatient when faced with problems and think that life should be easy. But "nothing is gained without effort". As the Qur'an says, life on earth is leading towards an end and we should be living towards that end. As a **marabout** I once consulted said to me: "Help yourself, and heaven will help you."

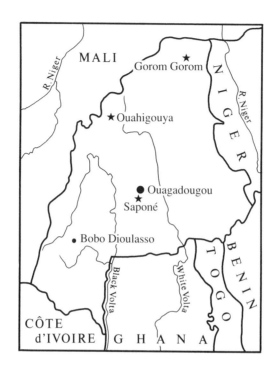

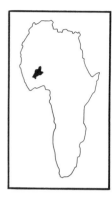

Country Profile: BURKINA FASO

Human Development Index (UNDP): 154th out of 160 nations
Population (1990): 9 mn. **Growth rate (1990-2000):** 3%
Life expectancy at birth (1990): 48.2 years
Population per doctor (1984): 57,220
Adult literacy (1985): male 23%; female 6%
Labour force employed in agriculture (1985-1988): 87%
GDP from agriculture and livestock (1988): 39.2%
Principal exports: cotton, gold, machinery and transport equipment, leather and skins, livestock

1919 French create colony of Upper Volta. **1960** Upper Volta becomes independent state, with a civilian administration and Maurice Yaméogo as president. **1966** First in a series of military coups. National Assembly dissolved and constitution suspended. **1983** Captain Sankara and National Council of the Revolution take power and rename country Burkina Faso, "Land of the People of Integrity". **1985** Five-day war with Mali. **1987** Sankara assassinated, Captain Compaoré's Popular Front assumes power. **1991** Plans for constitutional referendum and multi-party elections.

BURKINA FASO

At Ouahigouya, in the north of the country, interviews with settled farmers were conducted in Mooré by **Camille Bernard Kabor**, a researcher from the Institute of Human Sciences, Ouagadougou, and by **Mariam Maiga**, women's officer with the organisation Six S (Se Servir de la Saison Sèche en Savane et au Sahel). At Gorom Gorom, in cooperation with the Union des Groupements Villageois d'Oudalan (UGVO), interviews were carried out with pastoralists and agro-pastoralists in Peulh and Tamashek by **Abdoulaye Diallo**, a researcher at the Institute of Human Sciences, and by **Alimata**, a local woman. The third site, Saponé, is the base for an integrated rural development project run by the Association Vive Le Paysan. Two extension workers from this project, **Ilbouolo Yabré** and **Adèle Konseïga**, conducted interviews with local farmers in Mooré. Work in Burkina Faso was coordinated by **Rhiannon Barker** and **Rosalind David**.

Kabré Gomtenga (F, 70 years), Saponé   B4
Samné Goama (F, 140 years)
Roamba Tampoko (F, 40 years)

During our lives there have been many changes. It does not rain as much as it used to and the harvest from our fields is not as large. Farming has become much more intensive and people have claimed larger areas for cultivation. Now one person may have the area that five people would have farmed in the past. This has been made possible by the new labour-saving equipment, such as animal-drawn ploughs. Those who cannot afford this equipment can farm only about 30% of the area farmed by others. Grain has become much more expensive. When we were young you could buy a huge amount of grain for 50 **CFA**. Now the same amount costs 1,800-2,000 **CFA**.

We can't use fertilisers since we have no means of transporting them to the field. The only way in which we try to improve the fertility of the soil is by each year changing the crop variety in a certain field. When the soil was more productive this was not necessary. We could plant millet for up to 10 years on one plot of land without the soil becoming tired.

A number of weeds persistently appear in our fields and can seriously reduce the yields. They include *wôgo, yodga* and *tim-timtinga*.

We have cut down all our trees and as a result the wind makes us suffer because it erodes the soil. We have been educated about this problem and now we build **diguettes** to try to reduce the damaging effects of erosion. We have plans to build shelter belts. Ravines can also damage our fields and to stop these enlarging we put stones in the path where the water flows.

We remember when, to find firewood, we only had to look behind our houses; today we have to walk up to 8 or 9 kilometres. The most important trees that we have in our area are the *karité* and the *néré*, while the most valued animals are goats and cows.

In the past we had various means of making extra money. We used to go to Ouagadougou where we would trade in a small way, buying and selling butter, kola nuts and wood. Now we ask our children to do this for us. Unfortunately, if the child has to walk—or even if he has a bicycle but simply does not want to go—he may refuse.

Nutrition
In the past men and women took joint responsibility in some areas. When one of our children was ill, the man and his wife would take some water in a gourd and carry the child over 20 or 30 kilometres to the home of the traditional healer. Now a mother can go on her own with the child to the dispensary; the journey does not usually take more than 30 minutes or an hour. On the whole, the health of our children has improved since there is now a much greater variety of food for them to eat. When we were young we only had **tô**, fritters and wild leaves to eat. Now we supplement this with vegetables, fruit, rice and **couscous**. **Soumbala** has always been an important supply of vitamins. The most common illnesses that we suffer from are measles, tuberculosis and worms.

The health agencies have taught us about hygiene and the conservation of water. We know that water must be kept covered and should be changed after two days. During the winter we collect our water from the pond, a kilometre away. When this dries up we have to walk 5 or 6 kilometres.

The way we work has become more collective. When I was young, it was rare for people to meet up except on festival days or when the chief asked for a collective effort to be made in somebody's field. Today men and women help each other. We have a number of collective fields in our village where we work together for the development of our area. In this way we progress faster and exchange ideas. When our neighbour is in difficulty we are always ready to help.

Our young people are shrewder than we were

We can see with our own eyes that the population in this village has grown during our lifetime. In 1930 there were only about 20 families here. *Men no* Since then this has more than doubled. We believe it is good to have large *longer have* families so that there are plenty of children to help us in our work. *such power*

The number of animals owned has also greatly increased. In our day *over women* there were only two farmers who kept animals, whereas now there are more than 10. Our young people are shrewder than we were. They go to Côte d'Ivoire where they make enough money to buy more animals. Some peasants manage to earn enough money from selling rice to acquire livestock—only the richer ones who own a lot of land.

Movement around the countryside has been made much easier by motor cars. Before there were any vehicles we would walk up to 25 kilometres at a time before we took a rest. We would carry water for the journey in gourds on our heads. Today it only takes about one hour by car to get to Ouagadougou, whereas it used to take us over a day.

Before development schemes started in the area we were without a dispensary, a well, a main road or a school. Now a lot of improvements are being made and this should encourage people to come and settle here. Our life is good.

Changing relationships

In the old days, it was the elderly people who gave us our education. If you wanted advice, for example if you wanted to leave your husband, you would go to the old people in the village to ask for counsel.

If a woman was stubborn and did not obey her husband then he would punish her by giving her maize to crush or perhaps by beating her. Now the men no longer have such power over the women, who are freer than ever before to do what they want. Men and women still have a definite division of labour. Men build the houses and do most of the farming. They look for straw to make the grainstores. Women grind the millet, cook the food, collect the wood, help with the harvest and have children. Women also have a small plot of land to farm themselves. They play a supportive role in community work and administration. For example, we have helped our husbands get medicines to stock the dispensary.

Circumcision was once seen as an important event. There were lots of festivities and people played the **tam tam** in the bush. Today the operation is no longer treated with much ceremony. By contrast, marriages are more lavish affairs than they used to be. The bride used to receive a **calabash**, a plate and a traditional straw basket called a péla-wê. For the last 10 years or so people have had to spend much more money, as the bride is not satisfied unless she receives many dishes and many **pagnes**. Funerals are the same. In the past a bit of **dolo** and **tô** was enough but now you need a whole bag of rice, lots of **dolo** and lots of **tô**.

We have no methods of contraception other than abstinence. Women try to wait three years between each child. If the woman has co-wives then this is easy enough. If she is the only wife and refuses to sleep with her husband, then there is a danger that he will take another lover.

B5   *Fatimata Sawadogo (F, 62 years), Ouahigouya*

A frail woman, Fatimata was sitting on a woven mat in the middle of her courtyard, rolling out balls of kaado which she then laid in the sun to dry. Kaado is made from sorrel leaves and is used for flavouring food in the Yatenga region of Burkina Faso. Fatimata sells the kaado in the local market to earn a little extra income. Her courtyard was enclosed by the walls of neighbouring houses and even at this early hour the heat was bouncing off the red sandstone. We sat on a second rush mat, in front of her kitchen and in the shade of the millet granary.

I was born and brought up in the village of Songondin in the Zogou area, which is in Yatenga province. I received the same education that most Burkinabè farmers gave their children. At an early age I learnt to farm as well as to spin cotton, weave baskets and carry water on my head.

I earned my living from weaving baskets. At one time, I could make more than 30 a month. Now I only spin cotton. I have given up weaving —and farming—as I am quite often ill.

One of the things that most dominated my life was my marriage. I didn't want to stay with my husband because he was too old for me. I often used to try to escape but my parents refused to let me leave my husband. I had four children with this man and when he died I was left alone to bring them up. They often used to go to sleep at night without any supper. Sometimes we would only be able to eat one meal a day. During the drought of about 10 years ago, we would sometimes resort to eating wild leaves, like *eligo* and *keglu-vando*. I never turned to stealing or lying—just struggled even harder to survive.

Silent women

Before, it was a silent life between men and women. They never spoke to one another, not even husband and wife. Neighbouring women would pass the evenings chatting and spinning, and you would talk with other women at the wells or at the grinding stone. Women never spoke in the presence of men: they'd be ashamed and above all scared that they'd be beaten by their husbands on returning home. So women kept their ideas to themselves, even if these would have been a help to the community. Women are never allowed to inherit the land of their husband. As this is normal here, women never complain, thinking "that's how things are". Nowadays, the radio is a major source of information. This keeps women up to date with all the news from the area, the town, neighbouring countries and overseas. *Development projects have helped women*

We now have women who preside over meetings in the villages, in the local area and even in the towns. They have all been democratically elected by village groups and through other political structures. Development projects have helped women greatly in their work, through meetings and by helping them to visit different areas and exchange ideas about different social structures.

Migration

The Burkinabè people have always liked to stay in their area. They value the elderly people in their families and don't want to leave them. However, sometimes lack of food forces people to leave. Generally, it is only the young people who are able to move. It's too difficult with old relatives. In this area, women go along with their husbands if that's what their husbands want. There's no such thing here as single women migrating.

Whenever I had a child I didn't mind whether it was a boy or a girl. The essential thing was that God might bless the child with a long life. I prefer a large family. If some children die, there are still some left to help you when you are old. To help ensure I have enough to survive on—both millet and money—I have worked hard to bring up my grandchildren. Sometimes my brothers, who live in Côte d'Ivoire, send me the odd present but it is a hard life for an old woman.

The dishes that we prepare are **tô, couscous**, haricot beans and leaves and sometimes rice. Only rich families can eat rice. I cook everything on a wood fire. Before, a family would eat only one main meal a day, in the afternoon. Anything left over we ate the next morning. Now almost all families prepare food twice a day.

The division of work between children is important after they reach 10 years of age. Then the young boys are put in the care of their fathers to learn about men's work, while young girls stay close to their mothers to learn about the type of work that women do. In some ways the behaviour of children has changed. Old people are not satisfied with it; they think children now are impolite and don't have enough respect for their parents.

There are four of us who cultivate the land for our family. We store the harvested millet in granaries and dry our groundnuts and peas. There

A Mossi village

are times of difficulty when you can't work because you're sick with malaria or some other disease and so the amount of work the family can do diminishes considerably.

Climate change

It used to rain a lot. From planting to harvest the soil would be moist. The trees were thick and full and the countryside was rich with wild animals. People were content because it was never hard to find food. Now the soil has dried up and people are unhappy and worried about the future. The degradation of our area has taken place since about 1970. It has been caused by lack of rain and by men cutting down the trees. The number of wild animals has decreased considerably. You can only find rabbits, porcupines and big rats these days.

It's now begun to get hot and dry in March, April and May. It's hot and humid from June to October and then dry and cold from November to February. The dry season has begun to dominate the year and the various seasons have become less obvious. Sometimes it is hot when it should be cold.

There used to be huge trees and abundant grass and everything was green. Firewood was always near and easy to find. Now, when you leave *Poverty* Bobo Dioulasso in the south and travel north to Ouahigouya you can see *meant that* how the vegetation has changed. We buy firewood in Ouahigouya because *women did* otherwise we'd have to walk about 15 kilometres to find any. *not really*

Soil erosion has made our land far less fertile. To protect the top-soil *enjoy sex* I use manure and the waste from my family. We spread manure three times each year. We try to leave the earth fallow for three or four years. We also rotate the type of crops grown. At the moment, in the Yatenga, agriculturalists are looking for seeds which grow quickly and mature before the end of the rains. It is possible to cultivate the same piece of land for 20 to 30 years, but to maintain the yield you must put on a lot of manure. You must also build **diguettes** to stop soil erosion.

Traditional remedies
Traditionally we have many uses for our plants. On the seventh day after the birth of a child we use various preparations to ensure that the child develops properly. We use *wolzare*, to guard against any hereditary diseases and *banguedéré* if the child cries a lot. To relieve congestion we give the child *zaaga* leaves boiled in water.

When I was younger and fitter I would make baskets out of fibres from *tansalga*, *kango* and *peleiga* trees and from the stem of a plant called *kougaré*. It is difficult to find these today.

Families use different types of wood as **totems**. We are not allowed to use *pousga* trees because they are used by bone-setters. We don't cut the *kango* tree as it is sacred. Certain families used it during the tribal wars to make shelters and so managed to survive.

There are no plants which we use as contraceptives or for abortions. In the past poverty meant that women did not really enjoy sex. They were too tired and didn't have enough to eat.

Haoua Ouédraogo (F, 62 years), Ouahigouya B8
Lizèta Porgo (F, 65 years)

The interview took place in the courtyard of Haoua Ouédraogo's house. Beside us was a water filter made from two **canaris***. The one on top was perforated and filled with layers of gravel, sand and carbon, which cleaned the water as it passed through. A piece of white material covered the top of the jar. Haoua was a frank straightforward woman, Lizèta was shy and quiet.*

To have a second child before the first one was three brought shame to the family

Haoua: Although I am quite old I still farm the land, just as my parents always did. My parents taught me how to fetch water, cook food and weave cotton. We used to have great respect for those who were older than us and knew more than we did. I have been the mother of nine children myself, though of these seven died so I am left with just two.

Lizèta: I am a farmer, as my parents were, although I also do a little trading in the market. Of the 12 children I bore only three are still living. The death of my boys was one of the worst things that has happened to me. If my boys were alive today they would be married and I would be benefiting from their wealth. I would suffer less than I do because my daughters-in-law would be there to look after me.

When I had my children I did not mind whether they were girls or boys. We like both sexes, although in my opinion boys are more difficult to educate and train. I am in favour of big families. There is a better atmosphere when there are more people, everyone exchanges ideas, and the children grow up in a stimulating environment.

Even if we had wanted to control the size of our families, we never had any form of traditional contraceptive. The only form of family planning we knew was personal restraint. To have a second child before the first child was three years old was a practice which brought shame to the family.

Changes for women

Haoua: Today, the position of women has improved. Before, we would only meet our neighbours at ceremonies such as marriages, baptisms and funerals. Now we work together on projects and have frequent meetings with other women in our **groupement**, in which we all discuss ways of overcoming our problems. Generally, I am most satisfied with the advice that I receive from these women. The only thing I regret is that women are no longer as warm and welcoming as they once were. In the past, if I had a problem I would go and see a wise old women from my area of town. She always gave me very good advice.

As for the division of labour within the family, it is the job of the women to spin and weave the cotton, fetch the water and grind the millet. The cotton cloth is then given to the boys in the family. If they are intelligent, they sell it so that they can build their future. As soon as the daughters are old enough they help their mother. Boys stay with their mother until the age of 10, when they begin to work with their father.

Modern women are much freer than we were. Twenty years ago a woman had to marry and care for a husband chosen for her by her father or brother. If she didn't like the choice she just had to put up with a miserable existence. Women today do not accept such subservience, and refuse to accept what they do not want. They are better provided for and better organised. For those who cannot read or write there is the opportunity to join a group run by the Union des Femmes du Burkina, which educates women and is a forum for debate and exchange of ideas.

I think that, on the whole, women are happy with the present political situation where there is one party. Before, Ouahigouya was full of so many different political groups that women's voices were muffled by the rest and nobody listened to the demands that we were making. Now we are more easily heard.

In my youth the rain used to fall throughout the wet season, right up until September. The trees were dense and bushy and the weather humid. There has been a great amount of degradation because the rains have decreased. The soil is so dry that the trees have died.

Vegetation near our living quarters has become thinner, though you can still find thick green vegetation about 10 to 13 kilometres away, or nearer to home in our sacred areas where the trees are preserved for our traditional ceremonies. To find firewood we have to walk up to 10 kilometres, and those who are too old or infirm have to buy their wood in the market. We select different types of timber to serve different functions. For building we use *willimwiiga*, *kouiga* and *préferga*. Artisans carve their works of art from *koigo* and *tansalga*, whereas herbalists make medicines from *willimwiiga*, *kouiga*, *banguedéré*, *sourtoutougou* and *kiskinde*.

The lions, buffaloes and antelopes which 20 years ago used to roam through these parts are today nowhere to be seen. The only animals we see today are rabbits. Even the birds, such as the nomwalga, are now rare, because there are no big trees for them to perch on.

Migration

During bad agricultural seasons some of our people go to the south to farm. Some family heads search for land which they can move to permanently and send for their families. Some people move for social rather than economic reasons—for example, if they have had a serious dispute with a neighbour or a relative. As a rule, women do not move on their own. I must say that it is the people who stay, those who do not migrate, who have the most courage.

Most aspects of life today are easier if you have money. We used to get our water from ponds and from wells which we dug with our own hands, but these sources were liable to dry out. Today, those who have money can buy their water from a tap.

In this area we have benefited enormously from development projects

It is the people who stay, who do not migrate, who have the most courage

Animals are run by organisations such as Six S, Oxfam and **CRDA**. As a result, there
a source of is greater solidarity. We support each other and work together more than
immediate before. We have learnt a lot of new skills which have given us more
credit during confidence in our work.
hardship   Our field is big. Sixteen people work on it, including the two of us.
Although we will not inherit any of the land when our husbands die, we
work as hard as everyone else and, of course, we benefit from its produce.
To improve the quality of the soil we spread natural fertiliser on it and, if
we can afford it, chemical fertiliser too. If the soil is very poor we try to
leave it fallow for three or four years to recuperate. Ideally, if you have
two fields, you work one for three years and then switch to the other.
Sometimes we practise mixed cropping since we find that the nutrients of
one plant have a beneficial effect on another. The main crops are millet,
groundnuts and haricot. Our staple food is millet so we never sell it except
in exceptional circumstances. If we need extra money we sell groundnuts.

Traditional farming

We cultivate our fields by hand. In the past we used ploughs drawn by
zebu but unfortunately they all died in the drought. A traditional farming
practice called zai involves the digging of small holes, a few centimetres
in depth, in preparation for the sowing of millet. Our ancestors found that
the holes helped preserve the soil's humidity during dry weather and
therefore helped the millet resist drought.

After sowing, we have to weed and hoe the field. The worst weed is
wango, which attacks the millet stems. Our millet crop also suffers from
the wind. We have no shelter belts around our fields and the strong winds
can knock the plants over. When this happens we try to prop up the stem
by building up the earth round it.

After each year's harvest I save some of the grain in three large **canaris**.
These I do not touch until the harvest of the following year approaches.
If I need grain before this I prefer to buy it in the market. Of the three
stores that I save, I give one as a present to my children. The second I sell
and give the profit to community needs. The third provides the following
year's seed.

After harvesting we take up other activities while waiting for the rainy
season to come again. Those of us who have irrigated land do vegetable
gardening, while others spin and weave cotton to earn some extra money.

In our fields there are a number of ravines created by water running off
the land. To prevent these spreading and ruining our farmland we fill the
ditches with stones. We learnt about this from the development projects.

Of course, we like to keep livestock as well as to farm. Animals are a good source of immediate credit during hardship. If you are struggling for food you can sell an animal without much delay. But this is only a temporary answer. Agriculture, if it is thriving, is much more long-term. More family members can profit from a good harvest. There is no doubt that our millet is very precious.

The sad fact is that today everything is based on money

Food preferences have changed since I was young. Today the staple foods are **tô**, haricot beans, **couscous** (from the market) and the leaves of the haricot bean and *kénébgo*. In the past we used to eat a sauce made from the leaves of the baobab tree. It tasted so good, even without salt, that we ate it every day. Today, people don't think that the sauce is good enough unless a Maggi stock cube, meat, salt and vegetables are added.

With more variety in our food, we no longer see cases of malnutrition. Besides, people are more educated and know which foods to eat to avoid certain complaints associated with vitamin deficiencies.

Children have been influenced by modern values which seem to have made them disrespectful of their elders. When we were young we listened to what our parents had to say, whereas the young today refuse all our counsel. For this reason parents are not happy with their offspring. When we were small we had to work to find clothes to wear and food to eat. Perhaps children now are too spoilt.

In the old days funerals were occasions which brought people together, since neighbours would give help and support to each other. Today it seems that if you want a good funeral you must spend lots of money, since people will only stay in the house of the deceased long enough to arrange the funeral dances if there is food to eat.

Our marriages were simple and straightforward affairs based on good faith. Today, if the marriage is to be acceptable to the young wife a fortune must be spent on sheep, kola nuts and clothes. Baptisms are just the same. The sad fact is that today everything is based on money. If you give a gift to someone today, you expect to receive something of similar value in exchange. For example, if a woman brings you a piece of soap worth 150 **CFA** she will expect at least 100 **CFA** in exchange.

B6 Group of women, Ouahigouya

It is hard to say what types of soil we prefer because the most important factor determining the land's productivity is the rain. Those of us who have the opportunity to cultivate different areas do so. Some farm on the bottom of a valley where the land is wetter and they also cultivate an area with hard soils, and then another with sandy soils. In this way, they don't lose everything—whatever way the rainfall fluctuates.

B9   *Aminata Traoré (F, 50 years), Ouahigouya*

Aminata Traoré is a local government officer. She does a great deal of work with women and also has her own irrigated market garden. Her work is her passion and she talked about it with great enthusiasm.

By birth I am a Malian. I was born and brought up in Bamako and came to Burkina Faso after my marriage. I am a civil servant, although in my spare time I do as much work as I can in my vegetable garden. My father was originally a farmer although later he took up commerce.

I went to primary school for six years and then to secondary school for four years. After this I got a post as a teacher but didn't get on well in this profession so I opted for general administrative work.

My work is concerned with women, their position in politics and the more practical aspects of their lives, both in rural and in urban areas. We want women to progress, so it is important that we see to it their lives are happy. In the past all the heavy work was given to the women but they were given nothing in return. It was the man who dominated, who took the decisions, looked after the money and got to know the children. Women had practically no rights.

The Union des Femmes du Burkina, in cooperation with the government, has organised special activities for International Women's Day. This helps to raise awareness about important issues. Since 1980 the Union has also provided women with training, for example, in small-scale trade and commerce, to help give them more financial independence. Our government now gives us so much consideration that women are asked to participate in international conferences, where they discuss issues such as desertification and the education of children.

Changes for women

Women are delighted with the work that is being done for them. We have more freedom and can travel from village to village in a way that was once unthinkable. We've been aided not only by changing public opinion but also by new equipment, such as grinding mills, which have lightened our workload enormously. Animal-drawn ploughs have meant that much bigger areas of land can be cultivated, so our harvests have increased. And then there are the carts, which mean we no longer have to carry everything on our heads and can transport large quantities of wood and water at the same time. Of course the only problem is that this equipment is not handed out free although, if women are lucky, it may be loaned to them by NGOs who offer training in its use.

It is important to warn children, particularly girls, that they may face *Women are* various economic difficulties. Women have become more assertive and *the true* participate in a wide range of activities. They may, for example, buy *vehicles of* vegetables from people who run the gardens and re-sell them at the market *development* for a slightly higher price. So they gradually begin to save money and improve the life of their families. Another popular activity is to buy and raise chicks which they sell for a profit.

Children are a gift from God, so I do not believe that we should have a preference between girls and boys. I gave birth to nine children but only five of them are still living. I am left with four boys and one girl.

I spend a lot of my time working with rural women, showing them how to build stoves which are economical in their wood consumption. At the same time I raise their consciousness about desertification and the importance of conserving wood. I work under the auspices of the development project, Groupements Naam. Women are the true vehicles of development. It's nonsense to talk about development unless you are working through women.

Market gardening

I also work in the market garden in a team of women. I don't have any money of my own, which is why I see the importance of giving women who haven't been to school the opportunity to earn money of their own in the market garden. Prices in the market are competitive because there is a great variety of produce. I do not garden solely to earn money, but also to encourage other women and because I enjoy it. Market gardening has many positive side effects. For example, we give old cabbage leaves to our animals to eat. Younger leaves are dried and saved for when there are no other vegetables around. In this way we avoid malnutrition.

Market gardening and the introduction of imported foods are changing our eating habits. Our two most popular dishes are **tô**, accompanied by sauce made from *gombo*, baobab leaves or sorrel, and rice with a groundnut sauce. Our vegetable gardens have introduced lettuce, potato and cabbage into our diet. Today, most people can eat until their hunger is satisfied.

Our plot occupies an area of half a hectare. It does not belong to us directly but is partly family property and partly lent by friends or neighbours. The best soil for market gardening is one which is neither too sandy nor too clayey; our soil isn't ideal but it seems to adapt quite well. To improve its quality we lay down organic and chemical fertilisers. I prefer using animal dung to chemical fertilisers. If you want to be successful as a market gardener it's important to keep animals. Many women look after a few sheep which provide dung for the vegetables. I don't think it's advisable to use human excrement on the fields.

We have found that proper irrigation channels have proved more economical than spray and sprinkler systems. When the plot has lost its fertility we leave it fallow. I have already left one of my plots fallow for a year. In a week's time I'm going to apply green fertiliser to this plot to try to restore its fertility. We also practise crop rotation to help maintain the soil's quality.

We keep some vegetables for our own consumption, give some away to friends and the rest we sell in the market to raise the money to buy new seeds. Most of the vegetables are either sold by the kilo or by the **calabash**.

Most of the vegetables that we plant are new to the area. The most popular varieties include chinese cabbage, **caca cross** cabbage, potatoes, carrots and aubergines. Like everything else, young seeds have a tendency to be swept away by the wind, so it's essential to create some kind of windbreak. We do this by planting rows of maize around our vegetable patches. Some people also plant lemon tree hedges to mark their enclosure and to protect young plants from the weather.

During the rainy season I grow groundnuts. When I go to the field, the boys come with me to help while the girls stay at home to prepare the meal. We work until two in the afternoon and then we return home. In my house, boys and girls help cook the food. I think others should follow this example, since boys should be able to look after themselves.

The environment

Today there is no bush left, so there are no wild animals either. It's at least 30 years since we saw any animals here. Now the only place you can find them in Burkina is in the game reserves in Comoé. In the past, when the rains were regular and trees plentiful, numerous birds used to perch in the trees. There was enough to eat, the harvests were good and our feasts were generous. Twenty-five years ago it would never have occurred to people to leave their families!

The vegetation today is only thick after the rainy season in the winter; during the dry season the land is bare. Local people have been forced to move away from this poor region, in search of richer areas where they can find food and money. As a rule it is only the men who migrate. Burkinabè women do not move around much on their own—it's only the Dogon women we see coming on their own from Mali. They stay here for a short while and then return to their country. Many NGOs are currently fighting against the high levels of migration. The government supplies extension workers, like myself, who try to help the villagers find solutions to the

problems they face. Thanks to the work of these people, some of the young
are beginning to realise that it's not worth the effort of leaving for foreign
lands, since if you make an effort there is money to be made here.

A few of our trees have been preserved because they are believed to
be sacred or are particularly valued. The baobab, for example, is greatly

Diana East/Panos Pictures

Women, laden with goods for market, pause in the shade of a baobab.

respected, as is the *fromager* under which the village elders sit to discuss their problems. There are certain small trees which only the **chef de terre** has access to. Each is linked with a specific state of affairs or event, such as the health of the village, a good harvest, or protection from the spirits. Similarly, certain animals are associated with various human qualities. If you were to call somebody a lion, for example, it would mean they had a lot of courage, whereas the rabbit is associated with intelligence and shrewdness.

Even though some traditions may be dying out, our people still place a lot of trust in old practices. I know that many of my colleagues who work for the state occasionally leave the town and consult their parents in the village about how they can use traditional practices to improve their work.

Although our climate has been changing since 1970, we can still identify certain seasons. The hottest part of the year falls between March and June. The rains begin in July and last through to October. They bring with them a lot of ill health caused by mosquitoes. The coldest part of the year is from November to January, when illnesses are on the decline. Nowadays, because of desertification, the heat is more persistent and the winds carry large amounts of sand.

Everyone has equal access to the available water, regardless of their tribe. In some areas, where serious degradation and desertification have lowered the ground-water level, water is scarce and women have to travel long distances searching for supplies. In the past, the wells rarely dried up and women did not have to go so far.

In the town, more and more women get their water from the tap. We have a tap in our house which supplies all the members of my family, as well as neighbours who ask to use it. We have to pay for this water.

Urbanisation

The town of Ouahigouya is rapidly expanding. There are a number of reasons, in particular the new technologies and improved infrastructure which encourage people to settle here. The opportunity to acquire land which can be irrigated is a great attraction, as is the presence of development groups who can teach us methods of improving soil quality and tackling erosion.

As urbanisation has increased and our lives have become more sedentary, we have seen changes in family size. People used to think it a great asset to have a large family since children were viewed in terms of available labour. Today, with all the climatic factors affecting us, people have begun to realise that having fewer children makes better economic sense. The smaller the family, the better the education and training that can be given to each one. Men, anyway, seem to prefer small families. In urban areas women feel the same, though in rural areas some women still need persuading.

These days contraceptives are available from the SMI clinics (Santé Maternelle, Infantile). In the past, we tried to space the births of our children by practising restraint. Mothers know that spacing their children helps to protect them from illness, weight loss and even death. I would like to be able to have lots more children, particularly some little sons. The priorities in my life are to eat well, to clothe myself and to help my children and husband.

As far as development goes, I believe that the most important thing is for us women to participate in building up our infrastructure. We must replant the forest, protect our animals and try to avoid forest fires. We must plan our food resources for the future and avoid aimless wanderings.

Harouna Ouédraogo (M, 92 years), Ouagihouya   *B11*

I was born and brought up in the Bingkiengo area. I didn't go to school and at a young age I took up a small job at the local primary school. In 1914, when I was 17, I found myself in paid employment. I met my wife and we eloped together to Ouagadougou, where we married without the permission of our parents. We stayed there for nine years, then our families pardoned us. I was able to return to my own family and stay in the village next to that of my wife's family. With this wife I had just one son, who is now dead. When he died he left me responsible for his widow and their 11 children.

In 1914 there was a terrible famine which killed many people. I swear that at that time people walked to Bobo Dioulasso, seizing food along the route and risking their lives to try to provide for their dependents. Some years later there was another serious famine which to this day is referred to as Naba Koabga famine, after the chief who ruled at that time. After this, about seven years ago, there was another famine, but it was eased by **les blancs**, who provided us with enough supplies to survive. Or at least, those with money escaped death, though I cannot say the same for those with none.

We have seen many changes in recent years. The winds have grown very strong because of all the wide open spaces. There are no trees or tall grasses to block its passage. The disappearance of the vegetation has also produced hotter weather and relentless sunshine. There are no wild animals any more. If you want to see a **yâka**, **walga**, gnissini or an ostrich you now have to travel at least 40 kilometres. When I was young you could go 7 kilometres and you would see a lion. The main factors that have led to this are the increase in population and the lack of rain. With the growth in population the few trees which have survived the capricious rains are also being cut down. If you can imagine, it is like making someone who is already sick carry a heavy weight on his back. You can be sure that he will fall.

Uses of trees

Look at my roof! The big beams are made from a tree called a *siiga* and the rest of the wood, crossing the beams, comes from the *pimpirssi*. Neither of these trees can be found here any more. You need a vehicle to collect them because they are so far away. The same is true for *soug'dri*, *barkoudi*, *koanga* and others too numerous to mention. However, some plants have proved resilient to the harsh conditions and these have been grown more intensively. Trees and plants that can still be found in this area today include *taanga*, *taya* and *pousga* and others for which we have special uses. *Kandiga* (or *zambné*) is used for dental problems. The roots of the *sabcé* plant are soaked in water and the solution is used in the treatment of abscesses. *Pousse m'pougou* is mixed with butter oil from the *karité* and the mixture is effective in the treatment of wounds. *Waidéga* is combined with sesame to cure a wide range of illnesses.

I could go on, since in fact most plants, shrubs and trees have a number of uses. However, there are two trees which are never cut or used for firewood. One is the *widèg'zaka*, said to cause "the indiscriminate death of the heart" [heart attack] in anyone who cuts it. The other is *kongo*, which has the same name as our chief—because of this we have taken an oath never to cut it. During the major famines, we always gathered various wild plants to supplement our diet. These included *wan'dé*, *pousga* and *pénkidiga*, which grew in the lowlands, and *silikooré*, a thorny tree bearing edible fruits. We also use the food supply of termites, a millet and grass mixture. However, the new generation no longer eats these things because provisions can be more easily procured by vehicle. As long as you have money you should be able to find food. Unfortunately, for those without money, the plants I have mentioned can no longer be found in the area.

The *pousga* is an essential tree and brings us great profit. The *taya* and *kouka* are also important. As for animals, the cow, donkey, sheep and horse are all important. Horses are no longer raised just for prestige, since people have discovered their value in agriculture. Only the chief of the Yatenga still uses his horse for riding. The first time I witnessed the use of horses in agriculture with my own eyes was around 36 years ago.

Pastoralism

Drought has severely affected the pastoralists' way of life. In the past when the rains were good and there was plenty for the animals to eat, cows were easily acquired and raised. Today the Peulh have lost most of their animals. They have to drink milk and yoghurt made from powder bought in a tin. There is simply no longer enough grass for the animals to eat; you even see them eating earth.

During the last famine, cows which once fetched 30,000-35,000 **CFA** were sold at 500 **CFA**. After the animals were slaughtered the carcasses exuded a smell which the consumers found unpleasant. The few people who still practise pastoralism today tend to move their herds for part of the year to areas such as Garcy. This has two main advantages. First, the animals gain from the good supply of food and water. Second, the pastoralists themselves benefit because they can leave a reserve food stock in their village and maintain themselves frugally in the area of pasture, until they return home at the approach of the rainy season. In this way they fatten the animals while guaranteeing that a supply of millet remains at home.

I've already spoken of all the animals that have left the region. The same is true of the human population. When there is famine, people are forced to travel to the interior of the country, towards Bobo Dioulasso, in their search for food. Others leave for neighbouring countries—Mali, Ghana and Côte d'Ivoire—looking for paid employment. In both cases it's not the women who take the initiative but the men. Only the single men are able to leave whenever they like, without informing or getting authorisation from anyone. In rare cases a woman may decide to elope with a man, or perhaps to run away to escape from a forced marriage. In normal circumstances a woman cannot go anywhere without permission from her parents or her husband.

I feel that since it's the lack of rain which has caused the young to leave this region, it's necessary to control the water so that there is a supply even when there is no rain. We have begun to work on such projects and if all goes well I think people will prefer to stay here than move to Abidjan.

Land inheritance

The system of land inheritance has changed over the years. In the old days, when there was lots of space, the ownership of land was based on the order of people's arrival in an area. The first person to arrive on a piece of land was entitled to call it his own. After that it could only be taken by force

The Peulh have lost most of their animals. They have to drink milk made from powder bought in a tin

People today live without faith or laws

or during tribal warfare. When **les blancs** arrived they brought a new system of administration and the method by which land was acquired changed. Under the new system the person who farmed the land was entitled, after a certain amount of time, to claim the land as his own. So landlords largely lost their power since you couldn't own land that you didn't farm yourself. Concerning inheritance, land is passed from brother to brother. If, for example, I die then my younger brother will inherit the land and be responsible for providing for my wives and children.

Although my wife helps me in the fields her real domain is the home. However, the husband grants his wife a piece of ground which she cultivates with her own hands, planting whatever she chooses. In addition to her own harvest, a woman is given a small amount of millet by her husband, which she can sell to buy the things necessary for her work in the home, like pots for cooking or sheets for the beds.

Today, to meet our many needs, both men and women are turning to alternative money-making activities. Men may go to other areas to buy goods—such as cloth, batteries, cigarettes and cooking utensils—which they then sell in local markets. Women are more likely to practise small trading, selling tomatoes and peppers.

Men and women have their own clearly defined economic duties. Women take care of small domestic needs, while men are only concerned with the purchase of larger items. This is because women are not able to buy in bulk. In the first place they can't travel as easily as men, who can go to Abidjan [Côte d'Ivoire] or Bamako [Mali] and buy goods to bring home. Second, it's the men who possess sufficient capital to guard against the occasional misfortune when they are robbed by bandits or cheated. Women are not in a position to cope with this.

These days when you are a farmer growing crops it is very hard to look after animals. In the past, it was easy to maintain a herd of around 30 goats and sheep and to use their excrement in the fields. Now such a practice is out of the question. Even with only 10 animals I can't control their movements and am forced to keep them in an animal pen and pay someone to take them away to find pasture. The expense of their maintenance exceeds their real value. Pastoralists don't suffer this problem. It's only those of us who live in permanent settlements. For those people without children it is harder still, since they have no one to guard their animals.

Still, it is possible to make a profit from cattle. I had a small herd and sold some of the small animals to buy a calf which I kept until it had grown, when I sold it for 75,000 **CFA**. You have to agree that this was a good profit. Unfortunately the other animals were slaughtered two years ago, so that we could provide people with food at the funeral of my younger brother. I no longer have any cattle—they have all died. Even if I were to get more, since I have no children there would be no one to look after them. My two grandchildren who remain at home both go to school.

State support

The government has provided for our community in a number of ways. During the last famine they supplied basic provisions to keep us alive. About 12 years ago they built a number of small dams. The water system allows us to irrigate our vegetable gardens and grow lettuces, cabbages, tomatoes, onions carrots, radishes and turnips. With our improved infrastructure we are now better prepared for future famines. Today, it is only the lazy who should suffer from famine.

We are now able to get water from the tap, at a cost of 100 **CFA** a barrel. This has led to a marked improvement in our lives.

To try to counter the declining fertility of the soil we apply natural fertiliser. The fertiliser of **les blancs** [chemical fertiliser] is used only on humid ground because otherwise it tends to burn the seeds. Our predominant soil type here is laterite.

The increasing population size is a response to the wishes of God. At the time of our fathers you could not have as many as six wives unless you were a chief. The maximum for an ordinary man was two or three wives. Only very rich men or chiefs could afford to have more. Now, men

---

B23 Hamad Ahmed (M, 26 years), Gorom Gorom

I earn my living as a shepherd. Most people in the village do not have any animals left, since most died during the drought. It is not really worth their while going in search of pasture with just one cow, so they give it to me to look after. In all I have a herd of about 40 cows, all belonging to the villagers. They give me 50 **CFA** a week for looking after their animals, or they may pay me in kind with a bowl of millet.

I take the cows to the bush nearby, never going farther than about 12 kilometres. In the evening, I return the cows to their owners and they are given dried grass or grain husks to eat. They graze on *cram cram* or *fonio*. I know other shepherds who go much farther with their animals. Sackau, about 55 kilometres away, is a popular area to take cattle. Most of the shepherds stay there for anything between a few weeks and a few months, returning in the rainy season when they can find pasture nearer home. During drought years, when the normal water points have dried up, we dig the ground until water appears, so that our animals do not die of thirst.

I have to give some of the money that I earn to my mother and brother. My father is dead and, as the eldest son, it is my responsibility to support them. It is hard, since I have a wife and one son of my own to support. I can't see how I'll ever be able to save enough to buy a cow of my own.

are able to take several wives because there are more women than men.

Another reason for the rising population is the fact that some young girls today are burdened with unwanted pregnancies. I have known girls give birth in their father's backyard as many as five times. Neither boys nor girls seem to want to get married. The boys only want to play with the girls and the girls just encourage them, since they too want to lead the good life and to eat good food such as grilled meat. People today live without faith or laws. Before, all young people were married and they lived according to various rules and regulations.

Children's behaviour

Two different types of children can be found today: those who love and respect their parents, and those who have broken all links with their home. If I send a child on an errand he may refuse to do what I ask him. Even if he deigns to carry out the job, I cannot be confident that it will be done well. In my childhood, such behaviour was impossible. If I try to punish my children, by refusing them a meal, I know that they will find other means, even if they have to steal in order to eat. Formerly, my sanctions would have been respected by everyone in the village and the child would not have won his case. Children are no longer submissive. This change in attitude has taken place gradually over the last 50 years.

When I think about what has changed, the things that strike me most are the new types of food, the fact that everyone wears clothes, and the new materials used for construction: cement and corrugated iron. I am also struck by the fact that although we no longer suffer from certain illnesses, such as scabies, new illnesses have appeared. These include **zaa** and sudden fits.

It is true that conditions today are better than they were in the past, and this must continue. My priorities in life are never to go to bed without food, never to walk naked, to live honestly and proudly and, finally, never to steal or borrow.

B17   *Salam Sawadogo (M, 53 years), Ouahigouya*
Idrissa Sawadogo (M, 74 years)
Boureima Sawadogo (M, 65 years)
Hamado Sawadogo (M, 57 years)

> *The interview took place in Gourga, a large village of some 1,800 people, 5 km east of Ouahigouya. The group sat on a bank of earth, under the shade of a neem tree. On the other side of the bank was the*

entrance to the village's nutrition centre, outside which groups of mothers holding their babies talked together. The fields surrounding the village were full of millet and sorghum.

Our parents were involved in a number of different occupations including agriculture, pastoralism, weaving, dyeing of clothes and leather, and making guienda—the instruments which the women use to spin cotton.

Today the craft of dyeing has completely disappeared, despite the fact that women used to earn a lot of money from it. The first stage of the process was to dig a hole in the ground between 3 and 4 metres deep. Then they would make a rough cast from clay mixed with the hairs of sheep and goats, which they filled with potash water, itself obtained from cutting and burning very old trees. The trees were chosen specifically for their potash content, the most popular being *siiga*, although *taanga*, *pousga* and *nobcé* were also used. The women then added a mixture of ingredients to the water, including ground and dried *garga* leaves. The mixture of the plant and the potash solution produced the dye, which was stirred over a fire for anything up to a week to produce the desired depth of colour.

Dyeing and weaving were the most important economic activities in this village when I was young. The art of dyeing has become obsolete because there are quicker modern methods and in the market we can buy clothes made by **les blancs** which are already bright and colourful. Young people no longer have any interest in learning traditional dyeing techniques as they are quite complicated. The same applies to the art of weaving which now exists only as a symbolic activity. Market gardening has replaced these crafts as the main economic activity.

Famines worthy of names

Many of the significant events in our life have been marked by famine. The famine of Naba Koabga was one of the most important. If I try to give you a date for this famine, all I can tell you is that there was a man in this village who died very recently at the age of 103 and that during the famine of Naba Koabga this old man was already fully grown. To be more precise, 30 years after the famine of Naba Koabga was the famine of Piiss'Wai [literally "90"], which was exactly 51 years ago. Between these two great famines was the famine of Suya, which means "grasshoppers". For three consecutive years we were plagued by grasshoppers, after which our defences were so weakened that we were hit by famine.

There were other famines which were pretty well as bad but we did not give them individual names because by then the hardship had been alleviated by modern transport and other kinds of aid. During the previous

If it weren't for the hares, there wouldn't be one wild animal left in these parts famines which were worthy of names, we were so desperate that we used to search the bush for wild leaves and plants to eat. Some of us went for 10 to 15 days without one grain of cereal passing our lips. In order to survive we ate the seeds from wild grasses such as *lélogo, kièguèndo* and *titiko*. During the dry season we ate *silyingué* and *wan'dé*, whereas during the rains the leaves of *kamsaongo* and *poumpoumssé* were popular.

None of us have had the benefit of education—we can neither read nor write. Despite this we manage to earn our living. In addition to our income from agriculture and herding, we do some small-scale trading and some of us get salaried contracts in town. After the harvest, some men are able to find work in the restaurants or with the gangs who work on the roads. Others earn a good extra income from market gardening.

God is responsible for what has happened to our environment. We could say that it was the lack of rainfall, but you should remember that the rain is given to us by God, so this is the primary cause. But there are other factors, such as the rising population and the increasing pressure we are putting on our environment. We can convince ourselves that as individuals we hardly make an impact on our environment. But if you stop for a moment and count up the number of individuals who are each thinking the same thing, each cutting down the trees, one at a time, you soon get a true measure of the scale of destruction. To see how much damage has been done you only have to look at the wildlife. If it weren't for the hares, there wouldn't be one wild animal left in these parts.

Many of our animals are of great traditional importance. Among domestic animals there are the goats, which are perhaps most numerous. They are ideal for those who are learning how to herd and for poor people who cannot afford any of the larger animals. Sheep are also important smaller livestock. They provide a valuable credit system since they can be sold to meet the immediate financial needs created by funerals or marriages. Urgent needs for smaller amounts of money may be met by selling poultry—our smallest asset. To afford large herds of the bigger animals you need cash. Again the advantage is that in times of hardship these animals can be sold.

Environmental change

The climate has changed. It began with a lack of rainfall and now all around us is open space. The winds and the hot air all blow in our direction. There is nothing to block their path. It is the same when the cold weather comes; it seems to be more bitter than it was before. But at least we have blankets nowadays to protect us. When I was young we were lucky if we had one piece of clothing to put round us. People who had clothes were

"The winds and the hot air all blow in our direction. There is nothing to block their path."

usually generous with them so if someone had to go on a journey, or to a funeral or festival, they would ask their neighbour to lend them something to wear. Today we are all better off. If five people were to approach me, all completely naked, I could dress them from head to foot without running short of garments.

Our vegetation has quite simply disappeared! To find wood for construction, of good enough quality, we have to go and buy it in the town of Ouahigouya. We generally manage to find firewood 5 or 6 kilometres from our houses. There are some trees which to a certain extent we have managed to protect, in particular those which are valued in traditional medicine. If we see an important tree being abused we do not hesitate to reprimand the vandal.

Soil erosion

To replace the trees that have disappeared we have begun to plant a number of different varieties which are not indigenous to the area, including *neem*, eucalyptus, lemon trees, mangoes and acacias. We have chosen two other sites around the village where we plant local species such as *nobcé*, *sabcé*, *waidéga*, *gawo*, baobab, *néré* and *cailcédrat*.

Our soils are in a bad state of repair, so we have begun the fight to save them. We have constructed **diguettes** from stones, which slow down the flow of water as it runs off the land and allow the soil to absorb it rather than being eroded. We also use natural fertiliser and we have a new method for planting. Before we sow our seeds we dig holes in which we put layers of decaying vegetation and natural fertiliser. The holes are bigger and deeper than before and remain humid longer. With these new methods of maintaining fertility we no longer have to leave fields fallow.

Ever since my marriage, 25 years ago, I have gone on working the same plot of ground without it showing any signs of fatigue. At the beginning of each planting season it is like a brand-new soil. This is the advantage of using natural fertiliser. In contrast, chemical fertiliser dries out and eventually kills the soil. It is best used on humid soil, which we have not known since the rains began to decrease.

We have even been able to recover some of the land spoilt by ravines. As well as building **diguettes**, we make use of the soil's humidity by planting vegetables—sorrel and *gombo*—on both sides of the ravines. Sometimes we also plant lines of trees along the **diguettes**, which act as hedges and stop the ravines spreading further.

We have a good domestic water supply. There are five wells, two of which we dug ourselves and three with pumps built by the government. Access to water is free, although when the pumps break down, we have to find the money from within the community to repair them.

Changes in the community

When we first arrived in this village there were 40 couples living here, whereas today there are 300. Because of this we are facing a shortage of land, and each of us has to stick to his original plot. I suppose population numbers have risen because of our wish to have large families. As long as our health allows, I think that we would have a hundred children if we could.

People who migrate can be divided into two categories. There are the money hunters who go to Ghana or Côte d'Ivoire, hoping to earn large sums of money. The other sort are those who leave their villages to go *Only those* elsewhere in Burkina Faso as they are unable to survive on the meagre *who have a* harvest from their infertile soil. The density of population has led many *deep love* of our younger people to migrate. It is only those who have a deep love *for the land* for the land which they farm who are prepared to stay. *which they* Children have grown complacent because they want for nothing. Look *farm are* at that child sitting in the yard over there. Just see how he is dressed! *prepared* When we were young, until we were circumcised we didn't have so much *to stay* as a pair of underpants, or a blanket to cover ourselves with at night.

Today, even babies are dressed from head to foot. The result of this is that *If we were* when a child grows up he does not behave as we would like. He may *to show our* believe that he is the son of the chief, because he was never forced to face *children the* any difficulties. If we were to show our children the leaves we used to eat *leaves we* they would think we were mad. They have no understanding of why we *used to eat* used to eat such things. They don't know what solidarity means. They *they would* even refuse to help us, their own parents. *think we*

In my day if you refused to help your father in his work you worried *were mad* about where your next meal would come from. Today, somehow or other, children can survive for a whole year without eating in their father's house. They organise themselves on the basis of self-interest. If one of them wants what the other has, they cannot seem to sort it out between themselves. The most ruthless one wins. Age no longer has anything to do with it.

Djeylalli Hamad Daouda (M), Gorom Gorom   **B25**

The Peulh people, who are pastoralists, were happy when the rain came, since they worship it as if it were a god. They would hurry to communicate the good news to their animals. The animals had a perfect understanding of their language. Each animal had its own name, according to the markings or colour of its coat. When the Peulh called to them the animals would reply by bellowing in unison. They seemed to get on so well together that it made you wonder whether it was the cow or the pastoralist that was born of the other. There is a popular saying that the cow and the pastoralist have the same ancestor.

Women are largely dependent on men, who go in search of clothes and jewels. But with the move towards emancipation of women this is changing. Men and women work side by side. Women are involved in every type of activity and occupy posts of responsibility. Personally I don't like this state of affairs. Women are now so free that they have begun to dress like Europeans, with tight skirts and trousers, hardly hiding their nudity. It's shameful.

As for the children, they are the carbon copies of their mothers. They don't do anything to make themselves useful today. They have no respect for the old. Even your own son will refuse to run errands for you on the basis that all work merits a salary. If you chase him out of the house he will simply go and find another father and mother, who will look after him and put up with his every whim. Deserted, we are left to fight our hunger. That's what people refer to as civilisation!

B26   Hama Allahamdou (M), Gorom Gorom

I was born and grew up in Ménégou where my parents were courageous peasants. They raised a small number of goats and sheep but did not own any cows like true Peulh pastoralists. For the Peulh, the cow is an inexhaustible source of pride and happiness. My parents' fields stretched out so far you could not see the end of them. The seasons were good and the harvest abundant. The environment was benevolent and everyone knew they could savour the fruits of a few months' work in the fields.

When I was eight I went to school along with all the other children in the village. I had six years' schooling and then returned to help my parents in the fields and the vegetable garden. My father used to gather in a huge millet harvest. He had three granaries: each year he would fill them all.

My father decided to marry me to a beautiful young neighbour. I liked her well enough despite her shyness. My sisters and cousins made all the preparations for the wedding. There were plates of sweet and succulent food, from recipes known only to my village. There was traditional dancing to the music of flute and the **tam tam**. We were as happy as we have ever been or ever will be again.

As the years went by, our luck began to turn. The rains became rare and inconsistent, the ponds dried up, and the trees died. Suddenly our environment was a scene of desolation. How could I alleviate the crisis for me and my family? I could not contemplate emigrating and leaving my relatives in such a bad situation. But the ground was so poor that it produced nothing. I took my courage in my hands and left for the other side of Gorom where, after several months, I finally found work with a dubious merchant who did not pay me properly. Still, it was better than nothing. During this time my wife stayed behind, waiting for a message to come and join me.

The region used to be full of wild and ferocious animals, such as lions, panthers, buffaloes, hyenas and jackals—and less aggressive animals, such as does and gazelles. We were graced with almost every species of bird on the planet including wild ducks, ostriches, bustards and the crowned crane. Now these times have become something of a legend and the animals have disappeared as if under a spell.

In the past nobody would have believed that Gorom could grow into such a big town. People migrated from isolated rural areas during the drought, in search of jobs. They found themselves badly paid work and stayed, waiting for better days. It was not easy to live in the town. The mixture of different ethnic and social groups meant that people did not easily integrate and there were problems of communication.

For the Peulh, the cow is an inexhaustible source of pride and happiness

Women only moved if they came with their husbands. Divorced or single women stayed in the place of their birth, since to do otherwise was to appear coquettish.

Women's social position has evolved greatly during my lifetime. In the past, women stayed in the house to look after the children and cook. Now they participate in all forms of economic and social activity: in the office, in the factory or even in world affairs.

State support

The government has already made certain efforts to lighten our tasks, bringing improvements in health, education and literacy. There have been projects to sink wells, build dams and vaccinate the animals. The sick can now be treated here instead of having to go to Dori or Ouagadougou. We have also acquired grinding mills, animal-drawn ploughs and solar cookers.

Children present us with increasing problems which preoccupy us greatly. They no longer have any respect for the elderly. They have become naughty and intolerant, refusing to work and turning to a life of delinquency, drinking and drug-taking.

Our crucial problem is water. There are two sources of water here: the ponds all around the village, and the wells. Yet our needs are great and only the blacksmiths are satisfied with this quantity of water. Many of the ponds dry up as soon as the rains become irregular. Water is shared by the whole community and everyone is given free access, although we all pay a small contribution to the running costs and repairs of the well. Years ago our wells were only about 1 metre deep. The area we farmed was small but we always reaped a good harvest. Today a family of 10 to 15 people may have up to three fields but their needs will not be satisfied.

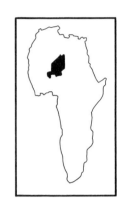

Country Profile: NIGER

Human Development Index (UNDP): 155th out of 160 nations
Population (1990): 7.7 mn. **Growth rate (1990-2000):** 3.4%
Life expectancy at birth (1990): 45.5 years
Population per doctor (1984): 39,730
Adult literacy (1985): male 32%; female 11%
Labour force employed in agriculture (1985-1988): 85%
GDP from agriculture and livestock (1988): 36.1%
Principal exports: uranium, live animals, cowpeas

1891 First French expedition arrives, and establishes Niger as a military territory by turn of century. **1921** Niger formally becomes French colony. **1960** Independence. Diori Hamani becomes president of a one-party state. **1973-74** Hamani toppled by effects of severe drought. Lt.-Col. Seyni Kountché takes power. **1974-79** Revenues from uranium triple. **1980-85** World uranium prices collapse. **1987** Kountché dies. Military council appoint Brigadier Ali Saibou as successor. **1989** Elections. Saibou elected president. **1991** Growth of opposition. National conference to discuss transitional government and new constitution.

NIGER

Four interviewing sites were selected in Niger, with the assistance of **Dr K. Mariko**. **Ibrahim Mamane** and **Zeïnabou Ba**, students at the University of Niamey, interviewed settled farmers in Takieta, near Zinder, on the proposed site of an SOS Sahel agro-forestry project. A second group of students conducted interviews in areas where projects had ended. In Abalak, a site where many pastoralists were settled after the 1984-85 drought, **Ibrahim Abdoulaye** and **Melle Ibrahim Habitsou** spoke to pastoralists and agro-pastoralists, and also to communities of small-scale irrigated farmers and fishermen. These interviews were conducted in Hausa, Peulh and Tamashek. **Kollo Mamadou Ousmane** interviewed a group of Hausa-speaking settled farmers in Tibiri. He also carried out work at the fourth site, Boubon, where he interviewed local fishermen participating in a fish-farming project, as well as sedentary farmers. Interviews were conducted in Hausa and in Djerma, and were coordinated by **Rhiannon Barker**.

Hadiza Hassane (F, 80 years), Djéouta   *N1*

> *Hadiza told her story sitting in the shade of a tree, her two 50-year-old sons shouting directly into her deaf ears and trying to take over the narrative themselves when their mother's memory needed jogging.*

I was born in Garagoumsa village, a few kilometres away. My parents were farmers and hunters. My father decided to leave and was the first to arrive here and dig a well. Thanks to his efforts, we were able to settle; and many of our relatives from Garagoumsa came to join us. When we arrived, there was nothing here but huge trees. The forest was so thick that, even in daylight, it was enough to scare you. As each relative arrived, they cut down trees to clear enough space to build their houses. So many trees were cut down that the forest began to turn into a field. Little by little the village grew and the beautiful big trees disappeared. Now we can no longer find the trees once used for traditional medicine, men have cut them all down. Baobabs are still grown in people's compounds and its fruits and flowers boiled and eaten. An infusion of the bark of the *yano* tree is drunk to treat haemorrhoids, and the very hard wood of one tree is made into pestles and mortars for grinding grain.

After the millet and cotton harvest, we would put some cotton aside to weave the wraps we wear. We we're really very poor. We had only one **boubou** between the whole village! If it came about that someone wanted to go to another village, the chief would lend him the **boubou**, which would have to be given back on return. So you see, my daughter, only one **boubou** between all the village! How could we have possibly survived like that? My father wove two **pagnes**. One was used to bury his father or mother; the other was given to me on the day of my marriage. It was with this cloth that I was joined to my husband. This tradition is now totally changed. My daughters spend lots of money on their children.

Unlike today, there were many animals in this region: doe, antelope, hare and gazelle. After harvest, my father would go off hunting. The family would eat some, the rest would be sold to our neighbours in the

"We would like a grinding mill—we women spend about three hours each day pounding grain to make boule.*" Group of women, Kongomé village.*

market. Sometimes he would go into the bush for weeks or even months, *The man* catching and selling wild game to make money to pay his taxes. If he did *has a right* not earn enough, he had to sell some of our millet. *to twice the*

The rights of wives

I was the first of three wives. When my husband wanted a second wife he *share of* said nothing to me. Husbands do not have to tell their wives what they do. *inherited* When our husband died, the other wives returned to their relatives. Land *land* inheritance follows Islamic law. When you live alone with your husband, sharing of land poses no problems because it all goes to your children. It is more complicated, however, when there are other children by other wives. Then, if the father dies, the land is divided between everyone. According to Islam, the man has a right to twice the woman's share.

(marginal note, right column: ***The man has a right to twice the woman's share of inherited land****)*

The weather is always unpredictable. One year the rains failed and it was very hot. Everything and everyone was thirsty. The ponds dried up. Both men and animals died. The soil cracked and everything had the pallor of near death. We resorted to going into the bush to gather wild baobab leaves to make soup. We suffered that year. Another year a terrible whirlwind blew off the roofs of our houses, broke the millet stems and carried animals away with it. It was a sad time. Another time, locusts destroyed our crops so badly that they created a famine. We tried to fight them in our traditional ways—killing them by hand and scaring them away—but, unfortunately, these "migrants" proved stronger than us.

Immigrants make up about half of the village. Since they have stayed here, we have become their relatives and live together. The village pastoralists never let their animals damage our fields, but migrant pastoralists really get on our nerves. They leave their animals free to damage crops. Sometimes, farmers and pastoralists fight each other over this. I remember when one such fight resulted in terrible injuries and someone even died.

Declining harvests

Farming has become more difficult. In my day, we had vast areas of free space and could leave fields fallow to revitalise the soil. Today, everywhere seems to be occupied and people have to plant the same land year after year, especially if they only own one field. This impoverishes the soil and results in poor harvests. In the past, we would get 100 to 150, sometimes even 200 bundles; nowadays, we can hardly manage 60 to 80 because the soil is so poor. Those with money try to improve the situation by buying chemical fertilisers. Some wage labourers in the area, called **baremas**, will work in the fields for 80 **CFA** per hour. During the famine,

One year the they worked for millet, not money.

rains failed.... We have no vegetable gardens because there is no permanent or
The soil reliable source of water. Nor is there anywhere to fish. The fish which
cracked and people eat are brought from Nigeria, which has good markets. After a
everything had good harvest, our men sell some of our millet and buy **pagnes**, soap and
the pallor of **boubous** for themselves, their women and children.

near death The recent introduction of farm machinery, locust control and chemical
fertilisers has greatly helped our children. We had none of the advantages
of these modern methods in my day.

Wild dogs for sale

*It was clear that Hadiza was tired with the strain of having to listen
and respond to our questions. The clear sounds of a flute filled the air
and Hadiza's son went and found the flautist, who told us his story.*

My name is Maima Dau Sarkiu and I left my village in Nigeria 13 days
ago. I walk from village to village in search of wild dogs. Here, in Niger,
people do not sell dogs, I am given them as presents. On this trip, I have
collected 13. In Niger, I have to walk everywhere with my dogs because
drivers refuse to take them on their buses. When I reach a village, I tie the
dogs up outside, then enter and look for new ones. I carry this leather sack
of traditional medicines with me everywhere I go. When walking round
the bush, one must always take such precautions. When I have been given
a dog, I like to do something in return, such as supplying a remedy for a
certain ailment. If I get hungry along the way, I kill and cook one of the
dogs: they are delicious! My father and my grandfather used to do this,
so why can't I? When I have collected enough, I go home. In Nigeria I
can find cars or lorries which will take them to my home village where I
sell them, using the money to pay for my education.

*Maima then picked up his hollow bamboo flute and began to play a
tune to call the wild dogs to him.*

N3   *Fauré Maussa (F, 90 years), Djéouta*

I was not born here. I married young and came here, to my husband's
village. I am a Tuareg, the daughter of pastoralists. My father owned one
of the biggest herds in the region: maybe between 200 and 400 cows,
goats, camels and sheep. Each species was the responsibility of a different
shepherd. My mother and the rest of my family moved around with my
father, unless he was going very far, in which case we stayed at our base.
During these long journeys, my brothers helped my father pasture the

---

N2 Zauley Souley (F, 78 years), Djéouta

The *tanwa* is a little plant whose leaves are shaped like a rose. If a woman is having a difficult labour then the plant is put in water. If the woman is going to have a long labour, then the leaves of the plant will close up, whereas if it is only going to take "one second to the next", the leaves open.

N20 Issoufou (M, 66 years), Garagoumsa

I think improved communications would be an important development. We need to be able to see and hear (but particularly to see) what is happening in other parts of Niger and other countries in the world. We have no televisions here, which is a shame considering their importance.

---

herd, while I stayed to help my mother with domestic work.

Our animals were all marked, so we could identify them if they were lost or stolen. It is best to have a ratio of four females to one male in a herd, though not always so good to keep them together, because they fight. Males are bigger and sturdier, so raise more money when they are sold.

Animal reproduction

My father regulated the timing of the animals' births by tying the males' testicles—a technique only really possible on goats, as other animals are too powerful to hold. It is better for animals to give birth during the rainy season, when vegetation is plentiful and the young receive enough milk. Thus you take account of the gestation period when calculating when to untie the testicles. Camels, horses and donkeys have the longest gestation: 12 months. Donkeys are the most regular, they are as good as a calendar. If you show a female donkey to a male, you can be sure that, 12 months later to the very day, she will give birth. Sheep take seven months, cows nine and goats six. Chickens and guinea fowls are much quicker: chicken eggs take 20 days and guinea fowls' eggs take 26 to hatch. Knowing this, we used to take fresh chicken eggs and put them under a guinea fowl that had already been sitting on her eggs for six days, and she would sit on the chicken eggs and nurture the offspring as her own.

When a Tuareg man dies, his animals are given to his wives, who decide how to distribute them among their children. Boys and girls are both entitled to some inheritance. Following Islamic tradition, males receive twice as much as females. If a man dies who has more than one wife, a **marabout** is called in to apportion the inheritance fairly between each wife.

A pilgrimage

Once, my husband and I decided to go on a pilgrimage to **Makkah**, the birthplace of Mohamed. In those days, there were no cars or planes. We

We travelled for days, months, years... had to do the journey on foot. Thousands of us, many with children, set off on this trek. We prepared for our departure: I sold all my animals to raise money for the journey; my husband bought lots of millet, maize, oil and other commodities; I pounded grain to make enough flour to keep us going for a month; and I bought eight donkeys. We needed four to carry our provisions, such as food and cooking pots, and four to ride. Every two days, I swapped the donkeys' burdens: those carrying provisions then carried us. In this way, we travelled for days, months, years...walking, walking, walking...men, women and children alike. Allah alone knows the number of deaths that occurred during this long journey. Sometimes we stopped to cook, rest—and bury our dead.

Occasionally, we fought powerful bandits—for up to a week or more. They stopped at nothing to steal our possessions. Thankfully, among our group there were some important **marabouts**, who could make us disappear from our enemies. As the enemy approached, he lost his sight and so we could pass by unnoticed with our possessions. Only after overcoming thousands of difficulties did we arrive in Sudan, where we travelled by car and foot to a large town, where our hardships were finally over and we caught a plane to **Makkah**. Once there, we made ourselves at home and practised some small-scale trading. When we arrived back in Niger, we realised we had been away for seven years. It was a terrible journey.

I had four children born in **Makkah**. My oldest son is still there and refuses to come home. He is married with three children. He wrote, saying that he had decided to come and look for us this year, so that he can take us all to live with him. We are waiting for him.

A traditional skill

Fauré became lost in deep thought. Her friend and neighbour, who was sitting in our circle and had been trying to interrupt throughout, could be restrained no longer.

I am the village **coiffeur traditionnel**, responsible for the tribal markings on the children's faces. To become a **coiffeur traditionnel**, you need to be taught the art by someone with years of experience. After being trained, you need his permission before you can practise. If you don't seek his permission, then your art is doomed to failure. I knew a man in Koundoumawa who marked the face of a one-week-old child, but he had omitted to ask permission from the old **coiffeur traditionnel**, so the cuts became infected and the child died.

Children are marked with a hot sharp knife at the age of one week.

Boys and girls are given the same markings as their father. In the past, this was done because intertribal wars were frequent and children used to be taken hostage during raids. The marks were important to help identify the area from which the child had been taken, enabling its parents to buy the child back, if they so wished. I remember my grandparents talking of such events but I have never experienced them myself. Today, the custom is beginning to die out, since there is no longer a practical need for such markings. I also practise traditional medicine. Look at the scars on the back of this boy.

As he spoke, he pulled one of the young boys to the ground and, lifting up his shirt, pointed to some patches on his back where many tiny slits had been made with the edge of a heated knife. Taking a hollowed-out goat's horn from an old leather sack, the **coiffeur traditionnel** *placed the larger end of the horn against the cuts. Then, putting his mouth to the thin end, he sucked hard to build up pressure and draw blood out of the cuts, filling the horn. As the blood is drawn out, it is believed, illness is taken away with it.*

The **coiffeur traditionnel** *also circumcised boys, usually between the ages of seven and nine, although recently some families have taken their children to the dispensary. Enjoying the chance to demonstrate his skills, he grabbed another unsuspecting young onlooker and, pulling down the boy's shorts, displayed his delicate work.*

Of course, circumcision hurts a bit because you take a knife to it. After circumcision, the child is given a special meal of chicken, fish and chips. The good food ensures that he is quickly healed. After this feast, he goes back to eating from the family plate.

Group interview with five women, Kongomé   *N4*

We talked with the women under the shade of a tree. A bowl of boiled beans was placed in the middle of the circle, so people could eat as they spoke. This small village was unusual in that each person's house touched directly on to their field.

For many years, Kongomé village had no chief, but the colonial government persuaded us to elect one. As the village was large and well-populated, we decided to elect two chiefs: one for the Hausa and one for the Tuareg. Today, both chiefs live closely together and always consult each other carefully before taking any decision. They only have one place for their meetings and one school. Taxes can be paid to either chief. The

Traditionally, contraceptive methods were sought by asking the marabout for advice

chiefs tell us that they are like real brothers and that only death will separate them.

Mixed marriages

Most villagers are Hausa; traditionally, sedentary farmers. The Tuareg are nomads by birth. Both races get on very amicably in the village. The children all play together. If you go to the home of a Tuareg, you will find children with a Hausa mother and a Tuareg father or vice versa. Mixed marriages have brought the two races surprisingly close together. This good rapport goes back to our grandfathers' time: the first two village chiefs swore they would never betray one another and lived according to their vow. One of them told his sons and men:

> Do not forget the oath taken between the two parts of the village. Whoever takes over from me is worthy of your respect, and you—you must be sure that the day never comes when somebody says that you have worried your brothers. If you manage this you may always remain justifiably proud.

With these words, the old chief died but we still respect his wishes. So, if an adult is walking along and finds two children arguing, he will correct them and reason with them without trying to find out whose children they are. We teach them to like and respect each other.

The chief nominates the president of the village women. Her job is to keep them informed of decisions and to mobilise them for community labour. When visitors come to the village, she has to organise the cooking and to welcome them; if there is a festival in a neighbouring village, to which Kongomé's youth are invited, she has to provide for the event. Also, she is our representative at meetings in Takiéta which concern women.

Midwives

There are two women midwives in our village. One stays with the women for the first week after the birth of the baby: the other stays for a month. One is Tuareg and the other Hausa. Mothers are the ones who pay the midwife and they can choose either of them. If it's a boy, they have to pay seven blocks of soap, a **calabash** full of millet and 500 **CFA**. If it's a girl, they might buy a **pagne** for the midwife. The midwives go together to Takiéta, where they receive products to help with their work.

This village has no water, no pump and no well, so we cannot have a market. The ground is so rocky that we cannot dig traditional wells. Young people have to walk 6 kilometres to fetch water in the dry season. They leave at six in the morning and don't return until midday; sometimes they have to go again in the evening. Before a well was built in Djéouta, we

used to walk 10 kilometres to a never-failing pond. It was very punishing. *Unless you*
Much has changed. Not one of us five old women chose our husband. *are rich, it*
Perhaps that explains why four of us were so unhappy that we got *is difficult*
divorced. Divorce is not difficult but you have to return the bride-price to *to get*
your husband's family. Today, we let our children decide whom they *married*
want. The problem is that young girls tend to be disobedient and do
whatever they want. To afford their marriage, we have to sell everything
we own to satisfy them. Unless you are rich, it is difficult to get married.
As yet, we have no modern means of contraception, but we did once ask
our president to bring us back some contraceptive pills from Takiéta.

In Kongomé, we cultivate everything we can. Millet grows for four
months, groundnuts and maize for three months, and haricot beans take
40 days. This area is just wet enough for sorghum, which is well adapted
to the cold. Sorghum harvests are normally plentiful and in a good year
we employ **baremas** to help us on the land. One weed persistently resists
annual weeding: it is a wicked thing that reduces our harvest. If you know
any way of getting rid of this plant, then please help us. In the lowlands,
the soil is rocky. There is a seasonal pond down there but these days it
doesn't last more than three months. Many centuries ago, the sea came up
to this spot. We believe this because we find fossil shellfish in the ground.

We are very poor here. Many of us cannot afford to buy meat for
months on end. Some of our men go to Nigeria or Zinder to practise petty
commerce. Others earn money by making mud bricks for houses.

We would like a grinding mill. At present, we women spend about
three hours each day grinding grain to make **boule**. Look at these big
callouses on our thumbs, developed over the years from all the pounding
we have to do!

Assalama Abdau (F, 70 years), Koundoumawa, Zinder   N5

*Assalama first said she was 30 but her one surviving daughter, who
looked 60, argued that this was impossible. Intense debate followed
and finally 70 was agreed upon. All this seemed to be unimportant to
Assalama. She seemed happy to accept any age her younger relatives
gave her. Throughout the interview, Assalama sat without moving,
her feet lame and swollen.*

I was born here. My father was a farmer and blacksmith; every day, after
working the fields, he spent some time at his forge. He had apprentices to
help him. Lots of people placed great trust in my father and sent their
children to be taught by him. In his youth, he spent many hours collecting

iron ore, which he smelted. Today, this takes too much time and scrap metal can easily be found from cars abandoned on the roadside.

Being a blacksmith, my father knew about fire magic. If people were badly burned, more often than not they were taken to my father to be cured. In serious cases, he applied a special powder to the injury and gave the patient a solution to drink. The treatment continued until the wound healed. As part of the cure, he also recited verses. He was known for his powers throughout the region, recognised as an expert on burns. People brought the sick to him from far away and he let them stay, since they could not return home the same day.

My father taught me verses to recite and gave me some very effective powder for treating wounds. Everything had to be very clean before being applied. Once, a child of eight months put his hands in boiling oil. All the skin came away but, with Allah's help, the wound healed in two weeks. I still have that powder but things have changed: modern youth prefer to go to the dispensary. I can't force anyone to come to me, but I am always available.

Faith and fire

My mother was a **marabout**'s daughter from the Hausa sherifi, meaning "someone who does not get burnt in the fire". She had such strong faith, she could put her hand in the fire or a pan of boiling water without scalding it. These powers were a gift from Allah. All the children of a male sherifi take on his powers, whereas only the first children of a woman sherifi do. In my family, not all of my mother's children are sherifi: I do not have the powers, whereas my brother does. He proved this once, when he took some meat out of boiling oil with his bare hands.

On their wedding day, my parents gave a display of their great powers. They threw petrol on a house, shut themselves in it, then set it on fire. The house burnt with my parents inside. They emerged when the fire faded, alive and unharmed. After that, whenever there were fires in the village, my parents were called upon to take people's possessions out of the burning houses. Everyone had great respect for my parents; they were honoured people. When my father died, my mother spent her last years far from the village, with one of her sons and his two wives.

I grew millet, and gave away any surplus to the needy rather than selling it. I also grew, spun and sold a lot of cotton to weavers, using the money to pay for livestock, houses and many of my children's marriage expenses. With the residue and with cash raised from selling animals, I could afford to make a pilgrimage to **Makkah**. Thus I do not regret all the time I spent working with cotton. The work was very hard but I am thankful that I had the strength to do it. Now, I am tired and cannot work, so I look after my small granddaughters when their mother is working.

Young people go to the pharmacy. They don't use the natural chemist of Africa!

The natural chemist

When working with cotton, I used a special concoction against fatigue. I gathered roots, bark and leaves, especially from *kirné, dâni, nonbo* and *kalgo*. When I came home, I put whatever I had collected into a dish with lots of water and left it to infuse. Then I drank the infusion throughout the day to give me energy for my work. Only *kalgo* and *sabara* remain. The forest is poor. Some trees have been cut down by man; others died in the drought. Young people are not as badly affected as we are, because they go to the pharmacy. They don't use the natural chemist of Africa!

Cooking wood is brought from far away and so is very expensive. It is hard to find wood, or even a dead tree, within about 30 kilometres. To make matters worse, if we cut down trees, we risk a heavy fine.

In my time, when a young bride was brought to her husband's house for the first day, her parents bought her the basic necessities for married life. These consisted of one mat, three **calabashes**—two for work and one to hold **boule**—and three clay water pots: one to keep drinking water and the other two for use in the kitchen. There were no plastic plates or cups then. All were made from wood and I still use mine today.

I was 12 when I was married and my husband, who was my cousin, was 14. I was his first wife. I did not know him before my wedding day and I did not want to go through with the ceremony, so I ran into the bush and somebody had to come and find me! When I returned, people began to play music and my husband gave me a cow. Later, he took two more wives but one divorced him and the other died. My husband is now dead, too. He had 19 children in all: 11 of them were mine but nine died, mainly of fever when very young. Only the youngest child lives and eats with me here. It's because of me that he hasn't left the village after the harvest to find employment elsewhere.

Malnutrition

Children are breastfed with no additional supplements until two years old, then they are fed off the family plate. Today, there is much malnutrition.

Look at this baby: you can tell from its hair colour and thin arms that it is ill. Eye and skin complaints are common. We used to prevent our children becoming ill, and heal them, with herbal medicine. Today, mothers don't have this knowledge and so they wait until the illness has considerably weakened the child before running left and right to look for a remedy.

I can remember three main famines, during which our animal herds were wiped out. The first was caused by grasshoppers and locusts; the others were caused by drought. During the first, I sold the cows I inherited; in the second I sold my sheep; and during the third, my goats. The second famine was the worst in terms of livestock deaths from hunger and thirst. Before the famines, I had over 100 head of cattle, producing so much milk that I gave it away to friends. I did not sell it. After harvest, we kept our animals in the fields to manure the soil. Occasionally, I sold one of my animals to pay for a marriage or to build a house. This house and my son's house cost 10,000 **CFA** to build from mud bricks, and took about a month. It was not cheap.

Locusts

Grasshoppers and locusts cause us many problems. We have no traditional methods of fighting them, although children catch them to grill and eat. Running through the thick grass to catch them, many children have recently been bitten by snakes. Only yesterday, a girl from this village was bitten. She did not tell her parents but her hand suddenly became very swollen. Her father had to search for the leaves to apply to the wound and cure it. Today, Allah be praised, she has recovered.

In my day, nothing was taken as a contraceptive. We did, however, have traditional methods of family planning. After a woman gave birth, her husband waited two years before sleeping with his wife again. Now men only wait 40 days before returning to their wife's bedroom. I have heard about a birth control pill on the radio but it has not come here.

We would benefit from new technology, such as carts. Young people would like to work with better equipment, but all they have is hoes. They don't have the means to buy anything else. They can't afford to buy animals to pull ploughs, because they have taxes to pay.

The villagers asked us if we would like to meet a village woman with fire powers. We agreed and were led to an old woman, who hurried off and came back clutching a pile of glowing coals in her bare hands. After much pleading and assurances that she had demonstrated her skills adequately, she was persuaded to put the coals down. She held out her palms. They looked remarkably unscathed by the experience.

Kouré (M, 65 years), Takiéta   *N17*

I was born in early colonial times. The colonialists explored in around
1900 and started ruling by about 1914, when our country was struck by a
terrible drought and pitiable famine. Before they succeeded in installing
themselves, there was local resistance and fighting. Sultan Amadou
Kouren Daga resisted in Tirmini, Damagaram region. In the face of the
superior fire power of **les blancs**, he could not hold out for very long and
was eventually killed in Turmuji, his home village. Dan Basa took over
as sultan but the colonial administrators replaced him with one of his
servants, Ballama. He reigned for about 20 years until overthrown,
because servants or slaves have no right to usurp a chieftaincy. Our social
structure is not egalitarian, it is organised into groups and sub-groups—
castes. These groups interact, but do not intermarry. Most people here are
Hausa-speaking Kanuri from Daura, Tuareg, and minority groups, such
as Peulh-speakers.

Examples of harsh treatment during colonial times included the
imposition of taxes and forced work. Many of us men were forced to build
roads. We had little equipment. We had to walk long distances in our bare
feet, to carry heavy stones and baskets of sand or pebbles, to cut trees and
to dig the road, all by muscle power alone. Numerous cattle were needed
to feed all the workers.

Also, local people had to grow cash crops—groundnuts and cotton—to
satisfy growing overseas needs for raw materials. People had to do hard
work on administrators' and traditional chiefs' fields, each one several
square kilometres. The tragedy was that the poor working on the fields
never benefited from the crops they harvested, even during famines, as
the crops were sold secretly. But good things resulted from colonisation
as well: new systems of education and social justice were introduced, and
there was a new emphasis on equality of men—a concept the local
community found difficult to accept.

A merciless famine
The famine coinciding with the rise of the colonial powers was known as
Kakalaba, owing to its merciless and ruthless character. In 1927, the Mai
Bouhou famine hit the population, so called because people wandered
from village to village with empty sacks, looking for food. Later, the Mai
Amaro and Mai Zarara famines did little damage to the population. During
these famines, the administration reputedly confiscated grain, so some
people buried their grain in small holes at a number of different sites,
hoping that the soldiers would not find it. As a result of these famines,

about 38 years ago a system of grainbanks was instituted. Each family head gave some millet, sorghum and haricot beans to the village chief after the harvest. Those experiencing difficulties during the year, would ask for a share of the grainbank. The next year, any unused grain was returned to the donor.

I remember when the bush was denser and better stocked than today. This area was full of acacia trees. Among other plants were tamarind trees, shrubs and *sodom apples*. The bush was full of antelopes, gazelles, hyenas, monkeys, big wild cats, guinea-fowl, squirrels, rabbits and hares. Now these animals live far away in areas free from drought and man's destruction, or else in the mountains. Even there, though, they are rare. The main factors responsible for today's degradation are the successive years of drought, and population growth with its consequent pressures on land and water resources, such as the uncontrolled clearing of bush for agriculture. Animals left these clearings to look for new homes where there is little or no deforestation. In trying to tackle this deforestation problem, a few new kinds of tree species have been introduced, including eucalyptus and *mesquite*.

Trees are crucial to our life. We feel their loss in different ways: soil fertility is reduced because there is less leaf litter and wood-ash, and wood for fuel or construction is lacking, as are the leaves, bark and roots variously used to treat specific ailments. The drought has destroyed much Sahelian vegetation, killing people and animals in large numbers. Many trees have gone because of excessive cutting down for fuel and for the construction of roofs, fences, sheds, mortars and pestles, hoes, ploughs and works of art. Forty years ago, the colonial government was aware of the negative impact of deforestation and introduced a law requiring people to have special tree-cutting permits. However, the Department of Water and Forests and the Department of Fauna and Flora only began enforcing it two years ago.

Strong winds

The strong winds often destroy our grainstores or blow hot ashes about which set fire to the grain. Forest fires are also aggravated by windy conditions. And if the wind blows sand over the young crops before or after their first weeding, it hinders their normal development. We have no traditional methods to protect our crops against the wind's ravages. Recently, though, people have begun to plant trees to lessen the force of the wind and there are shelter belts in some areas. Winds today are perhaps not as violent and dusty as they were. When I was young, a wind storm completely obscured the sun for three days and people had to cling to trees

Uncultivated land is now hard to find or non-existent

to stop being blown over! This rarely, if ever, happens now. Now, as we have no trees, such winds would blow away the whole village!

It is hard to compare past and present soil fertility. Our fields used to produce more because there was enough free space to allow us to leave our fields fallow every one or two years. Now yields of our traditional species are much lower than before, even with chemical and organic fertilisers. Our fields are dead. To try and improve the situation, I practise mixed farming, growing different crops in the same field. I believe that, despite the shortage of financial and material resources of many peasant farmers like myself, we have benefited to some degree from modern farming methods. Few have the means to use ploughs and carts drawn by animals, or chemical and organic fertiliser or pesticides, but quick-growing crops introduced include four different millet varieties: *zango*, which takes 80-90 days to mature, *dan tchima, dan heca* and *gundu gundu*, which all take only 70 days. There are also two types of sorghum: *biririhouta* and *el bazanga*, which take 70 days; and haricot beans—*babarbare*—which take 40 days.

> *Land was a natural phenomenon, a gift God gave to all living beings*

Today, pastoralists cover large distances to find suitable pasture because of extensive desertification and the change to farming by more and more people. Uncultivated land is now hard to find or non-existent. Here, in Takiéta, pastoralists now have to take their animals 400 kilometres away to Aderbissinat. When I was young, they could find suitable pasture here.

People have a greater spirit of free enterprise, individualism and materialism. This has eroded the past strong community spirit. I remember when the welfare of any individual was everyone's concern. This changed with the colonials' introduction of money. People now like to buy animals because they are a good investment. We raise them, sell many at a profit, then use the money to pay for our basic needs, such as food, clothes and marriage or baptism ceremonies.

Land ownership
Once, nobody claimed land as their own. Land was a natural phenomenon, a gift God gave to all living beings. No one sought permission from anyone to clear the bush for farming. This is now changing, as more and more fields become private property. Division of labour and share of the harvest are determined mainly by family size and composition. Our fields are cultivated collectively and the produce stored in grainstores owned by the whole family. The store's use is monitored by the family head, who has the last word in all family affairs. Since all agricultural produce is shared, land ownership presents few problems.

Land used to be considered almost sacred... today, fields can be sold as if they were just another item of merchandise

Land is passed on from father to son. Women do not own land themselves but benefit from land inherited by their husbands. If women inherited land, then land would move from her family into her husband's. This would conflict with our traditional system, which ensures that land is not transferred between families. Unfortunately, this system is gradually being eroded because of the increasing importance that people attach to money. Land used to be considered an almost sacred family asset; today, fields can be sold as if they were just another item of merchandise. Land is only sold by men. I don't know why women are not allowed to sell land, as they need money just as much. The practice of selling fields became so corrupt that the chief ordered a moderate percentage of each field's monetary value to be granted to any women concerned. Before my father died, I gave a field to my brothers, because I already had acquired one in the bush outside Takiéta when land was plentiful and free.

Traditionally, women obey men; the destiny of society is in the hands of men. When a man worthy of being a man spoke, women never contradicted or disobeyed him. Sadly, our women have changed. They are emancipated. They believe more and more in equality with men. It's a bit as if the world has turned upside down! The same is true of the youth: they no longer respect their elders. They all want to be modern, so reject traditional values. Our own daughters no longer ask our advice: they think they know all there is to know. They want to choose their own husbands and some don't want to marry at all—the towns and villages are full of bastards! After going to school, boys no longer want to work the land. Even failed scholars with no qualifications think they deserve a salaried job; they grow fat on the blood of unemployment and delinquency.

N19   *El Haj Chaïbou Bagouma (M, 87 years), Takiéta*

Bagouma was a stately old man, composed and gentle. As the right-hand man of the **chef du canton**, *he spent his days sitting in the chief's courtyard, from whence he could be easily beckoned to do whatever the chief required. He is the most senior member of the chief's staff, who acts as his secretary and intermediary, and has the power to settle certain cases or disputes after full consultation with the chief's son, Ibrahim.*

I am from the Zarma tribe and have spent the last 67 years here. Before that, I was at Fandou, Fillingué district, Niamey département. When the colonial government arrived, I was too young to be recruited into the army

but was employed as a "boy", cooking in a colonial household. The family employing me lived in Damagaram, Zinder, which is why I am here today.

Afterwards, I joined a team of 600 to 700 men conscripted for road work and was put in charge of them. We worked with the bare minimum of equipment, carrying all raw materials—water, sand and gravel—on our heads to the site. **Les blancs** lent us horses to travel into town to find the labourers needed. To feed this big workforce, they also bought many hundreds of animals.

In those days, we detested military service—compulsory for most men—and hated the schools of **les blancs**. The authorities ordered the chiefs to send their children to these schools but, initially, they were reluctant and often sent their subjects' children instead. These educated children then rose rapidly within the administration and soon were giving orders to their chiefs! The traditional hierarchy was being overturned. So chiefs now send their children to school.

Raiding and plundering

My parents were agro-pastoralists but also practised commerce and warmongering! In those days, there were wars between Tuareg and

Zarma, among the Zarma themselves, and between farmers and pastoralists. It was an age when courage was highly esteemed. Some men were so brave that they could fight a whole village on their own. My grandfather, Issa Korombé, was a famous fighter in his village. He was one of those warriors who resisted **les blancs** when they came.

Much raiding and plundering went on during my youth; the Tuareg were particularly notorious. The colonial administration's law and order put an end to such villainous activities. It also introduced social justice, peace and security. In those days, shame fell on the whole family of those who went to prison. This is no longer the case. **Les blancs** also broke "the yoke of ignorance" which bound us. Despite making us suffer with enforced road building, they brought us many things and helped us. The journey between Zinder and Niamey took 37 days by foot, now it takes just a few hours.

The value of money

The value of money has multiplied of its own account. Not only has there been five-fold inflation, but so much money is circulating that even small children can be seen clutching it. In the past, it was quite unusual to sell anything. Goods were bartered: your millet was exchanged for your neighbour's haricot beans, sorghum or even livestock. Money had very little meaning to most of us, which is why it is so difficult to estimate the price of grain then. Famines and food shortages were two of the rare times when goods were bought or sold for cash. At such times, grain prices soared. After the 1984 drought, a measure of millet costing between 125 and 150 **CFA** rocketed up to 500 or 600 **CFA**. This is not unusual. Prices always rise after any bad harvest.

It is difficult to estimate past crop yields, because we used different measures. Grain was stored either in tchukurfas, sacks woven from *dom* or *borassus* leaves, or in taikis, containers made from cowhide—those made from goatskin or sheepskin were more often used to carry water.

I first had to buy millet 30 years ago, when a bad harvest forced us to sell our domestic animals to buy grain. Those without sheep, goats or cows resorted to small-scale trading or to selling wood and hay. Some found employment with the more affluent; others migrated to find work elsewhere and earn money to feed their hungry families.

So much money is circulating that even small children can be seen clutching it

Without irrigation, we have not been able to practise dry-season vegetable gardening. We hope to, though, because it would supplement our income and give us some security in years of poor rainfall. At present, we wait for the rains before planting our staple crops: millet, sorghum, haricot beans and sorrel. In good years, any surplus is sold to buy other essentials, such as clothes and livestock, or to pay taxes or for baptism and marriage ceremonies.

We sell cereals only in exceptional circumstances, although cash crops—groundnuts, haricot and sorrel—are regularly sold to increase our income. A few years ago, the government introduced a grain bank, to give food security during famines. Every year each peasant puts millet and sorghum or, in rare cases, haricot beans into a grain bank under his chief's safekeeping, taking it out when the rains come the next year.

Famines and food shortages were two of the rare times when goods were bought or sold for cash

We still use the traditional farm tools used by our parents and grandparents. Although we would all like to use draught animals, few of us can afford oxen to pull ploughs. We maintain soil fertility with manure and chemical fertilisers. We used to leave the stubble to sustain the soil, but recently, agricultural extension workers have shown us that the stems hide all sorts of destructive pests. We now cut down the stems as soon as the harvest is over.

Land shortages

In the past, there were fewer people and the land was free. Even strangers could ask the chief for land. Land was inherited, was loaned to neighbours, but was too sacred to be bought or sold. Today, the ground is no longer respected: it has become just a saleable product, like any other. Our monetary economy has reduced our land to common merchandise. The "population explosion" has aggravated the problem, creating land shortages. When I was young, the bush seemed so vast that we never believed our fields would exhaust it. It was full of wildlife—some of it dangerous—and farmers had to keep constant watch to ensure their fields were not damaged by monkeys, birds, antelope or guinea-fowl.

Today, because there are so many people, our fields have shrunk. Those which once belonged to one person are now used by five. As population grows, soil productivity and yields decrease. To compensate for this, trees are being savaged to clear ground for agriculture. That hill, 300 metres away, could not be seen through the thick vegetation in the old days. Some village people's only means of income is to sell wood for

---

N38 Gawa Assoumane (M, 85 years), Tibiri

It is never a good idea to keep money, it is better to turn it into some sort of concrete object. Animals in particular are a good investment because you can be sure that you will never have any difficulties selling them.

In a group of children there will always be some who are lazy and do nothing to help. If, therefore, you have a lot of children you can maximise your chances of having some who will be useful.

---

fuel or construction. When the government realised how many trees were being cleared, they passed a law. Now, permits are required to cut trees. Without this law slowing down the rate of clearance, there would be no trees left in our country. As it is, *dargaza, dilo, zouré* and *hano* trees have completely disappeared, and *leyara, raria, gamba, nobi, tsabre* and *zamarke* grasses are decreasing.

Cleaning out a granary, Djéouta village.

Garba Adamou (M, 38 years), Abalak   *N27*

In Tamashek, "abalak" means "an abundance of water" and the
village is named after the big lake next to it. Lake Abalak has proved
ideal for fishing and fish farming.

My parents come from Tamaské but I was born and spent the first 13 years
of my life in Nigeria. Twenty-five years ago, I came to Abalak. My main
job was fishing, which I had done since I was 10. I also did a little farming
to supplement my income but very much as a secondary activity.

I have travelled widely, working on the Senegal River near Gaya, in
Nigeria, and in Chad. I decided to leave Nigeria to visit relations in
Adouna, near Tamaske. I stayed there until the Ministry of Water and
Forests told me about Lake Abalak and I came to see if a fisherman could
make a living here. The quality and quantity of fish are high and I am now
head of about 30 fishermen, who have great respect for me and ask my
advice about problems with money or the authorities. Fourteen years ago,
les blancs helped our fishing business get off the ground by providing
materials and training. We would benefit from more of this kind of help.

At present, we are organising a fishermen's cooperative to help us run
our own affairs, and this seems to be working very well.

I have no relatives here and my parents are dead. I am head of my
family, with three wives and some children. It is hard to live here, because
many people have taken up fishing and none of us can catch many fish.
Also, bandits add to our hardships: while fishing in Lake Chad, I had
400,000 **CFA**'s worth of equipment stolen. Our **pirogues** are the most
expensive and precious item, worth 40,000 **CFA** or more, but nets, fishing
lines, hooks and **calabashes** are also crucial to our work. We buy **pirogues**
in Yaouri, Nigeria, since there are none in Niger. Boats are best built from
the hollowed-out trunks of red *mad'âtchi* wood, but we are forbidden to
cut down this rare tree in Niger. A well-made boat lasts seven years.

In Lake Abalak there is a great variety of fish: long guechi, flat spiney
bokon, rambouchi, **silure**, herring, kouma, konkoura and the largest fish
of all, the **capitaine**, known as "the elephant of the water". Of these guechi
and bokon are the most common. The most profitable are the **capitaine**
—a large fish can fetch 5,000 **CFA**—and the guechi, which reaches 1,000
CFA per kilo. Some **capitaines** are more than 2 metres long; other fish
rarely exceed 1 metre.

We used to take the catch to Arlit, Agadez, Niamey, Maradi or Nigeria,
where we normally found a good market for fish. Today, our market is

Fish did not sell well. People considered them to be like snakes or frogs and hated the smell very secure and traders from these towns come here to buy. Our regular clients have risen from two to around 100. Sometimes, I take fish myself in a lorry to Nigeria. The journey takes two to three days but you can be sure of selling the fish at the end of it—even if it is rotten! The Igbo people of southeastern Nigeria have a particular taste for it.

Sometimes, if I can't sell the fish immediately, I dry them. I learnt this simple technique in Chad. I gut the fish, coat it with salt, then lie it in the sun to dry. The Chadians, Malians and Senegalese are good fishermen and taught me much about good preservation techniques.

Fish: an acquired taste

When I first came here, fish did not sell well. People considered them to be like snakes or frogs and hated the smell. It was not easy to introduce my trade. Even though I began by asking very low prices, only workers from other parts of the country bought fish. Gradually, however, others became accustomed to the taste. I spent a long time giving free fish to people hoping to convert them, which was not very profitable as the Tuareg were so repelled by the smell. But I felt there was no other way to encourage them to taste fish. Now the Tuareg like fish, but put perfume on their body to hide its smell when they eat it!

I use the same fishing methods here as I did in Nigeria. Little children use hooks and lines with bits of meat to catch small fish for their family. We fishermen take our **pirogues** to the middle of the lake and drop big nets, capable of catching many fish. The Ministry of Water and Forests sets no limit on our catch size, but we do have to pay a tax: 40,000 **CFA** for those selling fish in Nigeria and 11,000 **CFA** for those selling fish in Niger. Even children using lines from the shore have to pay tax.

Environmental degradation has caused rainfall to diminish which, in turn, affects the lake's water level. This is unhealthy for the fish population and so, to help maintain a natural equilibrium, we plant trees. As a rule, the water level falls in December and gets higher from July to November. During the 1973 drought, there was no water at all left in the lake: we had to dig holes in the lake floor to make small ponds for the fish. We put cow dung in the holes to help the fish to breed. It was a terrible year. We suffered great losses of fish, animals and trees. During the drought, when the water level was low, it was easier to catch the fish as there was so much less water. However, we could not sell them here. They had to be exported to Nigeria for money to buy grain for our families.

The year 1984 was another difficult one, when the water level fell dangerously. If fish die during droughts, we introduce new fish stock for breeding. Since 1984, things have returned to normal and now the lake has enough water, being 6 to 8 metres deep in the middle. The water is of a good quality and bilharzia-free and we can drink it—something impossible in Nigeria.

Fishermen's secrets

We have secrets of our trade, but do not put our newborn infants in the river to see if they will live, like some fishermen do. Some say this is the only way to test whether the child is really a fisherman's son. The child is left in the water for a week. If it is still alive when its parents return, then the father can be sure that it really is his son or daughter. The truth of the matter is that the parents leave a **genie** in the water with the child, who guards the baby until its parents return. This practice still exists in some areas but we do not do it ourselves.

I possess a special magic which means I can go into water where hippos lurk, knowing that nothing will hurt me. Some medicines can only be given to our own children. We also have secret medicines to administer when someone gets a fish bone or spike stuck in their throat. I could give you medicine to let you eat whatever fish you liked without any danger.

Group interview with four Peulh pastoralists, Abalak   N33
Aicho Benno (F, 40 years)
Jima Bello (F, 42 years)
Ibrahim Karu (M, 50 years)
Mamane Dan N'anto (M, 46 years)

The **chef des bouchers** *buys meat regularly from the Peulh and has built up a close friendship with them. Whenever the Peulh arrive in the village, they always go directly to the* **chef des bouchers***, who looks after them. Pastoralists are particularly keen to sell their sick animals to him, at a reduced price, before they die. He has better facilities than they have and can treat the animal or keep it for a while before slaughtering it.*

We were born in Madaoua département, near Abalak. We came to Abalak four years ago after being forced to move from Madaoua, because there was no more free grazing land. Everything has been taken over by the Hausa, who have turned our grazing land into agricultural fields. They were making us pay to keep our animals in the fields after the harvest, even though the fields were free land. That is why we came here, where there was plenty of free pasture and few farmers. Also, we had the free use of a pump for the animals' drinking water. Unfortunately, after we arrived, large numbers of Hausa people took a new interest in the land. Today, it is nearly all occupied. To make matters worse, they have taken up vegetable gardening and use so much water from the pumps that we now have to pay for our animals' drinking water. We do not have an amicable relationship with the Hausa: they treat us badly.

On the move

Until 1984, we moved around with our big herds. When we found an area with thick green vegetation, we would stop for six or seven days, until the grass was so trampled, dirty and stinking of urine that the animals no longer wanted to eat it. Before we changed pasture, one or two men would go ahead on the back of a camel or donkey to inspect other areas, always somewhere there was either a pond, lake or well. Having found a suitable spot, the men returned and the group packed up their possessions and moved on. We stayed together as we travelled. All our goods were carried by camels, donkeys and cows but you would never see a Peulh pastoralist separated from his staff. It was as important as a gun is to a soldier, being his main means of defence and his companion on the road. Generally, men rode camels and women were happy to travel on donkeys or cows.

We were content with this nomadic way of life and enjoyed moving on from place to place. As long as our animals had enough to eat, we had no worries. We were so attached to our animals that we could not stand to see them suffering: sometimes we could not even eat the meat of a cow that had died. We were sentimental about them. We had grown up together and had a parental bond with them—it is difficult to explain exactly.

In those days, we lived on milk, cheese and cereals. To buy the grain, we sold two or three animals, or milk and cheese. We have never done any farming ourselves. Our parents and their ancestors never did: they were pastoralists. Only in the last few years, with the terrible drought and famine, have our animals died from lack of pasture and thirst. Sometimes, we take sick animals to the Pastoralists' Service Centre, and pay for them to be cured.

We were so attached to our animals... sometimes we could not even eat the meat of a cow that had died

Loss of pasture

When we first arrived here, the vegetation was different. In those days, we lived in peace and abundance. Now our beasts are threatened by the poor vegetation: they have become feeble and thin. In our opinion, the main reason for this degradation is the lack of rain. On top of this, the increasing population ceaselessly exploits the land for agriculture. Farmers cut down trees, pull up grass and bushes, and clear more and more land. To enrich the soil, some of them burn over the ground which, *Increasingly,* stripped naked of vegetation, is then susceptible to wind erosion. *sheep, goats,*

All this has led to social and material poverty: juvenile delinquency, *cows and* prostitution, theft and crime are all on the increase. Certain illnesses, *camels are* particularly fevers, are more and more common, both among people and *being* animals. When we fall ill, we have to buy medicines, but it is hard to find *monopolised* enough money. We also have to pay for water. Everything has become so *by a few rich* much more expensive and we have less money than before. Solidarity, *people, who* once so strong in the community, has disappeared and has been replaced *own huge* by blatant self-interest. Our only hope is that life will improve and return *numbers* to what it was a long time ago. Most of all, we would like to be able to build up our herds, so that we can return to our nomadic way of life. We do not like to be in one place all the time. In order to achieve this, we ask for support from the government and from aid agencies.

Mahamadou Ibrahim-Mahamadou (M, 75 years), Tibiri   N41

I was born here in Tibiri in the reign of Chief Alou. I used to be a **griot**, but there was not enough work to keep me going, so now I practise mixed farming and pastoralism. I never went to school as a boy, my only formal training was in the army.

In the old days, life was harder due to famine: people sacrificed everything in the search for food. However, winds are stronger than before, because all the trees which act as a buffer against violent storms have been cut down. Valuable plants and trees include *kangna, aorawa, taoura* and *tchiriri*. We mistrust people who cut down *gawo* trees: these grow in our fields because we feel that they benefit our crops.

Quality of soil
We use manure to improve soil quality. We encourage pastoralists to put their animals on our fields, but if we can't manage this, then we carry the

N44 Kaka Bouchia (M, 40 years), Tibiri
The first times we heard a car we knew it was the man coming to collect our taxes, so we would run into the bush, or under our beds, to hide. My grandfather used to say to me that a day would come when women would be able to overtake men. He was right, because since the car was invented they have been able to do this!

In the past children used to constitute our wealth, but this is not so much the case today, because we have a number of labour-saving devices that do the jobs that children used to do.

A wise manure to the fields on our heads. In my day, charlatans gave farmers a
old man medicine which supposedly increased yields.
would   We no longer dare to leave land fallow, since we fear that it will be
never claimed by someone else. We plant our fields with one or two strips of
lie...even millet, then a strip of groundnuts; sorghum is planted under trees. We eat
if he was most of our crops, although the surplus in a good year is sold for money.
mad A sack of millet fetches 5,000 **CFA**. Once, we only planted millet, but
now the climate has changed so much that other crops can grow.

Migration

During the dead dry season, some people trade, others sell **banco** to build
houses. Pastoralists make contracts to provide manure from their animals.
Those with nothing else to do migrate to Kano [Nigeria], Niamey, Benin
and Ghana. Women rarely migrate, unless they are escaping from an
arranged marriage or their children have nothing to eat. Unsuccessful
migrants resort to delinquency and prostitution.

Fields are prepared for replanting before the rains. Fences are put up
round the fields and the weeds that cause most damage—*kassaoura,
kiassoua, bilbilwo, koumoudoua* and *kirikiri* —are regularly pulled up
and burnt. Women are busy with housework, although most also grow
groundnuts.

Today, we are much better supplied with water. Free wells were built
all around the village and this has greatly reduced women's work. They
still have to get wood, which they may collect secretly from the bush. It
is harder to find now than it was in the past. So some wood is bought,
collected by lorryload from far away.

Pastoralists cause farmers many problems by driving their animals into
their fields. Sometimes, the ensuing dispute can be resolved by the chief,
who decides on the level of compensation to be paid. At other times, the
issue may escalate into a bloody battle. I am a farmer, so I entrust the care
of my animals to my son and grandchildren. If I had no children, I would
have to keep a section of my field free for my animals. Increasingly,
sheep, goats, cows and camels are being monopolised by a few rich
people, who own huge numbers of them.

Education and social change

What I find most astonishing about our society is the way in which
traditional chiefs succeed each other: one dies and one of his descendants
takes his place. Our social structure has been turned upside down by the
increasing emphasis put on education. Once, old people were considered
the wisest and were always consulted. They were well respected: one

knew that a wise old man would never lie. Even if he was mad, he could not be contradicted. If you spoke against him, it was like placing a death threat upon yourself. Nowadays, because of education, people listen to the young. Modern schools have rapidly replaced Qur'anic schools.

Nowadays, because of education, people listen to the young

When I was young, strength was everything. Wars were won by force. If someone came from another country with a great fortune, you killed him and took all he had. It was good. The only problem was that his relatives sometimes got wind of the atrocity, then came in a group to take their revenge on you and your family. Now customs officers ensure the security of our frontiers and enforce law and order.

Sicknesses are caused by the cold weather or, occasionally, by the devil and can be very dangerous. The most common are haemorrhoids and swellings. Venereal diseases are particularly bad and result in swollen testicles and impotence. A dispensary has recently been built in the town, so people place less emphasis on traditional medicine, although those in rural areas continue to take herbal remedies. Two of the most popular traditional medicines are made from the roots of *anza* and *agadjini* trees.

My main hope for the village is that they should have a good rainy season. My dreams for my future are that I have enough to eat and drink and stay in good health. Now that I am old, all that I need is my health, so that I can appreciate the last years of my life. I want to die in my village.

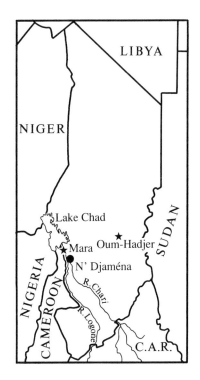
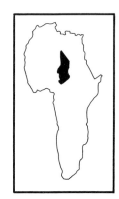

Country Profile: CHAD
Human Development Index (UNDP): 152nd out of 160 nations
Population (1990): 5.7 mn. **Growth rate (1990-2000):** 2.6%
Life expectancy at birth (1990): 46.5 years
Population per doctor (1984): 38,360
Adult literacy (1985): male 34%; female 13%
Labour force employed in agriculture (1985-1988): 83%
GDP from agriculture and livestock (1988): 46.1%
Principal exports: cotton, livestock

1890s Chad was one of the last territories to form part of French Equatorial Africa. **1960** Full independence. **1962** President Tombalbaye bans all political parties and creates one-party state. Country subsequently divided by recurring civil wars, in which France and Libya support opposing factions. **1975** Tombalbaye killed in army coup. **1987** Libyan troops expelled. Hissein Habré assumes presidential power. **1990** Dec: Habré flees country after three-week war. Idriss Deby establishes Conseil d'Etat and pledges a pluralist democracy.

CHAD

Interviews in Chad were all conducted in Arabic. The first group of interviews were collected from Mara, a fishing community on the River Chari, north of the capital, N'Djaména. **Albertine Ndonadji** and **Abderaman Issa Youssouf** interviewed fishing people and farmers. The same team also undertook interviews at Oum-Hadjer, 650 km east of N'Djaména, the site of an Oxfam/SECADEV (Secours Catholique et Développement) project supporting agro-pastoralists. The work was coordinated by **Rhiannon Barker** with **Mahamat Ahmad Alhabo**, a research associate at the Institut National des Sciences Humaines in N'Djaména.

Nizela Idriss (F), Alhi-bel, Koundjar   *C1*

As her cows drank from the watering holes which the men kept full of water pulled from the well, Nizela Idriss talked to us under a shelter. She was a small woman with a warm smile, preoccupied with making sure her visitors were fully covered by the

small area of shade provided by her shelter. Each time she noticed the sun creeping on to one of our limbs she would tap the exposed area with her stick, urging us to move into the shade. Despite the rain which had fallen the night before, the sandy soil was parched and the watering holes soaked up the water almost as quickly as the men poured it in.

We have been living in this camp, Alhi-bel, for about four years now. It is an hour's walk from the nearest watering hole. When the rains start we will move away to find new pasture for our animals. In this camp there are six families, who always move around together. When my own children marry they will choose people from our camp; that way we stay together.

Since my youth I have lived under the threat and insecurity of fighting. The first problems I remember were tribal; between the Masaguete and the Ratamine. It must have been a dispute over rights to water or to land. These are the only things that neighbouring tribes argue about. As for the war between Chad and Libya, I never knew why they were fighting, although of course I saw the planes fly over and knew that our sons were dying. My own son went to join the fighting, and now he lies with many others, buried in the ground.

When I was young I never had the chance to go to school. I wanted my children to learn, but when my son was educated he decided to join the army and now he is dead. That has discouraged me from seeking education for the rest of my children since I cannot bear to lose any more. One of my younger sons is with his aunt in Mongo, a few hundred kilometres from here, and attends the Qur'anic school. I need the help and support of my children. I am an old woman—do you think that I can look after my animals on my own? No, it's my son who does that for me. He is only 10 years old, but he is not afraid of his job and does not fear spending a night or two in the bush with his animals.

Today we have about 10 cows, two of them mine and the rest my husband's. It doesn't matter who they belong to since we all benefit from them. We do not sell their milk since our herds are not large and their productivity is not as high as it used to be. I value my animals more than anything else.

Before the drought of 1985 we had about 20 cows, 30 goats and three donkeys. Some of these died and others we sold to buy food. Since that time our animals have reproduced steadily, but the herd has not increased in size because we have had to sell some animals in order to buy other essentials. When my parents were alive they had over 100 head of cattle. Then my father died and my mother left the country to go to Sudan. She felt that life was more secure there and moreover it meant she was able to avoid paying taxes.

"The time we sold our necklaces"

In 1985 the big famine came upon us. We called this Laïtche: "the year when everyone fled from the area"

We have suffered four major famines during my lifetime. The first was called Amzaytone, meaning "the time we sold our necklaces", in the 1950s. The second, about 10 years later, was El Harigue, "the year when everything burnt", when our crops shrivelled under the heat of the sun. The third, in 1982, was Alchouil, "the year of the sack", when traders came with sacks of millet for us to buy. As long as you had the means, you did not starve during this famine. Finally, in 1985 the big famine came upon us. We called this Laïtche, meaning "the year when everyone fled

Nizela Idriss pauses to talk, while her cattle drink nearby.

from the area". At other times of difficulty, the men would go and leave the women behind. We would supplement our diet with wild plants. We picked the leaves from the *savonnier* tree and the *amuzba*, boiled them in water and mixed the solution with any millet flour that we had. We also dug the termite mounds to unearth the grain they store. To make extra money we sold firewood and our jewellery in the market. When we had used all the money we had, we would be forced to sell one of our animals. If our animals died we would eat the flesh left on their bodies, not by choice, but because the famine forced us to do this.

I farm my own field which is separate from my husband's. We both do all the work. Before the rains we put our animals in the field to improve the fertility. Those who have no animals of their own ask their brother to bring his animals into the field. This is something that's done as a favour, not for payment. This keeps the fields so fertile that we can continue to cultivate year after year. Before the rains we plough our fields by hand and sow the crops. We plant sorghum, millet and *beri beri*. We used to plant groundnuts but the grasshoppers attacked them so voraciously that in the end we stopped.

After the drought of 1985 we lost all our seed, so the following year we had to use seed collected from people who had come from other parts of the country, even from Sudan. These days productivity is much lower. In a good year, before 1985, we could produce eight sacks of grain from our field; today that has fallen to three sacks. However much we produce we don't sell our crops. We keep them for our own consumption or we share them.

Modern life

What strikes me most, when I think about how life has changed since I was a child, is that people today all wear modern clothes, and that women have more freedom than they did. Little by little men have begun to expect women to participate more equally in their activities and jobs. Nowadays, if we don't go to help men in the fields they will say: "Eh! Why do you not help me plant my crops?" Those people in the village of Koundjar can afford to let their women sit and grow fat, but we do not have the luxury of choice. We have to work, and through our work we have gained more freedom. So, there have been some positive changes, but overall I yearn for the past when we had big herds, lots of milk and food in plenty.

C2   *Ashta Ahmat (F), Adirté Sabana*

> *Ashta Ahmat is president of the **groupement** féminin, a group of agro-pastoralist women who participate in a credit scheme run by Oxfam/SECADEV. On the day of our interview the group was meeting to discuss new developments and to look at the credit situation of individual members. Ashta took us into her tent, made from a framework of strong, flexible branches covered in matting, and gave us a drink of milk, millet and water. We wandered down to the dry river bed, and sat talking in the shade. Ashta's two-year-old boy, who cried incessantly, stared glumly at the mango we gave him and was only pacified when his mother tied him firmly to her back.*

My life has been long and God has been generous. I have given birth to 10 children and thank God that six are still living. The others died when they were babies, weakened by diarrhoea and other diseases.

I can remember several periods of famine. Ajaradie was "the year of the grasshopper". In fact, they fought against us for two years in a row, eating the crops we had struggled to grow. Amhanzine was the year when a **koro** of millet cost 250 **CFA**—in a good year a **koro** only cost 30 **CFA**. The last major famine was the "Great Famine" of 1985, when most of our people were forced to migrate from this area.

I stayed here, raising a small amount of money from selling some of our male animals and the milk from our cows. I carried on making and selling mats but I had to lower the price a bit to encourage people to buy them. Today I sell a small mat for 165 **CFA**, whereas during the famine

Interviewer Albertine Ndonadji (left) with Ashta Ahmat in her tent.

it only fetched 75 **CFA**. In the end I was forced to run away too. With my husband and children I embarked on a 12-day 300-kilometre journey to Bidkin, where we had relatives who we knew would do all they could to help us.

Before 1985 I had 18 animals of my own. It is true that my husband owns most of the cattle, but when a woman marries she receives a number of animals from her husband as a bride-price. I have eight cows left now and my husband's herd is reduced too.

My husband has a field which I help him to farm. Our main crops are millet and sorghum. The clay content in the soil varies considerably in this area. In some places it is almost all sand and can only be ploughed if the rains have been very good. Recently we have begun to plant tomatoes, melons and *gombo* in the rainy season. Our neighbours have planted mangoes which they irrigate with water drawn from a well donated by Action Contre la Famine. Some time ago I planted cassava, but the seeds were not disease-resistant so I copied some of my friends and turned to sugar cane. I dug my own well, about 4 metres deep, which I use to water my crops. We cannot dig a well in the camp because the water table is too low, so we move down to the dry river bed but even here we have to dig deeper each year.

Of course We keep our animals in our fields to fertilise the land before the rains.
everyone At planting time we usually move our animals about 1 kilometre from
should be the fields. In very dry years we may have to go further but rarely more
circumcised. than 20-30 kilometres. One of our problems is the increased competition
It is our for land. Large herds pass through here on their way to seasonal pastures,
custom eating our pasture as they go.

The **groupement** helps the women by providing credit to buy the materials to make mats. I wouldn't say the project has altered relations between men and women. I command the same respect as before, but now I know that I can rely on my own income, and this makes me stronger. Other things are easier for women. We have more mobility and it's easier to find food for our families. If something is lacking, we can find vitamins at the pharmacy.

Circumcision

Women and men are both circumcised. Circumcision marks the entry of a child into the adult world. It is a time of celebration. We slaughter animals and dance, perhaps with more energy and vigour for a boy than a girl. A girl is circumcised at home when she is 7 or 8 years old. Her labia are cut with a knife by a woman who is skilled at her job. There is nothing to kill the pain, so we just have to be brave. If the wound goes septic we rub hot oil on it with a piece of cotton. Then we burn and grind cow dung and sprinkle the powder on the wound. It should heal within 7-8 days. Today the operation is less prone to problems, since at the first sign of infection we go to the pharmacy and buy tetracycline. Of course everyone should be circumcised. It is our custom. It's natural to be frightened, but it is simply something we have to bear.

C48 Abdoulaye Issaka (M, 65 years), Koundjar

There has been a change of mentality between us—the young—and our parents. The parents would never have taken the initiative to learn the methods of vaccination for the animals; we, on the other hand, have done it. When our parents were confronted by some difficulty imposed by nature, they used to seek immediately to leave the area and go elsewhere. But we, we try to resolve the problem and struggle to resist, to stay put at all costs. So there you have the difference between us.

C22 Madeline Koubou (F), Mara

I split up with my husband a long time ago. I don't expect I will ever go back to the home we had together . Sleeping on the same mat as him is not my idea of paradise because he used to treat me like a slave, an animal. I know he is the father of my children and for this reason if something happened to him I would, of course, offer him emotional and material support—but not as the husband of my heart.

Mariam Madra (F), Ad Djob, Koudere   *C3*

My husband died many years ago, leaving me to look after my children in these difficult times. I don't know if things are harder simply because he is no longer with us or because the land and climate seem to fight against us. Today, the only way I can make money is by grinding millet and weaving mats which we sell in the market.

We suffered a lot in this area from fighting between different ethnic groups. Armed bandits would come to our village, demanding money and animals. I had to give them the equivalent of 30,000 **CFA**. Of course, I didn't have this money and had to give some of my animals instead. It was Arabs from the south who terrorised us in this way.

In those days we had enough animals. Today I look around me and wonder where they have gone. When I married, my husband gave me a few of my own animals as a bride-price, which I was able to build up into a small herd. All I have left is one cow, some calves and three donkeys. I have a few chickens as well, but what is the value of those? They are not livestock.

Our fields are next to the camp. We no longer grow cotton because it was particularly susceptible to grasshoppers and because we can buy cheap ready-made clothes. Millet seems to grow better and is our major food crop.

Mariam Madra and her son outside her home.

Pests
One year the grasshoppers were so bad that we had to ask the state for assistance. They gave us powder to put on the land but it didn't kill the pests. The men also went to the **marabout** for help. He would beat his drums and cry to God but even this did not work. The only thing that was really effective was when the women themselves went to stand in the fields, from dawn to dusk, throwing stones and shouting to frighten off all the "intruders" who tried to snatch a bite to eat from our crops.

When I was young, men and women used to farm together in the same field. Now the men spend so much time travelling in search of work elsewhere that it's more practical for the women to have their own fields. Our men are courageous—they go as far as Nigeria to find work—but sometimes I feel it is the women, who stay here with the children, not knowing where they are going to find the next meal, who are stronger. Women only ever leave the area during a very severe drought, if they can no longer find food for the family.

The first big famine I remember was Amzaytone, the name of the pearls in our necklace which we had to sell to raise money for food. Then there was the year when millet was brought from other regions on the backs of donkeys. The most recent was in 1985, when everyone left the village. I left reluctantly for Abeche, with my children. We were gone for two months, and I found work grinding grain for women living in town.

When food is short we try to supplement our income by weaving mats. A good price for an average-sized mat is 500 **CFA**, or 450 **CFA** when they are not in such demand. That is what we get for about seven days' work, which does not include the time spent collecting and cutting the *rônier* plant and dyeing the straw. To make one mat you need about three bundles of *rônier* leaves.

We have to be resourceful since things do not come ready-made in this part of the world. The woven basket hanging on the wall was made by the blacksmith's wife—that work is too intricate for me. The grainstore in the corner of the room took three days to make from clay and grass. Last year our seeds were wasted as the rains came early. This year I pray that God will provide me with enough grain to fill two grainstores, since this is the amount that I need to feed my family without having to buy any extra.

I don't have any daughters, which means that some of the work that *Men and* girls would normally do I have to manage myself, even though I am *women used* growing old and weak. I have to grind the grain and go out with my friends *to farm* to collect wood. Although I have a donkey, I normally carry the wood *together...* myself since I like to accompany my friends.

The water supply is one of our biggest worries. We dig holes in the dried-up river bed, managing to get just enough muddy water to meet our needs. I don't know if this contributes to the diseases we suffer from. Many of us, both young and old, are plagued by health problems. I am sick myself. I have this swelling in my neck [goitre], and a fever. Some people say there is a plant called *terres azarack* which would help reduce the swelling. I have already tried to treat myself by burning the tips of my fingers and the ends of my toes—they are quite scarred now. It helped me a little, since at least now my appetite has returned.

...now men spend so much time travelling in search of work that it's more practical for women to have their own fields

SECADEV has greatly contributed to the development of the village, but there is so much that could be done. Improving our food would be one of my priorities. We women have no kind of formal organisation—we just work on our own as we have always done. It seems to me that women lack initiative and motivation.

There is no school in this village. Neither my husband nor I went to school, it is not part of our tradition. It's more important that my children learn the Qur'an. That is why I send them to be taught by the **marabout**. The best advice you can give a child is to work hard and value the productivity of the fields, and not to leave the place where they were born.

Haoua Talba Hadj (F), Mara   *C13*

I was born on the Cameroon side of Mara. My father was a fisherman who owned a dugout canoe and a net "en baguette", made from strips of wood. We used paddles, as there were no motors then. Today fishing is hard because there is not so much water in the rivers. We try to care for our environment, and since the big trees have disappeared we have begun planting *neem* and mango.

Fishing was once a profitable occupation. My father used to catch so many fish that he would throw some back. His catch included **capitaine, brochet, carp and silure**. Now these varieties are rare and some have disappeared altogether. Our existence as a fishing community has grown more fragile.

After a good season there is also some money to be made from the sale of crops. Before, there was always enough millet for us to sell some in the middle of the rainy season. Now the weather is unpredictable and we have to wait until the end of the season to feel secure enough to sell off the supplies from the previous year. When the rains were strong and regular the climate was cold and fresh. We were fortunate. Now the rain has been replaced by a heat which beats down with full force.

Today, we drink water which comes from the pump. Before, we never thought twice about drinking water from the river. The wells are dug by the state. We haven't done anything towards their construction. We used to have very simple wells, without any pipes like the ones we see today. We put shafts in the bottom to ensure that the sides did not cave in.

Of the crops we plant, rice is the most productive and the work is not hard. A sack of rice fetches between 2,500 and 4,000 **CFA**. Sorghum is another good crop, better than maize. After three years of sowing the same piece of ground, we give that area a rest and move on to another, where we burn the bushes to clear the land. We have neither ploughs nor tractors so we prepare the land with hoes. Of course, with tractors or ploughs our yields would be higher but we would have to be trained to use them.

We keep a few sheep, of "Peulh quality". As soon as we notice anything wrong with our animals we take them to the vet in the neighbouring village, about 5 kilometres from here. During the dry season we supplement their diet with millet husks and other products that we buy in N'Djaména.

Food aid

Life seems to be full of difficulties which multiply all the time. Even looking after a child, from infancy to adulthood, is a terribly difficult job. Famine can be a great trial. One famine lasted for four years. Throughout that time we managed to grow produce in our vegetable garden and sold it in order to buy staple foods. At the height of the famine the state provided us with sweets, semolina, red millet and rice but over the last few years it has given us nothing in the way of food. It is only groups such as widows who may receive a sack of grain between them. When the state stopped giving us food aid we went back to working on the land, planting maize twice in one year. The state gave us cattle-cakes, which improved our yield. After the harvest we gave a percentage of our crops to the state in payment for the cattle-cakes.

We take our fish to Yaroua in Cameroon where we buy cereals. Even the women have begun to make this journey. In the past none of this was necessary. If one year there was not enough rain, the following year would bring a lot of rain to relieve the suffering.

I never got the chance to go to school. I didn't even undergo a proper course at the Qur'anic school. I went for two years to learn how to pray but then I gave it up. All my children, except the youngest one, have been to school. Of the seven I brought into the world, three gave up their education, but the other three have carried on.

When I was young the women would rise very early in the morning to go and look for water. On their return they would sweep the area in front of their houses. Then they would remove the husks from the millet, grind the grain with a mortar and pestle and make **boule** from the flour. While we were busy with these chores our husbands would go out fishing, bringing back their catch for us to treat and dry. When the fish had been prepared, we tied them in a sack, ready for our husbands to sell to the traders who passed through Mara. Our husbands gave us a share of the money to meet our own needs.

Desertification

One thing we do not sell is firewood. We use all that we can get for cooking. If it was only us using the wood there would still be trees around us, but people come from far afield and destroy our vegetation. They come from as far away as Farcha or N'Djaména on the backs of donkeys, in lorries or pushing carts, piling the wood on to their various forms of transport. This is what has turned the land into desert. In an attempt to stop the practice a number of forestry guards have come to live with us in Mara.

Women belong to the house. Children should support their parents, the girls helping their mother and the boys their father. They should be given the utmost encouragement to go to school and should only be expected to help their parents in the holidays.

Jeremy Hartley/Panos Pictures

"People come from far afield and destroy our vegetation....They come from as far away as N'Djaména on the backs of donkeys, in lorries or pushing carts....This is what has turned the land into desert."

A woman's cooking pot is never far away from her. The basic dish I give my family is rice or **boule** with a sauce made from onions, oil, salt, water, *gombo* and a bit of hot pepper. In addition to housework a wife may also be called upon to help her husband, just as the man may help his wife.

There is a group of women here who carry out certain collective social activities. For example, they welcome all strangers who come to Mara, and they offer support to bereaved villagers. We all put money into a fund to pay for social occasions such as these. People simply give if and when they are able.

C18   *Elisabeth Nadjiyo (F, 45 years), Mara*

Our presence in Elisabeth's compound caused much hilarity among the family and friends who looked on. Although reticent at first, Elisabeth was encouraged and greatly amused by the sound of her voice on tape. A burning hot wind, and a goat which had taken a fancy to the plastic cover of the tape- recorder, soon drove us into the shelter of her hut.

Nadjiyo, the name given to me by my parents, means "survivor from death". I was born in N'Djaména and grew up there. When we were very small, our mothers or older sisters would carry us on their backs. As we grew older we wore cloth to hide our nakedness and put smaller pieces of cloth across our chest to protect our breasts. We tried to make ourselves look beautiful by smearing our bodies with cream, hoping that we would turn the eyes of the young men as they walked by.

Courtship
My husband came to my home to court me. It was important that we should do our best to look good, since looks were the basis of our choice. The pleasure shared between a boy and girl was based on observation of each other. Young men are like goats looking for grazing on the banks—you see them roaming everywhere, looking for girls.

Young men are like goats looking for grazing—you see them roaming everywhere, looking for girls

My husband always had to come to my home with a companion. When a suitor arrived at your house you had to go out and welcome him. It was acceptable to chat together but you could not draw close to each other. When your visitors wanted to leave you had to accompany them as far as the path. At this point it was up to your suitor's companion to impart the reason for the visit. Once the marriage had been agreed between all the parties concerned, the bride-price had to be arranged. The first night of marriage was always hard for the newly weds, since to enter into a sexual relationship the man has to fight for, and win, physical dominance over the woman.

As young people we would sometimes refuse to help prepare the evening meal because it was more exciting to go out with our friends. As a punishment our parents would not give us anything to eat, or at best they would leave the millet for us to grind ourselves. Today, if a girl cannot get the food she wants from her parents, she can buy it from the shop or the market.

I have had six children—four girls and two boys—although death has taken three of them from me. Just as it was God who was the instigator of my marriage, so it is God who decides how many children are born to us. Today I am divorced as a result of a domestic argument. I could no longer tolerate what was expected of me. Perhaps one day I will go to my husband's house to seek his pardon.

Our ground never refuses to accept what we plant. Even if it is tired it still does its best to produce a small amount

Brewing

I like to use a lot of oil and onions in my cooking. Of course, during times of drought we have to cook very simply, using salted water and a tiny amount of oil. To make a bit of money and satisfy my friends I make alcohol and **bili bili**. It takes almost three days to make the alcohol. I grind the grain and make it into a dough which I then boil all night, before leaving it to ferment. Using a pipe I filter the mixture. The alcohol is produced in the vapours of the boiling dough. **Bili bili** also takes three days. I make a gruel from the grain which I then boil and ferment all through the first evening. It is heated to a very high temperature and then left to cool and ferment.

Today in Mara, although the water has dried up and the environment is seriously degraded, we are still able to feed ourselves. There are two factors at work here: the first is God. But God's help is never enough on its own. We must add our own contribution to His assistance. The woman should arm herself with an axe, and the man with a hoe, and together they must go and clear the land.

Men and women often share the work in the field. You have to clear the trees and burn the vegetation to make more space. We are discerning about the trees that we cut down: we do not touch those that give us shade or that bear wild fruit for us to eat.

Our ground never refuses to accept what we plant in it. Even if it is tired it still does its best to produce a small amount. When the yield lessens, we search for more fertile land. My grandparents used to travel huge distances, looking for new land to use. Other people stay in the same place but switch between different plots, leaving one fallow while they cultivate another. Once the seeds have been sown the soil has to be weeded to prevent *belbeshre*, *haya* and *shiga* from destroying the crop.

We drink the water from the river, in the same way as our grandparents did. Even now that there is a tap, I still prefer the river water.

C28   *Djimé Mahamat (M), Mara*

There was once a chief in the village who taught us how to catch crocodiles. I learnt with him for a long time, maybe seven years. He taught us all the tricks that we needed to know so that we could eventually catch them on our own.

The first night I was taken out by the chief I remember sitting in a boat, a torch in my left hand and a spear in my right. Another man sat at the front of the boat, moving it slowly forwards. The night was dark, so I lit a torch to help me see the surface of the water. Suddenly I saw a crocodile. We moved slowly through the water towards it and, when we were a certain distance away, I hurled my spear. The crocodile tried to flee but the spear, which was attached to an iron chain, had pierced its flesh. We moved the boat forward, dragging the wounded, struggling crocodile behind us. It was still alive, so we gave it a blow on the neck and at last it died.

"Crocodile hunting is not easy"
After killing a crocodile we would skin it. We sold the skins to white people who came specially to buy them. Crocodile hunting is not easy. You have to be brave and take a lot of risks. Each time we went hunting we would go to the chief who gave us a charm to protect us from the more dangerous elements lurking in the water.

One day a Frenchman turned up at Mara. He introduced himself to our chief and asked if he could employ a group of crocodile hunters. The chief agreed in principle and organised a team of six. We travelled in our boat to N'Djaména, where we were collected by the Frenchman in his car. Together we drove down to the south of the country, arriving eventually in the region of Kyabé, where there are known to be a lot of crocodiles. The Frenchman told us that he had to return to the capital but would come back to pick us up.

When he had left, we all went our separate ways, since we could catch more crocodiles, more quickly, if we worked on our own. We managed to catch over 50. We were very happy with our work but a major problem was that we had not taken enough charms to protect us over the course of such intensive hunting. We told the Frenchman about this problem and fortunately he was sensitive to our needs. He produced a number of new charms, which we found most effective. From then on we never encountered any problems with our prey.

Even now that there is a tap, I still prefer the river water
Elisabeth Nadjiyo

After six months we had a collection of beautiful crocodiles which the Frenchman came to pick up. For each skin we received the sum of 500,000 CFA. We returned with the money to Mara, where we spent some time with our relatives.

After a while we wanted another adventure, so we sought permission to hunt crocodiles in the Central African Republic (CAR). When we arrived there, we found that the crocodiles were not so easy to catch. When the Frenchman arrived to buy our skins he found us with fewer than he had hoped for. He was disappointed: he had been relying on our catch. He proposed that two of us should go to Zaire to try our luck there. We were a bit unsure and told him that we could not go there without a guarantee. Understanding our predicament he suggested that we go with him to Zaire to evaluate the situation. If it looked as if crocodiles were plentiful, then he planned to return to pick up the others in our group. If the animals were in short supply, he would bring us back to the CAR. As it turned out we spent a whole day searching for crocodiles without success, and the Frenchman kept his promise by taking us back to the CAR. We stayed there for another two years before finally returning to Mara.

A few months later, the Frenchman came to Mara and tried to persuade us to return to Zaire. Although some of us had misgivings after the last experience, we left for Zaire, where we were given permission by the authorities to hunt in a clearly defined zone.

We began the hunt in a little lake where the rewards of our labours were not great. We moved on to another lake, but once again we found hardly any crocodiles. Our boss advised us to go further afield and said we should not worry about what the authorities had said. So, as he instructed, we followed the lakes and the rivers until we left the zone within which we had been authorised to hunt. Unfortunately, we were caught trespassing and held by the authorities for 12 days, before being deported.

Before we left, we went to see our boss, to ask him to take us back to Chad. He refused to help us in our plight, so we left on our own. He has never set foot again in this village, even though he has children here by his Zairean wife.

C33   Abouna Ali (M), Mara

The water in the River Chari used to be so high that it came up to this spot—where today you can see some trees and bushes growing. In those days this area was like a forest. The men who cut the trees could be heard singing in the forest. It used to take us a whole day to walk to N'Djaména because we had to clear a path through the bush. Now there is nothing to block our way. It is a desert out there. The rain no longer falls and there are no longer any little streams where the fish can lay their eggs before swimming back into the main river. If there are no eggs, how can there be any fish?

Ceremonies cast aside

The fishing season began in June when the first rains started. During the rains, the fish would reproduce in large numbers. My parents used to sacrifice sheep or goats by the side of the river. The atmosphere was always festive. After we had eaten our fill we would throw the goat skins into the river. Only when this ceremony was complete could we begin our fishing. One year the **marabout** told us to stop this practice. He said we were following the path of the devil. Our parents were discouraged and they cast aside the traditions of their ancestors. I no longer asked my neighbours for a bowl of honey before going down to the river. That had been my custom. I used to bring a bowl of honey myself and ask each of my neighbours for a similar offering. Then I would buy a red chicken and make a sacrifice of these gifts to the river, before setting out to catch the fish. When I pulled in my nets I would always share the catch with my neighbours.

The two people in the little canoe beat on the water to make a kot kot kot sound—that is how the Kotoko got their name
Abba Adji

Our boats were bought from the Bagrimiens. They had big nets attached to them which would sweep through the water, dragging the fish into them. The nets we use today are lighter and more manageable. The boats were made from the wood of the *mourai* tree. This does not grow in our area, hence we were not able to make them ourselves. I know that the process of hollowing out the trunk and carving the inside and outside used to take about 15 days.

Some people fished with a rod and line, using hooks made by the blacksmiths. When **les blancs** appeared in our country, they brought hooks which cost as little as 25 **CFA**. But although some equipment has got cheaper, our life has not been made easier—since the fish have disappeared. We blame our suffering on the bad rains. The land dried up and the trees died. People who found it hard to earn a living began to cut down the remaining trees to make charcoal which they sold as fuel. In this way the environment deteriorated, and now the desert is advancing more quickly than ever.

Years ago our fish were in great demand. Some were taken as far as France. We sold a lot at the big fish market in Farcha. The Bornu people came from Nigeria with their donkeys to buy dried fish. They grew so rich that now they have abandoned their donkeys for modern vehicles. Even Chadian merchants come in their cars to buy our fish. If we have fish to sell during the rains, when the cars cannot drive over the muddy roads, we take them to N'Djaména by boat. In 1964 a Frenchman established a cooperative here, through which we could sell our fish at a profit. This venture lasted until about 13 years ago, when the climate began to deteriorate.

Lost traditions

Our traditions have been buried in the sand. The menace of famine looms over us. We, the Kotoko people, are a race of fishermen. Now that our fish have gone, what are we supposed to do? After the last famine we knew that fishing was on the decline, so we looked for jobs as labourers and mechanics. We began to rely more on farming. The pastoralists did not manage so well. When their animals died, all they could do was make charcoal to sell.

In the time of my grandparents, if we could not find work in our village we would travel to our neighbours and help them to weave cotton. My parents used to buy their own cotton supplies from the Bornu people of Nigeria. They used to make their clothes. Men were particularly skilled at weaving and could make a big piece of cloth in three days. Cotton cost 4-5 **CFA** per basket. In return the Bornu would buy our dried fish, which cost 8 **CFA** for one dried salanga. We used "English money" and other currencies and some people used beads.

In the past, hares, monkeys and birds could cause all sorts of terrible damage. To guard against them we went to the fields at six in the morning and did not leave until the sun had set. Today we have relaxed our guard since the animals are quite rare. In addition to my main crop of millet I have a small vegetable garden where I plant tomatoes, *gombo*, *karkadeh* and lettuce. I am able to supplement my income by making clothes and mending radios and watches. I can mend pumps as well, since I have a few mechanical skills.

There have been many changes. Now we have a primary school, attended even by the children of the **marabout** and the chief. When it first opened we did not think that it was wise to send our children there, so it was only orphans who were educated.

We used to respect our parents, because it was they who put our clothes on our backs. We washed their hands before they ate and respected their wishes if they did not want to eat with us. When we married, we no longer claimed a share of their harvest but gave them a share of ours. Today young people have their own ideas—but they still feel the pull of their ancestors and they do not leave Mara for long. There have been times when I left Mara, but I always returned.

C49 Adoum Mahamat (M, 50 years), Koundjar

When we were young we worked with our parents; it was they who bought us what we needed. Today the young people go to work in the towns and bring money when they return, and it is they who give money to their parents. That is how much times have changed.

C31 Fatimé Achoumboule (F, 50 years), Mara

We used to say that if you worked you could have everything you wanted. It was only those who did not pull their weight who found themselves struggling. Then a year came when locusts appeared from the skies and destroyed all our crops and we realised that this statement was no longer true. Something more than hard work was necessary for survival.

Thomas Maskemngar (M), Mara   C40

My parents came from Gabringolo. I was taken to N'Djaména when I was a child. Later, I did some travelling—but being a man who could not forsake his native land, I returned.

Before my birth my mother got divorced. My father's family were angry and cursed the place where my mother was, and when I was born I was very ill. I was laid by the river where it was coolest and given the traditional treatment for **mindakoro**. You can easily die of this if the symptoms are not recognised, but the people in the village are very good at identifying and treating such diseases.

Some of my relatives wanted to marry my mother after her divorce but they were afraid because my father was still alive. One of them put a spell on me and lodged a gaya—the fruit of the *dom* palm—in my armpit. It was one of my grandfathers who managed to cut it out and release me from the suffering.

I paid bride-price for a wife but my cousins wrecked the chance of this marriage because of an old quarrel between her family and my uncle's. I am looking for a wife at present, but I want a model wife.

Locusts

When I was a child there was a famine, caused by locusts swarming in such numbers that they turned day into night and destroyed everything edible. People in the village were forced to dig for wild tubers but some died trying doing this because the famine had made them so weak. Children were particularly liable to die unless given special care.

After that, people had to settle by the river so that they could get the food they needed by fishing. They would also wrap fish in *titimri*, a plant from the river bank, and take them to areas untouched by the disaster, where they exchanged them for millet. Some people from unaffected places came to the famine areas, bringing millet to exchange for fish, but then they promptly started fishing themselves.

As a child I went to school until I dropped out to join my friends and start fishing. In the past, people refused schooling out of ignorance, but these days everyone wants to educate their children. God willing, the wife I find will be able to read and write, so that even if I'm not at home she can write to tell me how the children are, or read a prescription if the doctor orders medicine. I will send my children to school and in the holidays I will teach them to fish, and that way they will get the best of both worlds.

I plough when there is a lot of rain, when it is not possible to fish. People grow maize, red millet and beans. We can only cultivate small

There was a famine, caused by locusts swarming in such numbers that they turned day into night

We have no means of knowing why it is hot or cold. Only God knows

plots because it is forbidden to clear the ground by cutting down young bushes. We grow maize twice a year and the other food crops just once. Women grow okra and sorrel, and men help them as women are not as strong as men. Women also gather firewood, fetch water, pick, pound and grind millet, make the food and brew **bili bili**, which they sell so as to buy salt. Men, too, have other work. After working in the fields they go hunting for small game to bring home for cooking.

We move from one piece of ground to another, and let the ground rest after it has yielded the harvest. Some very fertile land can produce yields for three or four years before it needs to lie fallow. We do not use any fertiliser. Our grandparents used to use animal dung on the fields.

The main problem over the loss of trees is that the herdsmen cut them down for animal fodder and we do not know where to find saplings with which to replace them. Trees growing wild in Mara include tamarind, silk cotton trees and *ndain*.

Fishing

Our grandparents used to make fishing nets such as kabra, mbende and soro, but now we use modern ones. At the moment there is not much water, so there are fewer fish. We catch pike, **silure**, **capitaine**; different kinds of fish at different times. Carp is the only one that can always be found. You have to wait for the river to be very high before you can catch big fish such as nyinr, wouya, ngonr, kaou and youa.

Most fishing is done with the aid of a canoe. The way to fish without using a boat is to dig a hole a short distance from the river, channelling water into it. Fish which swim into this cannot get back to the river and are caught.

We sell the fish at the market. As there is a lot of **silure** at the moment, we sell it quite cheaply, but we charge quite a high price for pike. The women, who are responsible for selling the fish, first preserve and store some for future use, and then sell what remains. Some women also fish themselves.

Most people quench their thirst with river water, although there is one tap. The river water is boiled, cooled and then poured into a jar. We have been given a great deal of advice, verbal and practical. We have been taught how to avoid certain dangers and if people do the wrong thing, they are severely punished.

We have no means of knowing why it is hot or cold. Only God knows about these things. People these days seem to be incapable of accepting rain when there is rain, and heat when it is hot. In the old days, our grandfathers prayed for rain and it rained, or if the river was dangerously high, they prayed for a drop in the level, and there was one. They accepted what God offered. Nowadays, it seems even children have become disobedient. A young boy will threaten you, shaking his fist. There is no understanding anything any more.

Our life is harder than it used to be but we manage by working together. Our community is divided into two groups, Muslims and Christians, and when we worship the Muslims cannot join with us, nor we with them. Among us Christians, if one of our brothers suffers some misfortune, we consult together at church and each will give what he can to help the person in difficulties. In such circumstances our Muslim brothers also give us financial help—there is a general readiness to help one another. It is just that we have different traditions.

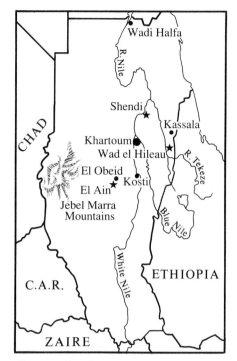

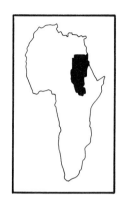

Country Profile: SUDAN

Human Development Index (UNDP): 143rd out of 160 nations
Population (1990): 25.2 mn. **Growth rate (1990-2000):** 2.9%
Life expectancy at birth (1990): 50.8 years
Population per doctor (1984): 10,100
Adult literacy (1985): male 39%; female 10%
Labour force employed in agriculture (1985-1988): 65%
GDP from agriculture and livestock (1988/89): 36%
Principal exports: cotton, sesame, gum arabic, sorghum, sheep and lambs

1898-99 Kitchener's defeat of Mahdist forces at Omdurman.
Establishment of Anglo-Egyptian condominium. **1955** Beginning of
conflict in southern Sudan. **1956** Independence. **1963** Anya-Nya
movement for southern independence formed. **1969** Colonel Nimeiri
takes power. **1972** Addis Ababa agreement ends civil war. **1983** Civil war
resumes. **1985** Nimeiri ousted. **1986** Civilian government. **1989** Lt-Gen.
El Beshir leads coup and sets up administration with backing of National
Islamic Front. **1991** New penal code based upon **Sharia** law applied in
all of northern Sudan.

SUDAN

Interviews in Sudan were carried out within three distinctly different communities. The first interviews were conducted in villages around Shendi, to the north of Khartoum, on the site of SOS Sahel's Village Extension Scheme. These were carried out in Arabic, among irrigation farmers, by **Abdel Salaam M. Sidahmed** and **Awatif Sidahmed**, both journalists. The second site was Wad el Hileau, a refugee camp in the east of Sudan administered by UNHCR. **Rukia Abdullahi**, a nutritionist, and **Habte Abraha**, himself a refugee, conducted interviews in Tigrigna, Tigre and Amharic with Eritrean and Tigrayan refugees of the Ethiopian civil war. Interviews at both these sites were coordinated by **Rhiannon Barker**. The third interview site was centred around SOS Sahel's Natural Forest Management Project at El Ain, near El Obeid, Kordofan. **Suleiman Haroun** and **Kaltoum Ahmed**, extension workers from the project, interviewed pastoralists, agro-pastoralists and settled farmers in Arabic. Their work was coordinated by **Gill Vogt**, extension coordinator for the El Ain project.

Sayda Hussein Agag (F, 56 years), El Shagalwa, Shendi   S1

I am the daughter of a boatman, who used to sail between Wadi Halfa and Aswan in Egypt. Later, he took up farming and moved to Shendi, where he was elected village **sheikh**. My family are members of the Konoz tribe, who came here with the Egyptian army during the war and settled.

My father had many cows, sheep and goats; he even had a horse- driven **hantour**. We hired a shepherd to take the animals for grazing. Today, our family has only one sheep and two goats for our daily milk supply. Animals have become very expensive. Twenty years ago, a sheep cost S£3; today one costs S£1,000.

My husband used to be a railway mechanic but he also took up farming later in life. People once grew a great variety of crops, including wheat, corn, sorghum, soya beans and oats. Today, fields are only full of onions and *barsim*. I don't know why this change has occurred. *Tormos*, once a popular bean, is no longer grown because higher temperatures have reduced yields. Traditional terracing systems were once used and sacks were filled with soil and put in lines to prevent soil erosion by the river.

Land shortages encourage crop rotation, but fertile land is being badly affected by shifting sand, by a creeping worm, and by the dramatic fall in rainfall levels over the past three or four years. Trees are drying up: date palms planted years ago have fallen down and not been replanted because so many young people have left. Up to one-third of the local population have migrated, though some do return to reclaim ancestral land. This was how my husband and my 50-year-old brother (recently returned from 15 years in Libya) got their land. In my tribe, land is passed from father to son, but never sold. Those not entitled to much land may have to rent from private landlords, often far afield, moving out of the village to plough and sow and returning home after harvest. Families finding it hard to eke out an existence from the soil may let their women work as cleaners and nurses in the village, but this is very much a last resort, as the Konoz disapprove of women working.

The SOS Sahel project arrived here a year ago to start a green belt. I know little about their aims and objectives, but I am suspicious of their activities. They will probably take our land and we may never see it again.

I have five sons and three daughters; four of them are working abroad. Looking back, I am fully satisfied. I have fulfilled my life's goal to see most of my children with a university education and good positions at work. The success and stability of my children are the first and final priorities of my life.

S3   *Hajeya Jumà Ahmed (F, 80 years), Shendi*

I was born in Khor Rahama, near the Sudan/Egyptian border. My father—a member of the Egyptian army—brought me to El Shagalwa when I was a few months old. I am illiterate, having had no access to any formal education. I had no children but if I had, I would have had a big family. Big families are better, because Allah may take some of them away.

Rain doesn't come now as before, and when it does, it devastates our homes and farms

When I was young, the grass was 3 foot high and included *siada*, *halfa*, *camal gesh* and *tabr*. There was no need to employ a shepherd to look after livestock. Rain doesn't come now as before, and when it does, it just devastates our homes and farms. This is God's will. What can we do?

There have been two bad floods in my lifetime: one 40 years ago, the other 10 years ago. I laid sacks filled with soil along the river banks to try to hold back the water.

I don't support the recent adoption of cash crops: it is the decision of young people. They wear us out and don't listen to any of our advice. When I was young, I used to work on my husband's farm but now women are just sitting at home waiting for their husbands and sons to bring them money. Yet young people have more hope and opportunity than before. With new technology, their chances are better. **Babor** pumps can irrigate vast areas, whereas we used a cow to draw water and could only irrigate very small plots. Men stuck to their land and farmed it; now they migrate or are interested only in getting quick money from selling onions.

Men stuck to their land and farmed it; now they migrate or are interested only in getting quick money from selling onions

Nutritional needs are harder to meet now because fewer crop varieties are grown. Also, with fewer animals, the supply of milk, butter and meat no longer meets demand. Much of the family income is spent on buying gasoline for the water pump. I preferred the old **sagia**: it was made locally, could be hand-operated, and lasted for ever.

Firewood used to be easily collected from the wide variety of local trees nearby. But it is all gone now—cut by the nomads and sold to the **kama'in**. I have three trees in my yard, which I have often refused to sell to nomads pestering me with requests to buy them. I want to leave them as shade for everyone who needs them: the reward from doing this is bigger than money, because money doesn't last.

Taha Hussein el Kashif (M, 83 years), Shendi   S15

I am an agro-pastoralist with a family of eight and innumerable grandchildren. My father was a soldier in the Egyptian army. I cannot read and never had any formal education. The most significant events in my life were the 1946 floods—when the banks of the Nile broke and crops were swept away—and the 1950 drought, when grain was brought from India to supplement the scarce supplies. I am despondent about the changes in our quality of life over the years. Although pump irrigation has improved agriculture, material costs and foreign imports have caused inflation to soar. Education is the priority that people should struggle for.

In the past, the rains were better. With decreasing rainfall came the disappearance of trees in the area around my village, which was once thick with *sellam*, *sidr*, *serreh*, *seyal*, *heglig* and *samreh*. Now, almost no trees or wildlife are left. Recently, I was travelling to a distant place and, believe me, I couldn't find a single tree under which to rest or from which to hang my sheepskin water container.

Today, orange, grapefruit, lime and mango trees are planted on

Foreign imports have caused inflation to soar irrigated land close to the Nile. Date palms, common in the past, are now scarce. The emphasis is also shifting away from grains towards vegetables such as onions, and corn and *barsim* for fodder.

I am concerned about pressures on the land caused by rising population. Now we can't leave any land fallow. Constant fragmentation by inheritance has resulted in over-intensive cultivation. This is why productivity has fallen. When I was young, 1 **feddan** yielded up to 5 tonnes of grain per year, compared to today's yields of 3 to 4 tonnes in similar climatic conditions. Our only benefit today is from cash crops, such as beans. Although soil fertility has clearly deteriorated, I don't blame wind or water erosion. Chemical fertilisers have been used to boost production and can be bought from the Agricultural Bank or the government for about S£85 a sack or S£120 on the black market. People prefer chemical fertilisers: they require less labour and are more effective in the short term. Manure makes vegetables tastier but is hard to find as there are fewer animals. My family only keep a few. Sheep and goats provide milk, meat and other products. Cows are used as draught animals; donkeys are ridden to and from the fields. Generally, animals are less important now than in the past.

I am resigned to the exodus of village youths to larger towns and cities. Although they then can no longer assist with agriculture, they can help by sending money. I have two sons: both have gone to work elsewhere.

S17   *Adam el Iman (M, 98 years), El Ushara, Shendi*

Like my father, I have farmed all my life. Today, I feel that the country is in better shape and life is easier. In the old days we lived a simple life, but food supplies were a problem in some seasons. We had to store millet throughout the year: now, we just buy enough grain for a few days.

Farming is the men's work here. Women never work in the fields. Intensive cash cropping employs some seasonal labour. This was not needed in the past, as farming always provided enough to satisfy family needs. We didn't have to supplement our income, though some people grew a little cotton, which women spun and men wove on looms made locally from *sunut* wood.

I used to cultivate about 10 **uds** of land—quite enough then, because our family was smaller. We grew grain in the summer, harvested it, then took care of our animals. We prepared for the winter season as soon as the river water changed colour and started to rise, flooding the land. That was about 40-45 years ago. We cultivated land once or twice a year, *Cash crop* depending on the river, land and **sagia** capacity. The new pump irrigation *incomes* was too expensive for me; the **sagia** was much better. *have raised*

Today, cash crop incomes have raised us out of poverty. In the past, *us out of* after paying taxes and the share of crops due to blacksmiths and **sagia** *poverty* carpenters, we were left with just enough to survive. I did not replace my animals after they died in the drought. They had been a valuable supplement to our food supply, but now we have to manage without. A few villagers keep camels for herding cattle in distant pastures, but this is not as common as it used to be.

The disappearing forest

There used to be many trees: *taleh, samreh, sellam, sunut, heglig, tundub* and further away *kitr* and *laut*. Thick forest surrounded the village. Stronger woods were used for making water wheels and roofs. Women used acacia wood for the "smoke bath". Married women make a hole in the ground, in which they put a small pot containing smoking wood and coal. They then sit over the hole, covered only in a heavy blanket, until their body has soaked up enough lingering scent from the wood smoke to treat their rheumatism. Other local remedies include **garad** from *sunut* to treat colds and fevers, and **lalob** from *heglig* for stomach pains.

When I was young, we planted date palms, but we do so no longer as their shade would inhibit our crops. Trees disappeared because the pump scheme encouraged people to clear land for agriculture. Also, nomads—eager for extra income—supplied brick manufacturers with many *sunut* trees. Now, only a few *sunut* and *taleh* trees are still standing, near the river. Since independence, people have planted fruit trees and a few date palms. Trees prevented soil erosion, sand movement and acted as a wind barrier. Due to lack of water, we cannot plant more trees. Rainfall has declined because of the loss of tree cover: in turn this affects the wind, causing clouds to move away and reduce rainfall.

In my lifetime, I estimate that the population here has increased tenfold. Many migrate seasonally for work in the fertile areas around Kassala, eastern Sudan. Others work on the railways in Atbara and Khartoum. Three of my sons have moved away; one is in the army, another is a merchant in western Sudan and the third is a merchant in Shendi. Relatives who migrate for seasonal or permanent work remit a lot of money back here.

The change which has had the greatest impact has been the widespread introduction of improved education—though I am not satisfied with what the government has provided for us in this area. This village has no government-sponsored development schemes; sometimes survey officers come and go, without us knowing anything about their work and its purpose.

S18   *Mohamed el Awad Ali (M, 70 years), El Ushara, Shendi*

I was born here and have been a farmer most of my life, except for a short time as a soldier with the Middle East forces during the Second World War. I married in 1942. I can clearly remember the floods of 1946 and the drought in 1960. I have four sons, one working in Saudi Arabia, one in the UAE and two others are traders in southern Sudan.

Since the Second World War, I have concentrated on agriculture, which is better now than in the past, because it yields money. My main crops are onions, okra, courgettes, tomatoes, grain for animal feed, and beans, which are grown on the cooperative agricultural scheme. Weeds sometimes pose a problem in vegetable plots irrigated by private pumps. I feel I have gained little from new agricultural and technical innovations: no tractors or other mechanical facilities are provided by the Agricultural Bank, as we have only a small landholding and it is too expensive. During the harvest, I employ people and that is also expensive. Labour was not needed in the past because people worked together, which benefited those without grown-up sons. The introduction of cash crops has changed things. The region is the biggest producer of onions and beans in the country. I used to grow cotton but found it no longer profitable.

Desertification and wind erosion are two major problems here. Wells around the village successfully irrigate new *mesquite* trees as they need little water, and these protect the soil from desertification and wind erosion. We didn't know of the advantages of *mesquite* before its introduction by the development project.

Knowledge of the stars
The stars play an important role in our agricultural calendar; certain stars help identify the seasons, which have their individual cropping patterns. El Dhura is the name given to the constellation indicating the coming of summer. The other seasons recognised by the stars are known as **El Tarfa**, **El Natra** and **El Habha**. Forecasting winds and rains is also done by the stars, but this is specialised knowledge, practised only by a few. The stars may even provide information about dates for important events, such as marriages and circumcisions. The accuracy of such knowledge is shown by a local old wise man, who was troubled by omens in the sky one night

as he was going to sleep. Asking who would be married that night, he then prophesied that the marriage would produce no boys. Villagers show no surprise that, to this day, nine girls have been produced from the marriage.

Sheikh Ahmed el Sigaydi (M, 70 years), El Meseiktab, Shendi   S19

I was a nomad, displaced by the 1983-85 drought—the final blow to our already depleted herds of cattle, camels and sheep. Nearly all have perished now. I was born in a neighbouring region, Bir el Sigaydi, and spent most of my life moving around desert regions with cattle herds. I support a big family: two wives and many sons. I am chief of my tribe, a branch of the Hasaniya Arabs. I am well respected and settle disputes among my people. All my settlement's 57 households (each averaging eight people) moved here after 1984.

I long to return to life as a desèrt nomad but, in order to pay taxes and obtain basic necessities, we have had to sell some old livestock, while trying to keep a high ratio of females in the herd for breeding. As soon as I have built up my herds, I will return to my nomadic life. My son

Nomad settlement, El Meseiktab, Shendi

Education is expresses grave doubts that this will ever be possible. At present, we have
the major no real means of saving. We survive by doing small unskilled jobs for the
advantage of villagers.
settling in
one place

Wells fall into disrepair

We are nomads, and I fear we do not know enough to start up settled farms.
We used to practise rainfed farming in such valleys as Hawada in the
Butana plains, and those with pack animals still go there in the rainy
season. Last year, my sons and I couldn't go, because we no longer had
such animals. We have problems with our valley wells becoming covered
with sand and earth and we have no animals to help dig new ones. The
last drought affected the water table, so that wells are now too deep to dig.
We asked the government for help but have received nothing yet. Wells
once lasted for many years but today, falling ground-water levels and
relentless sand movements mean they are harder to maintain. Desert wells
used by the whole community have to be dug to a depth of 15 men; each
settlement has its own and does not share it with other tribes. Water is
drawn up in a bucket with a long rope attached to a donkey, led by a child.
I want the government to help me build a diesel-powered artesian well,
like those in western Sudan, which use long tubes and diesel pumps to tap
artesian water into ponds from which livestock can drink.

In my first settlement, there were *samreh*, *sellam*, *heglig*, *sidr*, *seyal*
and *arak* trees and the vegetation was very thick. We still have a few trees,
mainly used for sheep, goats and camels to browse, as well as for firewood
and tent construction. We nomads are not used to planting trees. The
deforestation problem arose because the drought seriously depleted our

---

S22 Muzamil Abdalla (M, 96 years), Shendi

I spent my early working life as a merchant,
trading goods all over Sudan, travelling long
distances in camel caravans. I bought beans
and other products from western Sudan and
transported them to Port Sudan, from where
they were shipped to Saudi Arabia.
Twenty-five years ago we decided to give up
these adventures and to settle into
agriculture. In my lifetime, the quality of life
has changed enormously. In the past, our life
was simple in every respect. Today, by
comparison, people are living in paradise.

animal wealth, so we sold wood to villages and towns. One impact of reduced tree cover is the windier weather—which causes much more soil erosion than in the past.

Education is the major advantage of settling in one place. The younger generation sees a future in the new settlement, with chances for education and a better life. Yet children are not so healthy as before. Perhaps this is because they no longer tend animals, which gave them fresh air and plenty of milk. Livestock also suffer from a poor diet: unable to graze freely, they have to live on gathered grass.

Awad el Karim Ahmed Masa'd (M, 91 years), El Sayal, Shendi   S25

I started life as a farmer, turning to commercial activity when I was 27. I employed labourers to work on my land, while I concentrated on buying and selling goods in Khartoum. Now my sons work my land, though one left to find employment in Yemen. They are quite unusual in that respect, as most of the young generation is educated but not useful.

My family and descendants alone amount to 50 people. The pressure on the land, however, is not as great as might be expected, since many migrate for work or education. The lucky ones are those with sons or close relatives working abroad.

I have vivid memories of the 1946 flood, when many of my crops were swept away. Also the bad drought years of 1930-31 and 1960 meant I was unable to feed from my land the 10 to 12 members of my family whom I support, and I was forced to buy grain from Abu Dilayq and Shendi markets.

Irrigation

Until 1977, I irrigated 2 **feddans** of land using both a water wheel and Nile flood water. I grew beans, soya, onions, millet and wheat. In 1977, the new government El Sayal Irrigation Scheme increased potential farming capacity: my sons extended our farmland tenfold. We all agree that new methods of mechanised farming are beneficial. The government scheme has been a great help to us. Taxes and water dues are moderate. I must also praise extension workers, who have taught us about the value of trees. My family also practises some rainfed cultivation of millet in the valleys. We do not leave land fallow unless rainfall is low, in which case we limit the area planted. We use manure and chemical fertilisers wherever possible.

I once had four or five camels and some donkeys to carry food and other goods, but most died in the drought, as did my neighbours' animals. Reduced tree cover has not only caused firewood shortages but also reduced grazing. Natural vegetation used to be thick, the mixed forest trees included *seyal, sellam, taleh, sidr, haraz, sunut* and *samreh*. Most of these have now disappeared. Nomads cleared pastures and, as they desperately needed other income, sold wood to villagers, who used it in house building and as fuel. I fear the reduced tree cover will affect the environment. The drastic reduction in vegetation has resulted in soil erosion and accelerated desertification. Now 2 metres of sand cover some of the houses and the level is still rising. Although rainfall seems to have decreased in recent years, it still falls heavily sometimes and forms gullies in the soil. Usually water stays in well-worn channels but new gullies formed in last year's floods and damaged houses.

I do not regret the 1969 abolition of the traditional administration system—**Idara Ahliya**—whereby hereditary **sheikhs** were appointed and given administrative and judicial power to collect taxes and maintain law and order. Throughout the colonial period, "mayors" were appointed to local courts to preside over trials and law suits.

S37   *Nebiat (F, 50 years), Wad el Hileau*

> *Nebiat is a refugee from Eritrea. The walls of her home are lined with photos of her dispersed offspring and motifs declaring solidarity with the Eritrean People's Liberation Front (EPLF)—a testimony, perhaps, to her two children killed at the front.*

I am one of the traditional birth attendants in this settlement. During my life I have gained much fascinating knowledge. I have just returned from visiting my home at Deki Shehai in Hamasen, Eritrea. The journey, partly by armed convoy and partly on foot, has been arduous. I need to rest. I *War, not* made this difficult journey to pay my condolences to 38 relatives, who *drought,* had been burnt in one house by an enemy bomb. Their bodies were found *forced me to* one month after the tragedy; some of the dead women still wore their *move. You* gold jewellery. I was devastated by the sad scenes that confronted me *can't leave* in my home country. War has destroyed everything. There are mines *your area just* everywhere and people are scared to farm their land. *because of one*   I am employed by LALMBA, the American agency, who run the only *or two years'* clinic on the camp. Midwives at home have different practices to those I *drought* have learnt here. I used to watch them during delivery. When the baby's head started to appear, they began to pray and continued until the baby had completely emerged. I believed that this was the correct way, until I was trained to be a midwife by LALMBA and realised that there is more to it than praying.

Women used to be happier to have boys than girls. These days it matters less, though some still prefer boys. With 14 children of my own, I am not exactly short of personal experience in giving birth! Six of my children are fighting with the EPLF; two died while fighting; others are married and living in Eritrea. Only two remain with me: a girl of 16 and a young boy. The war, not the drought, forced me to move to Wad el Hileau. You can't leave your area just because of one or two years' drought.

In Eritrea, we grew *dagusha*, *ifun*, barley, *t'ef*, *intatie*, *dura* and beans. Vegetables included *adri*, cabbage, potatoes, tomatoes and hot peppers. Trees with edible fruit included *sagla*, *mileo*, *aaye*, *daero* and *chekomta*. We even used to eat fruit between our main meals. There was also plenty of milk and meat from the animals we kept.

A harsh environment

I used to get up very early every day to prepare the morning and evening meal for my husband and children. After that, I went to the field, one child on my back and one on my stomach. I would clear the land, preparing it for ploughing. On my way back, I gathered wood for cooking. I was strong in Eritrea because of the balanced diet: if you eat good food, you are healthy and can work properly. Here, I find even my basic necessities harder and harder to meet. See how my eyes have become sunken in this place! In Eritrea, mountains and trees stopped dust moving about; here it affects us badly. It is hard to adapt to this hot and harsh environment.

In Eritrea, we never had to buy anything. The soil was good and the harvests plentiful. Even our plates and dishes were made from free wood. We made clay saucepans and storage pots for water and milk and as much as four to six sacks of grain could be stored after harvest in **kofos** and used during the rainy season. We never sold any, but if somebody was poor and needed grain, I gave it to them out of my store.

Herbal remedies

I believe in using plants for medicinal treatment: for example, *leaw* could be smoked, infused—though it tasted very bitter—or simply bathed in, as a cure for fever or stomach problems. Popular herbal remedies often included *kihe* and *tambukh* leaves. Cows with blood in their milk are treated with smoke from *tambukh* and *shitora* plants. *Inchichi* and *shibti* plants are dried, powdered and used as cleansing agents.

S38 Halima Ahmed (F, 43 years), Wad el Hileau
I was born and raised in Eritrea. I was married at twelve years old. Nowadays, people marry at seventeen or eighteen. It is better to get married when you are mature. In 1979 the war forced me and my family to come to Sudan. I cannot compare my old life with the life I lead now. We were happy and simple then. Things that we used to get cheaply have now to be smuggled into the camp at a high price. Those who sell milk try to justify its price by saying it is expensive to get fodder for their animals.

The effects of war
Our self-sufficiency came to an abrupt end with the escalation of war between Ethiopia and Eritrea. Aeroplanes began a bombing campaign in the area and we were forced to adopt a completely different life. We worked during the night and hid underground in daytime. After much bombing, the enemy started a new tactic: they came with tanks and buried mines, which killed both grazing animals and humans. It was because of these atrocities that I decided to seek refuge in neighbouring Sudan.

   I disapprove of contraceptives. Our youngsters are away fighting, so are not able to have a family: it is therefore up to us to continue to have children. Divorce used to be rare, but the increasing difficulties men face in finding work create conflict between men and women. Women often resort to working in town, leaving their children to fend for themselves.

Zahra Idris Mohamed (F, 70 years), Wad el Hileau   *S43*

I was born in Amnayet village, near Hykota town in the Eritrean lowlands. I am a pure nomad of the Tigre-speaking Maria Telem tribe. In 1984, after all my animals had perished in the drought, I came to Sudan. Until then, we had only ever known a diet of milk, butter, meat and *dura*. Now, our diet has changed; we suffer from stomach problems and always seem to be ill because we can't eat what we are used to. Our skin is very dark now, but it used to be light. In our country, people died not from sickness, but when their time of death approached, a time known only to Allah.

We sold our animals to buy sorghum and other things, but we didn't have to buy wood, meat, milk and water. It was taboo to sell milk or meat. If we slaughtered animals, we had to give to those without meat or milk. We used to have goats, camels and cows. Camels ate big trees, goats ate almost anything, and cows would graze *almet* grass.

A milk-based diet

My family's diet was based on milk, which was put in an **amur**, which had been smoked both to give it a pleasant smell and to sterilise it. The milk was then transferred to a **hawat**, where it solidified into a mixture which was then shaken well to separate the curds from the whey. The curds—known as zibdet in Tigre or likhay in Tigrigna—were used as a hair oil or made into hesas by adding spices. Hesas was particularly important locally in the treatment of malaria. Sweet cows' milk often caused malaria and hesas, with its bitter flavour, was an effective cure for that and for constipation. An infusion of the *swhi* plant smeared on the body cured measles. **Sihnet** smoke ensured good, healthy eyes and head, and prevented vomiting or diarrhoea in children. Even the husbands of women who stood over smouldering, sweet-smelling *thahat* wood became strong and healthy.

The drought wiped out most of my cattle: the rest were taken by Ethiopian soldiers. I now have to depend on food rations. Many people are dying in Wad el Hileau because they have not adapted to the heat and the poor diet. I am thankful for my one remaining donkey. I let my neighbour's young children take it to the river to gather water and firewood for me; in return, they collect enough for their own family.

It was taboo to sell milk or meat. If we slaughtered animals, we had to give to those without

When we   When I was young, I used to grind sorghum by hand for the family.
couldn't   The boys tended the animals with my father, while the women cooked,
read, we   prepared hesas or zibdet, and collected water and wood. Girls do as their
were honest mothers, and boys accompany their father: this is important preparation
and in peace for later life. Girls are also taught to weave palm leaf mats, mattresses,
prayer mats and decorations. After marriage, a girl is not allowed to go
and fetch water or firewood. She stays indoors and should not even do
any grinding at home. Her mother or mother-in-law does all the domestic
work until she has had her first child—however long that might take.

When we couldn't read, we were honest and in peace; we respected
our parents and all our elders. These days people are educated but
dishonest and untrustworthy. However, education is important because
one must know about the good and bad things in the world.

S52   *Khedija Issa (F), Wad el Hileau*

I am an Eritrean of the Baria tribe. I came to Wad el Hileau from Geluj
with my husband, three daughters and son. We were forced to leave by
the war. Because my husband was Sudanese, we were given special
privileges. Unlike other refugees in the area, my family were allocated
farming land, which I had to work myself after my husband's death.
Farming needs money, so although I can farm some land myself, some I
have to give to other willing refugees, taking half of their produce.

Besides farming, I make **kisra**, the local bread, which my daughters
sell in the market. In Eritrea, my father grew millet and sorghum and
owned cows, goats and sheep. Whenever there was any sickness, we went
to the local **sheikh** and we got better because we believed in him. We also
used traditional medicines: for measles, we dripped an infusion of millet
and *leet* into the sick child's eyes. These days, our daughters prefer to go
to hospital. We believed that if a boy was breastfed for too long, he would
not grow up to be intelligent and would be slow at school. We breastfed
boys for 18 months and girls for two years. Girls are not born to go to
school and are naturally stupid.

Eritrean refugees have benefited the local Sudanese community, for
they arrived during a drought, when there was no food in the local markets.
They used some of their food rations to buy other goods in the market, so
increasing the supply of food as well as encouraging sales of goods. In
addition, Sudanese villagers now receive free medical treatment from the
Eritrean refugees' health centre.

Gezae Tewldemedhim (M, 50 years), Wad el Hileau   *S54*

Tukul, near Seraye in the Eritrean highlands, is where I was born. Before becoming a farmer, my father was a soldier in the Italian army. I began farming at the age of 14, but after a few years I left Tukul for Antore, in Gash province, in the lowlands. In Tukul there had been a seven-year drought; in Antore there were huge forests full of lions, tigers, elephants and monkeys. It was good new land to farm, although few did so, because there was gold to find and employment in a small factory run by an old Italian. Here I worked until he returned to Italy. Then we took up farming.

Farming was a lucrative business. I built up four pairs of oxen and hired men to act as share-croppers on my land. I took two-thirds of the harvest for myself and the rest was divided between the workers. Erosion was avoided by building fences around the fields, using piles of wood and large stones: wind storms were less of a problem than here because of the surrounding trees and mountains, although we did cut down small trees. I used no fertilisers. I grew *mashela, dagusha, t'ef* and *simsim*, rotating crops to increase productivity. My land was not irrigated. The only irrigated farm I know in Eritrea is Italian-owned, at Ali-Geder.

Women played an important role in farming activities around Gash: weeding, scaring birds, harvesting and cleaning seed. Weeds were a major problem, especially *hareze* and *muchuku*.

That area has changed little over the years. Vegetation is plentiful and wood readily available. No wood is sold because no one would buy it. Claiming land in Eritrea was easy, simply involving the payment of a government tax and an assurance that no important trees, such as *arcobcobai* and *gasa*, would be cut down.

Sudden changes in temperature, strong winds or sandstorms are given to us by Allah: we can only prevent them by praying to stop His anger towards His slaves. In Antore, however, the only problem we had was with weeds.

People at home used to give their land over to share-cropping and go to towns for a better life, to find schools or clinics and work in the offices or factories. However, when the war started, people left the towns because of threats of bombardment and persecution. In 1983, fighting between the **Dergue** and the EPLF intensified and I was forced to leave for the refugee camp in Wad el Hileau. The war disrupted all aspects of normal life.

In Wad el Hileau, my problems have increased: this place is the hottest hell in the world. There are neither mountains nor trees. When we came, the only tree we could see was *usher*—with its thick leaves and poisonous white sap, it cannot even be used as animal food. The soil is very light, has no water-holding capacity and needs a long fallow period. The only crops grown are *dura* and *simsim*, planted in alternate years. The village is affected by sandstorms and **haboubs**, which destroy the huts.

I am surprised that despite war, famine and epidemics, the population is growing. Perhaps it is because people now live to be 70 or 80 years old.

S58   Mohamed Salih (M, 60 years), Wad el Hileau

I came from a family of agro-pastoralists based in the Eritrean highlands at Adi-Keyih, Akulugezai area. I spent much of my time moving around with my herds. My family joined me if I was moving far and as long as the animals were healthy; otherwise they stayed in their summer camp.

The most serious animal disease was gulhay, recognisable by skin spots, diarrhoea and persistent bleating. Before the Italians brought veterinary immunisation, the disease was treated by marking the animal's abdomen with a hot iron and giving it an infusion of *klaiba* tree leaves.

My home was very rich in forest. You could not see from one end to the other because it was so dense. Lions, tigers, monkeys, snakes and other animals roamed around. The forest is still there but the animals have left because of the war.

A respect for trees

Trees were highly respected in Eritrea and had many uses: as shade for man and beast, and as an essential source of food and medicine. The *klaiba* tree was an effective prophylactic for malaria and yellow fever, while the milky sap of the *adgi zana* stops wounds bleeding. Trees were cut only when absolutely necessary: to provide wood for building or to clear land for cultivation. A place without a tree is like an ugly person without clothes. Trees brought water and protected the land from being eroded by strong winds. When we chose land for farming, we only went where the trees are small and useless. A forestry man in our area looked after the trees and wildlife, because where there was forest there was richness.

Our highland soil, called dukha, was fertile, rich in minerals and *Rural people* retained water well. The land was ploughed by oxen: tractors were no use *say that a* as too many trees and stones got in the way of the machinery. In my area, *person without* women do no farming or work with men, in line with Islamic law. *education is*

I cleared land for cultivation and marked my patch with a fence made *like an animal* from wood and stones. *Dagusha*, *mashela* and *nihuge* were grown for *without a skin* food and oil. A system of crop rotation was followed, as this enhanced soil fertility.

I moved to Wad el Hileau in 1984, forced away by the disruptive effects of war. Here, it is very hot and we suffer from terrible sandstorms: there are no mountains or trees to provide shade or shelter. I think refugees have had a positive impact on the Sudanese economy, providing a cheap labour force for many large eastern Sudanese farms—yet receiving little in return. The one thing I am thankful for is that, in Wad el Hileau, my children can receive a good education.

Girmay Gebray (M, 60 years), Wad el Hileau   S63

I was born in Tigray but when I was a child, a major famine forced my family towards the more fertile Gash province. I tended a herd of animals and farmed some land and was quite able to look after myself. Then the war came and the Ethiopian government claimed everything: men, animals, buildings, companies and the land itself. I was left with no more than a beggar. Because of such poverty, many have turned to armed robbery and theft has increased. When the military situation grew too unstable, I moved to this refugee settlement. I found evening work as a guard and, when available, some labouring in the morning.

Traditionally, women worked in the home, tending to children and cooking. They also helped on the farm by terracing, scaring birds and weeding (the worst weeds were *muchuku*, *kakito*, *kuanti* and *kurumtia*). Women's position in the household has undergone a dramatic change as a result of the economic situation refugees have been forced into. Women have found more ways of supplementing income than men: now they sell tea, beer and food in the market and even become prostitutes. Times are better for women than for men. Some even become head of the family.

Urban learning
The number of people in Sudan moving to urban areas astonishes me. Urbanisation is largely caused by people moving away to be educated. Rural people are saying that a person without education is like an animal

If we were given a letter saying "kill him", we would carry it to our murderer, because we are uneducated

without a skin. My sons and daughters all go to school. I don't want them to be ignorant like me and their mother. If we were given a letter saying "kill him", we would carry it to our murderer, because we are uneducated.

The climate in Eritrea was gentle and constant, protected by mountains and trees. It was not subject to the many fluctuations experienced in Wad el Hileau. Here, the temperature can change 10 times in 24 hours. Moreover, in Eritrea, there was plenty of water for washing and bathing; here we have problems simply finding enough water to drink.

There are three main soil types. **Whalaha** is the most fertile, though the Eritrean and Sudanese varieties differ. The Eritrean type is very heavy, strong, not easily eroded and retains water well, whereas the Sudanese variety is good but very light. **Keychtai** is used to make dishes and pots. **Husa** retains little water and is relatively infertile. At home, I used no fertiliser on my soil. I could cultivate one patch of land for 10 consecutive years, without suffering reduced yields. Each decade, I left it fallow for two years. I grew a wide variety of crops, including *dagusha, simsim, nihuge*, corn and different varieties of *mashela*, wheat and sorghum.

Soil erosion was no problem in Eritrea because the mountains and trees protected the land. In Wad el Hileau, **haboubs** cover fertile soil in sand. Herding is also more problematic in Sudan: neither man nor beast can find anything to eat. At home, cattle and sheep grazed green grass and dry *kancha*. Goats browsed on leaves and branches, and herdsmen took no **espeza** to eat when they went away, because there was enough food in the forest. Among the tree species were *awlea, haseba, anistayeti-andel, tebatay-andel, gollos* and edible species such as *sagla, leham* and *hawri*.

The Gash area was so thick with tree cover, it was difficult to move from one area to another. When checking a distant farm, we had to walk right to it: it was impossible to see through the trees. Wood collection was easy. In Wad el Hileau, by comparison, one has to travel many kilometres to find wood, and even that is useless for building or making charcoal. Wad el Hileau is like a bald man!

S69   *Ahmed Salih (M), Wad el Hileau*
Logoni Zogololo (M)
Mohamed Awed (M)

> *All three men were extremely jolly, laughing loudly every time they were asked a question. They were all fairly young, though they would not divulge their exact ages in case only the eldest was interviewed!*

We came to Wad el Hileau as refugees from Niger when we were young.

There was thick thorn scrub with lions, elephants and monkeys here. People worked more as pastoralists than farmers. Now their pastures have been claimed for farming and other businesses. When we arrived, we had had no experience of pastoralism and did not like the idea of being permanently on the move, having to leave wives and children. Instead, we settled by the Tekeze River, which became our most valuable source of income. The river was clean and full of crocodiles and fish. People did not have to worry about gathering wood because the river was like a train or cargo truck transporting large trees and branches to our door—now it just brings dead bodies....

Fishing was a lucrative and easy business then: no government regulations restricted us. We fished all day in a small **sumbuk** and sold the fish in the market. Like all other commodities, it was cheap. The widened river has become yellow and muddy. Fish cannot live in mud and most have disappeared, so fishing has decreased by about 70%. Even crocodiles are rare, yet a few years ago, if you just touched the shore with your leg, hundreds would run towards you.

Alternative trades

Many people have abandoned fishing. Some have become merchants, smuggling goods between Ethiopia and Sudan. They are happier and richer now than they were before. A few use their boats to ferry people across the river from Showak to Wad el Hileau. Others, like Ahmed Salih here, work as drivers. We two make our living from agriculture. When we first came to Sudan, we bought a sizeable strip of fertile land along the Tekeze River for S£300. Throughout the summer, we grow *gargir, bamia, bambei*, cotton, *mulukhia*, green peppers and corn. If the river rises and covers the farming land, then we cultivate sorghum further inland. We still use **selukas** to plough. Tractors can do a hundred times as much work in the same time, but the quality and taste of the *dura* is not as good as that grown in fields ploughed with a **seluka**.

When we first came to Wad el Hileau, there were no **haboubs**. The

S71 Yahya Ebrahim Ferez (M), Wad el Hileau
The world today is not suited to pastoralism or farming, but to education. An educated person can get a job wherever he goes at whatever time. But a farmer has to wait for the rains.

S32 Mohamed Fadelalla (M), Abdutab, Shendi
Environmental problems are not recent phenomena. As far back as 1946 our settlement was forced to move because of extensive soil erosion. Since then the village has been forced to move twice because of moving sand.

Now, trees protected us from these sandstorms; we only heard the movement of
haboubs the branches and saw leaves falling. Now, **haboubs** attack us because
attack us people have taken the place of trees.
because   I am proud of our position in the community. We are considered as
people have neither refugees nor pure nationals—quite self-sufficient, yet not troubled
taken the by the government, being left to do as we please. Our land is rich with
place of trees produce and the people of Wad el Hileau depend on us. I sell my produce
on the free market, tomatoes being particularly profitable. With some of
this profit, I spend time travelling around other African countries to see
how they live. This is a luxury of which my neighbours in the refugee
settlement, just a kilometre away, can only dream.

    Although not born in Sudan, we look on this as our home and have no
plans to return to Niger. We will stay here by the river until we die.

S72   Hamed Adam Ali (M, 57 years), Wad el Bacha, Kordofan

*It was difficult to find a good time for this interview as Hamed is very
busy: not only is he employed by a United Nations Sudano-Sahelian
Office (UNSO) project as a forest guard and worker in the tree nursery,
but he now has extra duties, which include calling the village to
prayers, and serving meals and tea to the numerous policemen
presently stationed at Wad el Bacha. Hamed was happy and animated
throughout the interview. We discovered the reason for his good
spirits: at the close of our meeting he was off to his home village of
Gaghrur to see his family.*

I was born in El Rehaid village in 1933 and I belong to the Gawama tribe.
My parents had three daughters and five sons. One of my brothers has
been working with the National Water Corporation and I work with the
National Forests Corporation. We now live together in this village of Wad
el Bacha, though my real home is in Gaghrur, 20 kilometres or so from
here, to the northeast.

    I moved to Gaghrur with my family when I was only seven months
old. We left my birthplace because my family was of a different tribe from
the El Rehaid people and my grandfather, Ali el Daw, decided to establish
a new settlement.

The community hierarchy

I have been the **sheikh** of Gaghrur for 10 years now. The role was passed
on to me partly by inheritance and partly by the votes of the villagers,
though it is the tradition for **sheikhs** to be elected from one family line.

My responsibilities include collecting livestock taxes from the villagers *It is the* and sending the money to the government, as well as controlling the *tradition for* division of available land between village farmers. All the land belongs *sheikhs to* to the government and therefore cannot be sold, but the **sheikh** receives *be elected* a small amount of money for supervising land allocation. There are certain *from one* boundaries to each **sheikh**'s area of control; knowledge of these is most *family line* important, in order to avoid land conflicts with neighbouring **sheikhs**. However, such conflicts do still occur, in which case the government is called in. If maps are available these are used to define people's territory; if there are no maps, disputes are generally solved through discussion and cooperation between neighbouring **sheikhs** and elders who know the boundaries well. The government, represented by the **umda** and **nazir**, are responsible for the keeping of the boundary maps, as well as for settling any other legal issues which cannot be settled by the **sheikh**.

The legal system works in the following way: each village has a **sheikh**, or an assistant **sheikh** if there is more than one village involved. Above the **sheikh** is the **umda**, who controls the settlements over a larger area. He is the first person any **sheikh** will approach during bigger disputes or issues. The **umda** is installed by agreement between the local people and the district level government. One **umda** may have as many as 400 or as few as 20 **sheikhs** under him, depending on how populated his area is. Usually he divides his area along tribal lines. A location takes its name from the majority of people living there. Higher up the scale of local government is the **nazir**. **Nazirs** have greater authority than **umdas** and are responsible for everything that happens over a very large area.

Movement forced by drought
In my lifetime this area has suffered three major droughts. During the first drought we moved to Nawa to be close to water. During the second, my family stayed near Hamadan. With the third, in 1984, we came to Wad el Bacha. I have stayed here ever since for work, although my family move seasonally between Gaghrur and here.

Before I came to Wad el Bacha I was a farmer in my village. My own family come and stay with me during the dry season, after the January harvest, and return to Gaghrur in June at the start of the rains. Sometimes I visit my village for a week or so. As the **sheikh**, I usually have to attend to many problems during these visits. My work is officially from six o'clock in the morning until midday, although if there is still work to be finished we have overtime.

I came to Wad el Bacha because of the drought. Wad el Bacha always has plenty of water because of the dams which supply the town of El

Obeid. Fortunately, I was then asked to join the UNSO Gum Belt Restocking Project, so I live here mostly. My job is to patrol both inside and outside the forest reserve of El Ain, to prevent people cutting down trees. Although people are allowed to cut or collect dead wood for their own domestic use, any that is cut for sale is confiscated. In the past we just used to confiscate any forest products illegally removed and release the person involved. But nowadays things are tougher: the person is sent to the court in El Banjidid or El Obeid and charged. The forest in this area has changed a great deal as a result of drought and tree-cutting.

I have been married for 30 years and have had 10 children: six daughters and four sons, two of whom have died. My remaining sons work, one with the army and the other in Port Sudan. Four of the girls are married and the others are still single and live at home. I haven't seen my sons for three years, but although they don't come home, they regularly send us money.

There are about 200 people living in Gaghrur village now. They are farmers who cultivate crops such as millet, sorghum, okra, groundnuts and water-melon and keep some livestock. Some people also move to the Gezira Irrigation Scheme during the early dry season, from November to February, to look for work, mostly bringing in the harvest.

Cultivation

In normal years autumn begins in June and continues until November. The cultivation season begins with land clearance and dry-season planting in May. Usually we weed our land twice a year, but if necessary three times. If the rains in autumn are good we only need to plant once, but sometimes the rains are poor or late and we may have to replant as many as four times in order to get any harvest at all. Millet is the only crop we plant early, before the rains, as it needs as much water as possible to grow well.

In Gaghrur we keep 250 goats, 200 sheep, six or seven camels and many donkeys for transport. During the rains, the livestock stay around the village but during harvesting they are moved farther away from the village and surrounding agricultural land. We keep the millet and sorghum for our own consumption and sell all or part of the other crops.

Our lives have really changed since I was young. In the past, sorghum was plentiful. I think this was because there were a lot of trees and grasses and the land was not tired, as it is now. The trees have been cut down or died from drought. With their disappearance, good grasses have also become scarce. Now it is difficult to find species like *el dambalab*, *el hasharat* and *abu asabeil* which were once plentiful. This area was

When I was young the grass was so thick that we could cut up carcasses on the ground without getting the meat dirty

Fatima el Mubarak

famous for its *tebeldi* trees but there are not many now; those that remain are very old. *Kitr* trees have suffered in the same way. We use *kitr* to make **sha'abs** and charcoal, and for firewood and building. *Sidr* trees are useful because we sell the fruits in the market for a good price.

Village buildings

The village buildings are mostly round huts, constructed from millet stalks and **hatabs** made from trees such as *kitr*, *babanous* and *underab*. We make the frame for the sides and the roof from the **hatabs**, and use millet stalks and grasses for thatch and to fill in the walls. These huts can last for a few years, with repairs every so often. Usually we build a new one every four to eight years, depending on circumstances, such as how much material is available. Sometimes we only need to renew the stalks or grasses, as the **hatabs** can last for 10 years or more.

For its water supply, my village relies on the **khors** and **fulahs** which fill with rain and last until around December. After these two sources dry

S35 Hawa Filli (F, 76 years), Wad el Hileau
When the military situation began to deteriorate in Eritrea, I moved to Sudan with my sister. I came originally from Maado village in Eritrea. At the age of thirteen, I married a soldier and spent many years moving around the country with him. In 1945, my husband died, leaving me to look after four daughters. With the help of my in-laws, I returned to my husband's land. Whilst living with my in-laws, all my daughters married. After the last one left, I was asked to leave my home. In our culture, a woman without a son is not entitled to inherit her husband's property.

up, some people move from the village to live near a good dry-season water supply. By this time—January— all the crops have been harvested. People usually return to Gaghrur around June, depending on the rains. Those who choose to remain in the village have to travel long distances to fetch water from permanent water supplies.

There is a small shop in the village selling some basic, everyday items, but we tend to go to Um Humeira market to sell crops and buy other items. As Gaghrur is small we do not have a grain mill ourselves. To grind the millet and sorghum into flour we go to El Gafeil or Um Humeira, both of which have mills.

The 1984 drought killed all our livestock; only a few goats remained. Luckily, the government was able to supply us with food. This food was divided and distributed by councils according to the village population.

The only [development] organisation that has ever visited our village was the UNSO Gum Belt Restocking Project, which started in 1985. When they first came they asked the people if they owned their land. Then they registered the names of some people and gave them *hashab* seedlings when the rains started. They give us 12 **ratels** of oil, 5 kilos of milk powder, 3 kilos of sugar, 1.5 **ratels** of tea and a large amount of sorghum once every two months, after they have ensured that the *hashab* has been planted. They now also give us training in planting the seedlings correctly, which they didn't do before. Unfortunately the *hashab* seedlings have all died because of the lack of rain. This year, 1990, is our last with UNSO as they stay in one village for only five years.

Customs and change

I don't think that our traditions and customs have altered very much at all. However, one big change is that now most young people tend to leave the village to try for work in the towns. Some settle there permanently, though others may return to the village after a long absence.

We still follow the traditions of circumcision for boys and girls, and of inheritance. According to Islamic tradition, your land and wealth are divided after your death between members of your immediate family, if you have not already distributed them during your lifetime.

Girls are not born to go to school and are naturally stupid
Khedija Issa

For happy occasions such as weddings, births and other celebrations we organise everything ourselves, using what is available at the time. Usually we invite people from neighbouring villages to attend. They stay as guests in our homes, so we must supply them with all their needs until they decide to return to their own village. The relationship between my village and neighbouring villages is good and we share both happy and sad occasions.

Marriage

In a marriage celebration, the bridegroom supplies the bride's people with everything. If you want to get married, the first thing is that your father and some friends from your village go to the father of the girl you want to marry and ask him for his daughter on your behalf. If he agrees, the custom is that there are certain things that you must pay for: the bride's mother tells you the type and quantity of gifts she requires in return for the loss of her daughter. After that you must take many things to the family of your bride, in certain traditional quantities—for instance, one sack of sugar, two tins of oil, 1 or 2 gallons of diesel, 45 pieces of soap for washing clothes, 15 pieces of body soap, 10 packets of **shireya**, 10 kilos of wheat flour, 10 kilos of rice, five cartons of cigarettes. These things help the bride's family to prepare good wedding celebrations to which many people, friends and relatives, will be invited. In addition, the groom must provide new clothes for the bride, such as two pairs of shoes, two skirts and two **tobes**, and some money—between S£1,500 and S£5,000—for her bride-price. While all other items are essential for the wedding, the quantity and type of clothes you provide for the bride is your own decision and made according to your means. The gifts are presented to the bride's family during a special ceremony known as sheyella.

Looking back at my own life, I am sad that I was unable to have enough education, but I thank God that my sons have had the opportunity to be educated in schools. I wish that all the members of my family were close to me, instead of all living apart...but life's circumstances have not made that possible.

A woman without a husband or a man without a wife is like trying to plough with only one ox
Sillas

Asha Mohamed Ibrahim (F, 70 years), Gahawa Hasabsidu Zeinab Mohamed Ahmed (F, 42 years)

S80

The interview took place in the early morning before breakfast, in the house of Asha's youngest son. As Asha was preoccupied with family problems and had difficulty concentrating, her husband and six other women, mostly family members, also sat with us to give her moral support and jog her memory. Asha's husband himself is reckoned to be at least 100 years old and, although frail, is still a lively member of the community.

I belong to the Dago tribe. My mother, who is still alive, is from the Gelaba Hawara tribe but her children all took the tribe of her husband, which was Dago. My mother is 150 years old and lives with us in Gahawa Hasabsidu.

For the past 30 years or so she has been very frail and can hardly leave her bed, but she can still eat and speak and up to now has had few health problems despite her very great age. However, for the past week or so she has not been very well and I am worried about her.

My parents had four daughters and two sons. We have all married and had children of our own. I myself had five sons and four daughters and they in turn have their own families now. I live with my middle son, and one of my daughters still lives here.

One of the major events in my life was when I had food poisoning. I was very sick and my family took me to the doctor in El Obeid. I still have a problem eating hot food because my stomach is sensitive. Later I started having very bad headaches and eventually the doctor had to remove all my teeth in order to help me.

I didn't go to school when I was young because there were very few schools around here for boys, let alone girls. No one had much education unless they were boys and were lucky enough to enter the khalwa, a special school for education in the teachings of the Qur'an.

Village buildings
In the past, all village buildings were made from wooden poles and cereal stalks or grasses. They haven't changed much, although if people get the chance they try to build with mud and make durdur, which are round huts with thatched roofs, and jalouse, which are square with both walls and roofs of mud. These last longer and don't need so many wooden poles.

Before we moved here, we lived in a village called El Dar, which is 11 or so kilometres to the north. The first person to come to this place was my son Adam, the present **sheikh** of this village. This area belongs to the tribe Gelaba Hawara, but Adam first used to come here just to herd our animals, because at that time it was a huge forest with good grazing and lots of water in the **khors** and **fulahs**. Many years ago, Adam's grandfather in El Dar, Mohamed Ahmed el Mistour, advised his family to split up and settle in different locations around the boundaries of our area so as to be able to control it in the future. As a result some of the family settled here and established Gahawa Hasabsidu in 1966, while others went to places like El Ain and El Hegena. I think there are about 220 people living here now, all from the Gelaba Hawara tribe. It is a good village and we have easy relations with neighbouring villages. Because of its rich resources this area was very attractive for settlement and the forest at the time was so dense that we had to clear the trees from a large area around our huts to avoid surprise attacks by wolves.

Water supplies

In the past, we used to collect our water from a place known as El Ain well, close to here. That well has now been abandoned because it was not very accessible and we had to work hard to dig out the sand every time. We also dug wells in the bed of the **khor**. But we used to take our livestock to El Banjidid and Khor Baggara during the dry season. Nowadays, we have two handpumps near El Ain railway station, supplied by UNICEF. We would have preferred these pumps much closer to the village but unfortunately when UNICEF tested this area, they found that there was no water under the ground. Although the supply from the handpumps is cleaner than from Khor Baggara, we still have many problems as they are far away and, worse still, inside the forest reserve. Recently the governor passed a law preventing us from entering the forest to take water, even for our own personal needs. The Forest Department now says we can enter the reserve with donkeys to collect our water but that livestock is still banned. So we have to take the animals to El Banjidid, Jebel Kordofan and El Jibna and this is a big problem. The handpumps belong to us, and two village men—Adam and Saed—are responsible for repairing and maintaining them.

In the past, we had very good grazing here and were able to keep many cows, goats and sheep. Most of our cows and sheep died in the last drought, in 1985, and though we now keep sheep and goats, we have few cows. They are expensive to replace and we no longer have the grasses to feed them. We have milk from our goats but we miss the old days when we had cow's milk.

Fires were a common occurrence here in the past but much less so now because there is no forest and few grasses left in the dry season. The last big fire I remember was about 50 years ago and it was started by some hunters who made a cooking fire in the forest.

At this stage in the interview it seemed that Asha was becoming tired and unable to concentrate well enough to remember things. As well as thinking about her mother, she was still mourning the recent death of her daughter's son who had died after being bitten by a dog. One of the women listening, Zeinab Mohamed Ahmed, who had previously been acting as Asha's prompt, continued the story.

We have many uses for trees, especially for local medicines. We use *tebeldi* fruits against diarrhoea and **garad** against malaria. Women use *subakh* and *taleh* as a perfume, especially if they have just given birth to a child. We burn *kelto* wood for people suffering from **ratoba**.

The last drought caused great suffering among the people, some of whom moved away from this area permanently. Although things were very bad, I did not move from the village. I came here originally to establish a **gahawa** on the main road that used to be close to the village, to earn some income for my family. We used to make tea, coffee and food for the many lorries which passed by during the dry season, but in the end we had to stop because fewer and fewer vehicles came by and we found that much of the food we prepared was just going to waste. Nowadays the old road between El Obeid and Kosti is hardly ever used because there is a new tarmac road to the north. Women don't go to the new road to work as it is too far from the home.

Food aid

At the time of the 1985 drought, one **mid** of sorghum, our staple food, cost S£5 and even that was too expensive for us. We received food relief from the USA which included things like rice, sorghum and milk. Later the price of sorghum dropped again to S£2.50 because there was enough on the market. Today, one **mid** costs S£50-60 and people are really suffering. Their crops have failed this year and they find it impossible to buy at that price. During the drought, the distribution people took special care of pregnant women and gave them milk, oil and yellow wheat flour mixed together. The children and babies were also weighed and if they were too light they were given extra milk and **the mixture**.

The area which is now called the forest reserve, belonged to our grandfathers in the past. In the 1950s the government Forest Department came along and took it, although they did agree to allow the people here to take firewood and building materials from it.

People in this village mainly work as farmers and livestock herders, though a few people now have work during the dry season at the new **gahawa**. In the past, during the dry season, we used to make charcoal and sell firewood by the road but that is forbidden now by the Forest Department.

A farming life

We cultivate the land by hand. Our main fields are mostly on sandy soil to the northwest of the village. However, we women have special, smaller fields in the small **khor** near the village. One family can cultivate 15 **mukhammas** for their main field. The crops we grow are different types of sorghum, sesame, *karkadeh* and okra. We also used to grow groundnuts, but we have stopped planting these because there never seems to be enough water for a good harvest. We sell our crops in the market and use the money to buy clothes, livestock, perfumes and our basic necessities. The sorghum is stored in pits in front of our houses, which keep it good and safe until we need it. There is enough land here to grow sorghum on a very large scale but we lack the capital to hire tractors and other machinery, so our fields are limited to what we can cultivate and weed by hand. We have no grain mill and have to take the sorghum to El Obeid, El Banjidid or Nawa to grind any large quantities. In the past, it was easy to catch a vehicle on the road to take us to El Obeid or Nawa in the dry season, but during the wet season the lorries could not pass this way and often we had to travel by donkey. For everyday amounts we used our own grinding stones, and sometimes still do so.

We keep the seeds from this year's harvest for next year's crop. Last year the government gave the farmers in this area special sorghum seed but it was not successful because the rains failed, so we don't know if it is good seed or not.

To the east of the village, we have some old *hashab* gardens where we tap gum arabic. We have tried to plant more *hashab* seedlings but the settled Hawawir nomads, who live on the Jebel, destroy the young trees. Our fields are about 3 or 4 kilometres from the village and our livestock pens, so we do not have any fencing around them.

Diet

In times of drought like this, when there is no sorghum to eat, the people collect the fruit of the *krusan* and make food from it. We have to prepare it by soaking it in water for three days to get rid of the bitterness. After that we leave it for some time to dry in the sun before grinding it into flour. We make our staple foods, **asida** and **kisra**, from it in the same way as we would with sorghum.

When there was good grazing and lots of livestock, we had a pleasant diet and ate mostly milk with other things such as rice, eggs, chicken, wild plants and fruits. It was good food and kept us strong and healthy. These days we miss the milk a lot though we still have some goats, and we eat sorghum, okra, vegetables and other things from the market when we can.

The clothes people wear have changed a great deal over the years, especially for women. When Asha was young, she would have worn only a skirt of leather and another soft leather skin as a shawl. Later, people stopped wearing skins and used cloth instead, though women still wore nothing over their breasts. The cloth that was wrapped around your waist like a skirt was called a tanoura, or furka if it was special cloth for celebrations. Another long piece of black cloth, called zarag, went over your head and covered your whole body, just like the many-coloured **tobe**

Nomads stay here longer, because of fighting in their grazing areas, and so compete with us for resources does today. The furka is still worn for special occasions today and is made of beautiful material: red, black and yellow with gold or silver threads running through it. Women wear it after giving birth, for their marriage and for circumcision, and it is very special and shows how proud she is at that time.

As well as working in the home and the fields, women are responsible for milking all the animals and looking after the young calves and lambs.

The war in the south has made life more difficult for us though we are not near any fighting. My sister's son was in the army but he was injured and now he is very sick indeed. The other problem it has caused is that the nomads stay around here longer than usual, because of the fighting in their traditional grazing areas, and so compete with us for grazing and other resources. Usually we have reasonable relations with them, but problems arise when they decide to settle or when their animals invade our fields.

Health care

I am one of the traditional midwives in this village and learned everything from my mother when I was young. At every birth I stay with the women in labour while all the other women wait outside the hut. As soon as the woman goes into labour I use a special knife called a moos el gadim to cut open her circumcision stitches and enable the baby to come out. Every now and again I feel the woman's stomach to make sure that the baby is in a good position and all the time I am comforting her and encouraging her to push. To give birth, the woman squats on a clean sheet on the ground with her legs apart. To help her push she holds on to a rope suspended from the roof of the hut. When the baby is about to come, I stand behind her with my arms held quite tightly below her breasts and above her stomach and I also squeeze to encourage the baby downwards. Once the baby is born, I use another round-bladed knife called a moos to cut the cord and then we bathe the new child with a mixture of oil and flour. Immediately after the

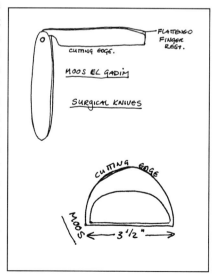

birth we give the new mother coffee and **nesha**. After she has rested a little, the woman washes her body with water in which *habeil* has been boiled. If there is no *habeil* available, we use tea instead.

I suppose the strangest case that has ever faced me as a midwife was when a baby was born with one leg and both hands coming out first. I kept hold of his hands and put my fingers inside to get a grip on his mouth and turn him round into a good position. He came out quite easily after that but unfortunately he was born dead.

As well as being a midwife I know how to treat broken bones in the traditional way and many people from villages around here come to be treated by me. If someone has a broken arm, for example, the first thing I do is check if the broken bone has made a wound. I feel the limb and decide how best to manoeuvre the bone into place again. I gently press and stretch the broken bone until I am satisfied that it is sitting well, after which I bathe it with oil and warm water. Then I bind the limb with clean cloths and place several sticks around it, which, when tied on with more cloths, help to keep the bone in place and allow it to heal nicely. If it is an arm that is broken, I make a sling to hold it safely against the body. With a broken leg or something like that, the person has to avoid movement for some time. Usually, after three or four days the sticks can be removed and the person just needs to take care not to do anything to hurt the bone for a while. Sick people with broken bones have to eat good food such as chicken, eggs and soup. According to our traditional custom, chicken bones left from a sick person's meal are not thrown away. Instead, we keep them and put them together under the shade of a green tree in the hope that this will ensure that the bone mends nicely.

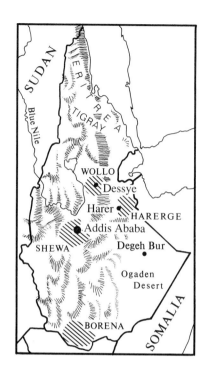
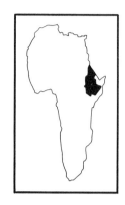

Country Profile: ETHIOPIA

Human Development Index (UNDP): 141st out of 160 nations
Population (1990): 49.2 mn. **Growth rate (1990-2000):** 3%
Life expectancy at birth (1990): 45.5 years
Population per doctor (1984): 60,000
Adult literacy (1985): 66%
Labour force employed in agriculture (1985-1988): 80%
GDP from agriculture and livestock (1988): 43.4%
Principal exports: coffee, hides and skins

1928 Haile Selassie becomes king, and then emperor in 1930. **1935** Italian invasion. **1941** Italian occupation ends, Britain assumes administration and Selassie reinstated as emperor. **1955** Independence. **1961** Eritrean war of independence begins, continuing until 1991. **1974** Revolution: Selassie deposed; the Dergue (military committee) take power. **1975** Tigrayan forces rebel against Addis Ababa, continuing until 1991. **1977** Lt.-Col. Mengistu Haile Mariam becomes head of state. **1977-78** Ogaden war with Somalia. **1991** Mengistu flees, opposition alliance promises fully representative democracy.

ETHIOPIA

The four areas where interviews took place were all sites of existing projects. Interviews with farmers in the central provinces of Wollo region were facilitated by the Italian NGO Ricerca e Cooperazione. The interviewers were **Yischak Tesfaye, Amelwork Tadesse** and **Andu-Alem Gubezie**, who also acted as a co-trainer and translator. Interviews in the Menagesha, and Yerer and Kereyu provinces of Shewa region were undertaken in cooperation with SOS Sahel and Farm Africa. **Andu-Alem Gubezie, Negash Yami, Walansa Fasil** and **Yeshiembet Chekol** interviewed agro-pastoralists, sedentary farmers and local traders. In Harer Zuriya and Gursum provinces of Harerge region, interviewers spoke to farmers and agro-pastoralists at the site of a project run by CARE International. The interview team was made up of extension workers from the project: **Habtamu Tadesse, Catie Leman, Mohamed Ahmed Dhag** and **Zufunworc Solomon**. The fourth interview area was in the southern province of Borena, Sidamo region, and was centred around a project run by Norwegian Church Aid. **Gimbe Borde** and **Tirunesh Sitro** carried out interviews with pastoralists and agro-pastoralists. The coordinator in Ethiopia was **Patrick Darling**; all interviews took place before the political changes of 1991.

Kebede Bantiwalu (M, 75 years), Cherecha, Adis Alem E5

I was born here in Cherecha and have never moved. I "served" my parents by looking after their cows, goats and sheep. From them I received all the experience I needed for my later farming activities. I still cultivate the same crops my father grew: mainly *t'ef*, wheat, barley, broad beans and the *zengada* variety of sorghum. I am the father of six children: four married daughters and two sons still at school.

I am very concerned about my crops being destroyed by wild animals, particularly baboons, monkeys and pigs. These animals are increasing because of a government ban on killing any wildlife here. In my youth, I hunted these animals with my friends, using spears and sharpened sticks, and so controlled those threatening our crops. According to Levitical law, it was forbidden to eat baboons, monkeys or pigs, but **dikulas** were hunted

By custom, anyone's animals can glean the field after my oxen have taken the first crop residues

for food. With the present ban on hunting, we farmers are having to stay around our farms the whole day long, just to protect our crops—because a herd of pigs or troop of baboons can completely destroy our fields in a few hours. During the night and in the early morning, it is too cold for us farmers to leave our houses: that is when most of the harm is done. Despite all the damage resulting from this government ban, we get no compensation for crops lost to wild animals, either from the state or the local **kebele**. I have also seen hyenas emerge from the forests on the other side of the valley—in broad daylight—to kill our animals. This is why I have stopped raising my own livestock.

When I was young, I built terracing to prevent top-soil erosion but I am too old to do that now. Being unfamiliar with fertiliser, I have never used it but I regularly applied manure. Now that scattered settlements are being concentrated together under the villagisation programme, there are no houses or animal stalls near my fields, so I can no longer easily apply manure. I have always practised crop rotation, growing barley, wheat and *t'ef* for many years, before leaving it under grass for two years. During the fallow period, livestock graze the land and drop their manure. The same is true to some extent on my croplands: by custom, anyone's animals can glean the field after my oxen have taken the first crop residues.

I was a tenant before the revolution and used to give one-third of my produce as rent to the landlord. My 2 **k'erts** of land used to produce 4 or 5 **quintals** of grain when I was young but now I only get 3 or 4 **quintals**. The reasons are partly my old age—I can't weed and plough at the proper time—and my inability to manure my fields properly following villagisation. My total production has also declined, because I am allocated only as much land as I can reasonably cultivate at my age: I am unable to till enough to make ends meet.

At a time when food is expensive and the status of farmers is higher than before, I am caught in a poverty trap: it is compulsory for me to sell my produce to the Agricultural Marketing Corporation (AMC). This places me in a terrible dilemma. I have to sell 2 **quintals** of *t'ef*, 3 **quintals** of barley and 1.5 **quintals** of wheat to the AMC at lower and lower prices almost every year. What is left over is insufficient to support my family. So I borrow money from those who can lend, or sell my livestock to buy grain. I have never had to borrow before. The loans can be repaid without interest. Now that my livestock is finished, I do not have the collateral to borrow any more. There is only one solution: I can only wait for my death. [Compulsory sale of grain to the AMC was abolished in March 1991, allowing farmers to keep their produce or sell at the current market price.]

Kenenet Mola (F, 52 years), Upper Kutaber Gorge, Wollo   *E18*

I cannot remember my parents. I was born in Ambasel and came here to be brought up by my aunt when I was six years old. My aunt had five women and seven men servants, so I only had to fetch water occasionally and never became familiar with housework. My aunt had three cows in the immediate farm area but I never knew how many livestock she had altogether. She had 1 **galameret** of cultivated land which she part rented out and part farmed, using her servants. She died six years ago.

I first married when I was 13. Since then I have been married five times but divorced due to disagreements. At the time of the revolution, I was farming with my last husband at Abaselama, 10 kilometres away. My husband had two cows, three donkeys and several chickens. Even then, we had marital problems and he used to stay in his farm area. We would only visit each other occasionally. After the famine, my husband came to Kutaber market and was forced by the police to go to a resettlement area. I no longer know his whereabouts or even whether he is alive or dead.

Since that time, nearly five years ago, I have earned my living brewing and selling **arekie**. Over the last year, Food for Work schemes have improved my situation as I obtain two sacks of wheat every month. This is enough to feed me but not enough to sell. I use the money I make from brewing alcohol to buy items such as coffee, butter, pepper, salt and soap.

I have one son: he is a prophet, a Qur'anic teacher under a vow of celibacy. He helps me in times of need. The government also helped during the 1974 famine, when I received 9 tasa of wheat and 8 tasa of flour once or twice a month, one can of oil or butter for every two persons, and also a blanket. But during the 1984-85 famine, I stayed here and received no help at all.

Eucalyptus trees were planted here before the revolution but their numbers have increased as each year we collectively plant more trees. Since the revolution, we buy eucalyptus firewood from the **kebele**: the wood from five trees is enough for my needs and that costs 7 **birr**.

There have been some other changes to my life. When I was young, I used to eat meat, but not now. I used to make **injera** using slightly fermented, ground *t'ef*; now I make them with wheat and maize, sometimes even barley. I still make a spicy **wat** from peas and lentils. For the last 10 years, I have had piped water. Overall, my life has improved. I particularly appreciate what the Food for Work programmes have done: now I can often buy what I need in the market.

E24   Yetemegn Damtew (F, 53 years), Lower Kutaber Gorge, Wollo

I was born quite near here, in Meskela village. As a young girl, I looked after the cows, helped to grind the grain, fetched water, collected firewood and prepared **injera** and **wat**. I did all this from such an early age that I cannot remember when I began. The main firewood then came from juniper, *muatie*, *kesie* and *embuacho* bushes. The wood ash was used as manure. Dried cowdung was also used as fuel. During the drought, the numbers of trees drastically decreased, though there has been a subsequent increase. Today, from the surrounding hillsides, I collect *woyira*, *bisana*, *digita*, *embuacho* bushes, and *imbis*.

When I was 15, I married and moved to Segeret village, 3 kilometres from here. I prepared **injera** from *t'ef*, sorghum, wheat and barley; I made **wat** from lentils, peas and cabbage; and I baked bread from wheat and oats—I prefer wheat bread. I used to farm, harrowing the soil to a fine tilth for the *t'ef*, weeding and digging it. We were particularly busy at sowing and harvest time. Today, my son takes care of the farm because my husband has a severe cough. Because of his illness, I am having to work to bring in income for the family—our four children live in different parts of the region. This is ironic, since only my husband knew the extent of our land and its yields. As the proverb goes: "Women and hoes eat whatever they are given." In other words, both do what they are forced to do.

I worked for Food for Work, on road construction, for three months but now I am too busy at home. From the Food for Work project, I received 90 kilos of wheat and 3 kilos of oil a month. We also had lessons on how to prepare **wat** and other forms of vegetable preparation but I was only able to attend one of the two days. I could not translate what I learned into action because I am so busy on the fields, although I do sometimes buy vegetables in Kutaber market. What I know about agriculture has not been gleaned from this project: I learned it from existing knowledge among us peasants and from growing vegetables in the other nursery further down the valley.

The oppression under the previous regime has ceased: now I am free to go out of my house and take part in organising and planning village affairs. I am chairperson of the Women's Association here, and learn much from joining in its discussions. The government has also given us the chance of education, although I am unable to take full advantage of this on account of my age. Today, too, I can take my grain to a modern mill: the era dominated by the backbreaking chore of grinding grain has come to an end.

Ahmed Elmi (M, 44 years), Degeh Bur, Ogaden E58

My mother died during childbirth when I was 12 years old. Within a few months my father and brother died of some disease of the lung. I was the oldest survivor but I could not look after the young family and our animals. We had been rich until then, owning 15 cows, 70 goats and numerous chickens. I could not even save one of them: they scattered far and wide and were killed by wild animals, such as hyenas. We used to have fields of sorghum and maize, ploughed with our neighbours' oxen, but someone else took over our crops and I could do nothing. My young brothers died one by one, until only my little sister was left.

I went to Dire Dawa to live and work in a hotel and then I became apprenticed to a tailor. After eight years, at the age of 20, I returned here to my birthplace: Degeh Bur. In the intervening years I had grown up. My physical appearance had changed and people did not quite recognise me. They remembered my parents but not me, so I never obtained the degree of help which I would have expected in my home area. This lack of support encouraged me to enlist as a soldier. By now I could speak Amharic, Somali and Oromigna, which meant I was easily accepted into the army.

Army life

Thus began a new life for me: I met many people, I learned about government work, and I earned enough money. I married and had eight children: three boys and five girls. Three of the girls and one of the boys died of whooping cough.

Then the Ethiopia-Somalia war broke out. Though a Somali speaker, I fought for Ethiopia because the Somali government came to take our land. We had plenty of food and medicine, everything was on our side. The government provided full support. For seven years I was in the war, but 12 years ago I was wounded. As usual, Somali forces hid on the ground or behind bushes as we chased them. Standing and shooting at them, I was hit by a bullet. It went through my neck and jaw, knocking out some teeth. For 18 days I was in hospital. My hair went white with the shock and I became like an old man. I have a pension for life, but nothing extra for being wounded.

E61   Atab Olad (M, 31 years), Ovale, Ogaden

I have lived in this village for about 20 years, keeping and trading livestock. I have 20 cows, 70 camels, 50 goats, 70 to 100 sheep and a few chickens. The milk from our cows and camels is very important. I have also borrowed some horses. Five years ago, I began to grow maize and sorghum. It's difficult here, as rain is unreliable, though it falls over about half the year.

When I was a boy, things were different. Livestock numbers have declined, because the lower rainfall has not produced enough grass for them. **K'ut**, **debrigor**, **abeb** and other diseases have stricken many of our cows. The rain has been decreasing gradually. There was some last night but not enough. We are expecting more before growing our maize and sorghum. Maize is better than sorghum in dry conditions. When crops fail to thrive, we feed them to our animals and these fattened animals are then sold in the town for money to buy food. We saved some seed from last year's crop: we always use the same short-season variety of red maize.

Atab Olad and his family

Last year, the government provided injections for our cattle and quinine *An advantage* for our fever but there has been no further help this year. *of having*

When I came here 20 years ago, livestock commanded better prices, *fields in two* and I did not need to sell any. There were more trees then, particularly *areas was that* galol and sogsog. Some areas round here were too thick to get through. I *rainfall was* do not know why the tree cover has become thinner. *sometimes*

When I was a boy, my family had three fields—two in Degeh Bur and *better here,* one here—with a total perimeter of over 3 kilometres: 35 hectares in all. *sometimes* Now I have two fields in this village with a total area of 20 hectares. The *there* fields in Degeh Bur did better. The soil there gave higher yields and allowed cropping for five years, whereas here one can only use the same field twice in succession before its fertility drops and it has to be left fallow for three to four years. One advantage of having fields in the two areas was that the rainfall was sometimes better here, sometimes there. We use animal dung to make our fields well again, especially for sorghum when we put dung specifically by each plant stand. Trees, not dung, are used for fuel, and the ash is thrown away. Trees are not food, therefore they are not good for us. We have enough food and enough animals to sell: we do not need trees so much now.

I have six children: four boys and two girls. One of my boys died when he was just 10 days old, so we do not know the illness. I married 10 years ago when I was 21 and my wife was 20. For the first three years we had no children: since then my wife has borne a child every year. I do not intend to let my wife rest. The babies are breastfed for four months and then given animal's milk. Our tradition is to have a child every two years, but my programme is for a child every year. After all, I do not know when my wife is going to die, so it is better that she has many children, so that—if she dies—her life will not have been in vain. Besides, I am going to marry another wife....

Abdulahi Osman (M, 70 years), Ovale, Ogaden   *E62*

I was born and brought up in Degeh Bur but I came and founded this village. I was 64 years old when Allah told me to settle here. Following my cattle about over the years, I had come to realise that this was a suitable place: there was enough grass for my cattle and enough rain, though both decreased from time to time.

It was always my ambition to have seven wives even when, at 19, I married my first wife. It is part of our culture. I achieved this ambition

and now have 20 children but am left with only two wives...and they both stay in another village.

When farming, I used to grow maize and sorghum. Everyone had different areas of land: I owned 20 **kotie**. In a good year, I would obtain 10 hundredweight [508 kg] of maize. I only grew sorghum occasionally. **Derkey**—a worm—used to destroy much of the crop, and there was trouble with birds. We did not report the worm problem to the government but went to a **sheki** who read the Qur'an and prayed. He used to give us a medicinal plant, but these days he prays in front of a vessel with water which is then sprinkled onto the sorghum. Sometimes the worm is killed; sometimes not.

The most abundant trees around here are *galol, sogsog, kansah, mara, hagar, obol, karasho, dirtab, mayo, delol, irgin, liby, bilil* and *kora*. None of these species has disappeared, though the numbers have decreased. Nomads clear trees when they settle somewhere, to make huts and charcoal. Refugees clear trees, too. Farmers have been ploughing more land, using camels—and oxen, which are better and more numerous. Finally, there is a change in the climate: it has been getting hotter over the last 15 years or so. Also the rain comes only once, between September and November, and even then is unreliable. There is sometimes a little between December and February; the rest of the year is completely dry.

The main changes that I have seen in my life are that I used to be healthy but now I am sick, that we used to travel around but now we must settle, that the government no longer gives medicine or food, and that our wealth has decreased.

Arden Dimo (M, 80 years), Arero Harodimtu, Borena   *E66*

Before the war, I was living in this area, near Arero, keeping 100 camels, 80 cows, and 30 goats and sheep. During the early part of the war, we became caught between the front lines. Both Somali and Ethiopian soldiers took our animals. I was left destitute. One day, Somali soldiers surrounded our village and shot anyone who ran out, killing many of our villagers. I kept inside our house with my wife and four children and we were captured.

We were taken away to a large detention camp at Surea in Somalia. There were thousands of other people there. We were given rations but no work and no animals. It was very hot and dry—impossible land to farm. The Somalis wanted us to join them, even though we were Oromigna speakers. They held us there for nine years.

Finally, the Somalis brought us back to the border for official release. Thousands of others still wait, as this process is being implemented only gradually. First, I went to Negele Borena for rations, then I was resettled here in my old home area. That was just four months ago. The government gave me some money for a few livestock and I have bought three camel calves, which are growing up nicely. In time, we will also try to grow some crops. Our main problems are not owning enough animals and an uncertain future. Now one son and one daughter are married, I want to educate my other two children. To do this, I will need to build up my flocks and herds to their previous numbers. That is my ambition.

When I was a child, we had the same amount of livestock as I had just before the war. Some people grew crops; others, like us, did not. Then more and more crops were grown for general food, additional to milk. I watched others cultivating, then I tried to practise it myself. When the war broke out, I had been growing maize, sorghum, barley and *t'ef* for five years. In the same way, I had been watching those who used manure on their fields. I noted how nicely the crops grew, their good yields and the way the land could be used more continuously. I, too, had begun to plough in manure before sowing, though I did not measure how much. Wood-ash was useless.

I lived on both hills and plains. On the hills, I used to keep my animals around the village and cultivate land down on the plains. When I lived on the plains, our farms lay near the village and our animals were all around, some of them being occasionally up on the hills.

Everything I saw in the landscape when I was young still exists now. The only difference as far as trees are concerned is that more have been cut because of cultivation and there are more villages around. I am unaware of any species having disappeared or of any new ones being introduced.

Before the war, there was every kind of animal around—leopard, elephant, giraffe, mountain nyala, zebra, wild goat and buffalo. We used to hunt the lions that killed our cows and laid traps for the bush fowl. Hunting and trapping are now forbidden. I do not know where all the big animals have gone; maybe the soldiers killed them.

E68   *Godauna Halake (F, 96 years), Kafate, Borena*

My parents owned many animals. Everything edible came from our livestock, for we ate mainly meat and milk mixed with blood, taken from a vein in the cow's neck. We knew nothing about crops or grain.

My husband, too, owned much livestock: cows, goats, sheep, donkeys and camels. He died 56 years ago, when Italy invaded Ethiopia. I have borne only one daughter and she is alive and married, here in Kafate.

As a child and as a married woman, one of my daily tasks was to collect water from the wells at Wachile, 17 kilometres away. I used a wooden container, smoked to seal any leaks. On the outward journey, I carried it over my shoulders in a wickerwork frame, all of which weighed about 10 kilos. On the return trip through soft sand, I carried the additional 20 or so litres of water. As I am now so old, I no longer have to do this, but my daughter and other women from this village still make such journeys daily.

Everything edible came from our livestock: meat, and milk mixed with blood

We collect firewood from the immediate locality. *Hale*, *sabansa*, *dadache* and *walchama* are preferred. They make good charcoal, burn slowly and consistently, as well as giving off a good smell. None of these species is in short supply.

The trees are less dense than before. We used to burn the forest to obtain fresh green grass for our animals. Where we burnt, usually without any control and well away from the village, the trees and bushes were further **Wars have** apart. If the fire approached the village, then it was controlled. Sometimes **taken a** we burnt back the bush around our village to stop it encroaching, as well **greater toll** as to kill insects—especially the tsetse fly—and to provide fresh grass for **of our** the livestock. Today, all such burning is banned by the government. **livestock**

The main pasture grasses are still the same as when I was young: **than drought** *mat'agudesa, alalo, alcheso* (which cures mouth infections), *hido, sericha* and *ilmogori*. During drought, the landscape goes dry. However, when it rains again, there is enough grass. I have not seen any big change in the rainfall pattern over my life.

Wars have taken a greater toll of our livestock than drought. Some of our livestock was taken in the Italian war; more was taken in the recent Somali conflict. It was impossible to hide our animals: the soldiers followed us and surrounded our village. We had to escape for our lives by night, leaving all our livestock behind. We managed to reach Wachile, where we stayed for 13 years. We had nothing to eat. We had to find roots but we did not know what was good to eat and what was bad. We survived. We ate *hargassa* grass, *gurisa* fruit, the boiled cabbage-like leaves of *rafu*, the ground tubers of *tuk'a* and the potato-like tubers of *white pear*.

My parents and grandparents taught me the medicinal use of plants. I could spend all day telling you of the hundreds of plants used in traditional medicine. Here are a few examples.

Medicinal plants

If the roots of the tree creeper, *hamaricha*, are boiled and the water drunk, it helps cure coughs and influenza. *Rericha* is a small plant, the roots of which can be boiled to cure coughs in young livestock and small children. Men also use this for gonorrhoea. I cannot count the plants that are used for this complaint: almost every medicinal plant is acceptable. If the roots of the low-growing *arsar* plant, the leaves of the big *k'obo* tree, or the roots of the large *awaicho* tree are boiled in water, like tea, for about 20 minutes, they produce potions against gonorrhoea. The *awaicho* potion is also a good remedy for tapeworm. Another cure for gonorrhoea comes from boiling the stems of *toticha* in butter. This small plant comes from a long way away, growing in very localised spots in Mega and Didleben, in Negele Borena.

Drinking a potion obtained by boiling the roots of the *ulicha* creeper will ease monthly menstrual pains. *Sabako*—a broad-leaved, small plant—has roots which yield a medicine to lessen the stomach cramps and morning sickness of pregnant women. *Anona* are big riverside trees and their bark can be infused in boiling water, for the same time as the leaves, to make a medicine to help parturition of the placenta in problematic post-childbirth cases. Only half a mugful need be drunk. For more normal deliveries, the leaves of the big *garse* tree are roasted and powdered to make them into a tea. Drinking this helps induce an early birth and ensure clean parturition. This is not done to induce miscarriages.

Stomach pain or gastric disorders can be countered with a potion brewed from the roots of the small *ubacho* plant. If wood-ash is drunk with water, this also relieves men's stomach pains. *Burate* creeper fruits are boiled and eaten to ease gastric pains and vomiting. The big *kuwa* tree has a white sap, which can be used to stop diarrhoea. Men who eat meat must not take this medicine. The white sap is dangerous for the eyes. This means that great care must be taken in its collection, preparation and administration.

By digging out and boiling the roots of the small *walda* plant, snake-bites can be cured—especially those of Puff Adders. The roots of the small *makofa* shrub and a different kind of *walda* plant can be brewed to help cows drop their milk. For cows refusing to release milk to their calves, another more specific medicine comes from bark infusions of *bik'a*, a big plant like a small tree. The small *butiye* shrub provides a paste, which can be painted on to animals' legs where they have been attacked by flies similar to the warble fly.

Internal or external pustules or swellings are treated by grinding the roots of the small *furza* plant to a powder, mixing that into an ointment and then applying it externally, like linament, to the cancerous sore or lump. The application is left to dry, uncovered. A powder to heal wounds on animals or people can be made from any part of the big *makanisa* tree. In cases where the infection is an internal one, a paste of ash and water applied to the swelling will help the pus to ooze out. From the spoil of some animal burrows, you can find suitable minerals for pasting onto surface wounds.

This is enough. Only a few men and women now have this knowledge. People travel up to 300 kilometres to see me. In Borena, they come from Teltele, Negele and Leban. I know of others who also practice herbal medicine, but they live far away and we have never met or exchanged information. The closest is my brother's son in Yabelo. The knowledge I have gained is difficult to pass on to others. I dispense my information willingly but no one has yet taken on my mantle. I am passing on the information to my daughter and her eight children; they are learning by fetching the ingredients.

Jirmo Buda (M, 80 years), Gabso, Borena   *E74*

The round homes of Gabso village, made from grass and the bent boughs of trees, were loosely clustered together in the empty bush. Women, adorned with bangles and neck bracelets, sat on wooden stools washing and pummelling their clothes. Men gathered around to listen, many standing on one leg as they leaned on their long sticks.

Dure, in the Mega area, is where I was born, though I spent the first 47 years of my life in Haraweyu, eight hours northeast of here. Even though only seven of its 17 wells are working, there was more water there than here. When I was a boy, we had 30 cows, 20 goats, one mule and four camels. Then I spent three years at Leban, Negele Borena. It was not a good livestock area, as sucking flies attacked the cows' shins and our cattle became thin and weak.

For the last 30 years, I have lived in Gabso, which has the same climate as Haraweyu and enough grass but insufficient water. When we first came here, we lived on milk and butter—food was no problem. Over the last eight years of drought and poor rainfall, our animals have produced little milk. So we are now having to buy food grain from Yabelo, 60 kilometres away, or Mega, 50 kilometres away, by selling livestock. Livestock numbers fluctuate with the rainfall. I now only have 30 cows and 15 goats.

During the drought, we dug ponds and built wells for Food for Work, obtaining grain from Norwegian Church Aid. We tried to find grass and to go where the grain was, but when the drought was hard, we shifted to Haraweyu. Afterwards, we moved back to Gabso, where the grass was better. There were other settlements here but this posed no grazing problems, as there is plenty of room to move about. Today though, we have nothing—not even grain from Food for Work.

There is a water shortage: we make a four-hour journey to the base of a small rocky hill to obtain water, taking the cows there every three days, while women go two or three times a week with donkeys to collect water for domestic use. When I first came here, the wells gave little water. Twenty years ago, two of the wells failed and more had to be dug: there are now four working wells. Up to six people are needed in some of these wells. One person from each herd meets on a set day and works with those from other herds in a cooperative. This labour custom has not changed over time.

Borena wells can be very deep and often have two working levels. A long, narrow cutting slants down to water troughs, 10-15 metres below ground level. From some 10-20 metres lower down, the herdsmen, perched on loose timber scaffolding in a wide well, pass water up to the troughs. Each herdsman takes a turn at being song-leader, telling of his cattle and his adventures, and the rest join in a chorus. Every now and then, they break into a rapid refrain and pass up the water twice as fast.

We know where to dig wells by looking around rocky hills for seepage and areas where grass remains green. Waterholes dug in the bottom of stream-beds soon dry up. During the rains, our livestock can get water everywhere and there is no need to travel far. Forty other villages use the same traditional wells as us. Well over 10,000 cattle are being served by these wells; 2,600 cattle are watered there daily! Usually, this just takes six to seven hours but, when the water level falls, it can take much longer and we work into the night, burning firewood to make enough light. The level of the spring water drops when drawn but then comes back up again; there has been no change in its recovery level from when I first came here 30 years ago.

E78   *Killoya-Silgo Ajambo (F, 80 years), Dillo, Borena*

Livestock converge on Dillo—a village in the crater of an extinct volcano—from far away, descending sheer basalt rock through great splits in the valley walls to reach the wells on the crater floor. Into this pastoral community came a woman with a different way of doing things....

I was born in Konso, Gamo Gofa region. I came here on my own— willingly—about 40 years ago. In Konso, I had been growing sorghum and soya beans. I had my own land, though I cannot remember its size or yields. I had neither cow nor ox; I just dug my land with my hoe. I worked on both red and black alluvial soils. Making bunds was a practical measure to protect the soil and some people terraced their hillside land.

I was married in 1935, aged 24, during the Italo-Ethiopian war and stayed with my husband for six years. During that time, I ground grain, prepared food, made beer from sorghum, and went to the fields to dig the soil. I used to make kurkurfa out of red sorghum, and mix it with boiled leaves from the *shiferaw* tree, which cures diabetes.

I started working early in the morning and stopped at noon. I collected *sabansa* and *deka* for firewood; I used no cowdung for fuel. I fetched water from the two local **elas**, which never dried up. I had one boy and one girl, but both died in their early childhood. I thought it was bad luck to live with my husband, for all my children died—and to be with him and just feed him was valueless. So I divorced him and came here alone.

I never married again. Here, I made **bordei** and **arekie**. I ground grain, fetched water from the crater and collected firewood. I had to buy grain—maize, sorghum, barley and wheat—from merchants, because the Borena people do not plough or grow cereals. Had they tried, they would have grown. I collected *sabansa*, *sirgirso* and *hamessa* for firewood. They can also be used for house construction. The trees and shrubs around here include *sigirso*, *hamessa*, *sabansa*, *dedecca*, *hidado*, *sukella*, *hagarssu*, *ballanji*, *ergenssa* and *oholley*.

There have been two droughts in Dillo. As I am not a pastoralist, I cannot recall exactly when they occurred. Those who have cattle will remember. We never had any drought in Konso. There have been no major changes in my life, though the vegetation around here has decreased. I prefer this area to Konso, and I prefer working to receiving aid.

Today, I am practising some small-scale agriculture, growing *shumbra*, pumpkin, sorghum, *abish* and a little maize. Borena people do not grow these crops. Ever since coming here, I have tried to teach the people around me about them. For years I failed, then—last year—I succeeded. I even have had to provide seeds to those trying to cultivate. The people around here are very happy with my efforts. They like me. They respect me. As I am growing older and older, the **kebele** provides me with 45 kilos of wheat and 1.5 kilos of margarine without my having to take part in the Food for Work programme. They gave these to me free, as a sign of their respect and liking, because they came to understand what my efforts meant.

E55 Nafissa Mohamed (F, 40 years), Ogaden
It is the man's job to seek new pastures where there has been rain. Today, our men are looking for **chat** and tea in town, not rain.

E50 Hasan Mussa (M, 56 years), Aubera
Chat is like a food to us: it takes away our appetite, yet gives us strength to plough.

E81   *Gorlo Jimo (M, 70 years), Ch'ork'asa, Borena*

I have been here four years. I originally came from Borbor, near Belale and Wachile. I moved here via Mega and Melbana because of the war. When I was younger, I had 400 cows, 20 camels, 200 goats, a mule, four donkeys and eight sheep. I obtained my food from this livestock. I had eight children to feed: four boys and four girls.

When I was younger, we used to catch giraffe, **sala**, hidi and **guguftu**. We hunted them on horses, spearing them when they became exhausted and weak. With giraffes, we first cut the achilles tendon in one of their back feet so they could not get up, then we struck them in the neck with big spears until they bled to death. Other animals we killed by striking them wherever we could. We also trapped some with a rope noose. The animals in the bush when I was a boy also included zebra, mountain nyala and others. The numbers of all the animals have gradually declined over my lifetime. People were hunting them more and more, so they escaped to the big forests and became scarce. During the war, soldiers went everywhere into the forest and shot the animals. That and the drought are the main reasons why there are so few animals in the bush today.

Every year in the dry season, we used to burn the dense, unwanted shrubs to bring up new grass. We did not burn near our homes for safety's sake. Burning is not good—it destroys...but the problem is that otherwise people do not get fresh grass. It also killed the insects that were bad for cows, and killed snakes—all the other animals escaped.

War

The war [with Somalia] started when I was at Borbor. Somali soldiers came to the village early in the morning, shooting and killing people. Some of us were captured, others ran and hid in the undergrowth and bushes. Borena people captured in earlier raids were fighting with the Somali soldiers against their own villages. God saved me. I picked up one baby; my wife took the other. I led the way without looking. I just ran...even through thick thorns. My body was badly scratched, but my wife and the other children could run after me down the path I made. Once out of danger, I left my wife and children in a safe place and, with a few other men, crept carefully back to our village. Nothing was left. Our houses were burnt to the ground. Our livestock had been stolen. We had saved our lives but lost everything else.

Some of our relatives in Melbe and Golbo helped us. They collected together a few cows for us to start a new life. Then came the drought. By then, I was staying at Dubuluk. The wells here are affected by the decrease in rainfall and the water was no longer flowing fast enough to water the animals every three days. Day and night the herdsmen toiled at the wells, but the water came slowly and the livestock only drank once every five days. On top of this, there was not enough grass. Our three milking cows died. Once again, we had absolutely nothing. This time, our relatives could not help us. They, too, were suffering. I moved to Yabelo to join Food for Work. It was then that my 20-year-old son fell ill.

If possible, I want to keep my children looking after livestock.... I want to depend on cows again

He was sick for over a year, during which a herbalist at Dubuluk treated him with boiled plants. I paid the herbalist with milk, coffee, and tobacco from Yabelo market. I was penniless when this happened. I had to join Food for Work to obtain grain, which I then sold to raise the money to buy the commodities to pay the herbalist. Eventually, my son was taken to Yerga Alem hospital and there he died.

New ways

Under Food for Work, I made roads, planted seedlings and constructed ponds. It was all new to me and it was good to learn new things. The work was interesting but exhausting. Today, I would prefer to rear animals, but I am still doing Food for Work. The ponds we make sometimes hold water, sometimes go dry. Some of the tree seedlings we plant survive, but most eventually die from lack of rain—they are only watered in the nursery and are planted out when the rain comes. Something else I have learned: new ideas about cultivating land. Maize, wheat, haricot beans, barley, sorghum and *t'ef* are some of the seeds I have been given by Norwegian Church Aid. There has been some harvest this year but some has been lost because of the lack of rain. When I say lost, I mean just the crop; the foliage is useful fodder whatever happens. The livestock prefer it to grass. I know nothing yet about vegetables—I have seen but not eaten them. Local farmers here have long experience of growing vegetables.

In my lifetime, there has been no change in the vegetation. The changes that have affected the lives of the people are the extra clinics, ponds and wells. Now I have two cows and four goats. Food for Work pays with both grain and with animals. I want to build up my livestock numbers again...maybe this will take up to 10 years or more. I have a son and a daughter working with me; the others are too young. I want enough milk for my children. If at all possible, I want to keep my children looking after livestock as the Borena people used to. Some of my children are now at school. I do realise that they may become interested in other things. I want to depend on cows again. For the moment, though, it is good to live in a new way...a change.

Further reading on the Sahel

Club du Sahel, *The Sahel Facing the Future*, OECD, Paris, 1988
Cross, Nigel, *The Sahel: The Peoples' Right to Development*, Minority
  Rights Group, London, 1990
Giri, Jacques, *Le Sahel Demain*, Karthala, Paris, 1989
Monimart, Marie, *Femmes du Sahel*, Karthala/OECD, Paris, 1989
Rahim, Nafissa et al., *Greenwar: Environment and Conflict in the Sahel*,
  Panos, London, 1991

GLOSSARY

abeb	foot and mouth disease
Ag	son of
ahofar	type of bread made from fruit of *Ziziphus spina-christi*
aich, el	gruel made from butter, flour and milk
alluxunne	fish: *Gymnarchus niloticus*
amur	container for storing milk
anjobe	fish: dog fish
arekie	strong alcoholic spirit made from dates and sorghum
asida	solid porridge made from fermented or fresh batters of sorghum wheat or millet flour
awasill	hand tool for tilling the soil
babor	diesel engine used in irrigation pumps
balde	fish: *Heterotis niloticus*
banco	mud and manure mixture used for building
bappoore	fish: Nile Perch
barema	wage labourer
bazdoul	fish: *Pomadasys rogeri*, type of carp
bili bili	non-alcoholic drink made from fermented gruel
birr	unit of Ethiopian currency
blancs, les	term used to refer to whites and also strangers in general
Bobo revolt	1913-1916, one of the last local revolts against the French
bordei	local beer
boubou	loose cotton cloak worn on formal or special occasions by men
boule	drink made from millet flour with milk or water
boyinaajo	wild dog
brochet	fish: pike
caca cross	local name for cabbage which can be grown throughout the year
calabash	dried gourd skin used as container
canari	earthenware jar, usually for water
capitaine	fish: Nile Perch
CFA	Communauté Financière Africaine: the CFA franc, freely convertible to French francs
chat	plant (*Catha edulis*), chewed as stimulant
chef des bouchers	head butcher
chef du canton	(Niger) traditional chief who has some administrative duties
chef de terre	one who allocates the land within a community
coiffeur traditionnel	lit. traditional barber; an expert on scarification patterns, circumcision and bleeding cures

courbine	fish: *Sciaena aquila*
couscous	crushed steamed wheat, eaten with broth, meat or vegetables
CRDA	state regional development structure in Burkina Faso
daba	hoe
debayë	agricultural tool for ploughing
debrigor	cattle disease affecting the back
dégué	millet gruel
Dergue	Ethiopian military committee, which took power from Emperor Selassie in 1974 and was deposed in 1991
derkey	larva of intermittent cereal pest
diguette	barrier of stones to stop soil erosion
dikula	small antelope
dolo	millet beer
duba	agricultural tool for ploughing
ela	pond dug to catch rainwater
emir	traditional leader
espeza	type of bread
etejhtan	Islamic burial ceremony
fanco	weaning food
fatiha, el	opening section of Qur'an
feddan	area of land approximately equal to an acre
fulah	natural pools of water
gahawa	lit. coffee; roadside café
galameret	2 acre plot of land
garad	pods of *sunut* tree used in inhalation as remedy for colds and fevers, and in tanning
genie	spirit being
griot	traditional musician or praise-singer, formerly attached to and provided for by a specific family or village. Although their livelihood is now considerably reduced, griots are often employed to encourage communal activities
gris gris	charm
groupement	traditional community group, often active in local development activities
Habha, el	Sudanese season
haboub	strong wind usually associated with thick dust
haj	pilgrimage to **Makkah**
haji, el	one who has made the pilgrimage to **Makkah**
hantour	wagon
hatab	wooden pole used in house building

hawat	goatskin container for making yoghurt
husa	sandy infertile soil
icterus	jaundice
Idara Ahliya	when **sheikhs** had the power to implement colonial legislation and tax systems, under the British administration
imam	Muslim leader who is recognised authority on Islamic theology and law; also the prayer leader of a mosque
injera	thin pancake of fermented *t' ef* dough
ivr	fish: *Pomadasys jubeliri*, type of carp
jakka	share of harvest paid as rent, a tithe
jamba	male wedding dance—known as the vulture dance
jujube	fruit of *Ziziphus mauritania or spina-christi*
kama'in	brick factory (pl. of kamina: brick kiln)
katikan	fine fabric
kebele	Peasants Association
kerba	goat skin
k'ert	area of land
keychtai	red clayey soil
khayma	tent
khor	seasonal water course
kisra	unleavened, fermented batter made from sorghum flour, cooked into thin pancakes
kofo	large barrel made of cow dung and ash
kola	bride-price
koro	enamel bowl used for measuring, equivalent to 2.5—3 kg
kotie	area of land equal to 3.2 hectares or 7.9 acres
k'ut	possibly rinderpest, contagious disease fatal to cattle
lalob	desert date, fruit of *heglig*
Makkah	(Mecca) the holiest city of the Islamic religion
marabout	Muslim prayer leader, teacher and sometimes healer, who is venerated locally for his spiritual powers
mid	local measure equivalent to 3 kg
mindakoro	chicken pox
Mint	daughter of
mixture, the	possibly Oral Rehydration Therapy (sugar, salt, water)
mukhamma	area of land equal to 7400 sq. metres
muude	measure of harvest
Natra, el	Sudanese rainy season; lit. the roar of the lion, ie. the period of thunder and rain
nazir	traditional leader of tribal group, now a district-level officer

nesha	nourishing drink made from local vitamin-rich fruit
niinan kande	basket of ground grain paid by tenant to land owner
Ould	son of
pagne	length of cloth
pain de singe	lit. monkey bread; fruit of baobab
phacochère	wart-hog
pirogue	small boat shaped like canoe, used for fishing and transport
pro'h	condiment
qadi	Islamic court judge
quintal	hundredweight
ratel	local measure equivalent to approximately 1lb (449.28 gr)
ratoba	arthritis
sagia	traditional wooden water wheel
sala	large antelope with long horns
segeremmes	guinea-worms
seluka	digging stick, with foot-rest
sha'ab	forked building pole
shaman	traditional healer
Sharia	traditional code of Islamic law, both civil and criminal, based in part on the Qur'an
sheikh	community leader
sheki	traditional healer
shekwa	sheep or goatskin containers
shireya	thin spaghetti, eaten with sugar
sihnet	"smoke bath" believed to make one strong, healthy and attractive
silanye	fish: *Bagrus*
silure	fish: cat fish
SONADER	parastatal organisation set up to manage irrigated agriculture
soumbala	seasoning for sauces made from processed locust beans *(néré)*
sumbuk	wooden fishing boat
tam tam	drum
tanin	product of *Acacia nilotica* used in tanning
Tarfa, el	period of light showers at end of Sudanese rainy season
tô	solid porridge made from millet flour, eaten with sauce
tobe	thin multi-coloured material worn by women over ordinary clothes
totem	animal or plant species with particular association to a human clan name

ud	lit. stick; also area of land
UM	In 1973 Mauritania withdrew from the French-backed West African Monetary Union and created its own currency: Ouguiya (UM)
umda	head of tribe with administrative and judicial powers, but subordinate to **nazir**
varou	large lambskin blanket
Walet	daughter of
walga	female deer
wat	vegetable or meat stew
whalaha	black fertile soil
xarannimbe	student followers of **marabouts**
yâka	gazelle
zaa	type of meningitis
zebu	humped domestic oxen

BOTANICAL GLOSSARY

It Has not proved possible to verify the accuracy of all local names, some of which may have been misheard or mistranscribed. Therefore this glossary represents, at best, a provisional list. No attempt has been made to check vernacular names against specimens, although wherever possible they have been checked with standard reference works.

A=Arabic; Am=Amharic; B=Boré; Bo=Borana; D=Djerma; Eth T=Tigrigna; Eth Te=Tigre; F=French; G=Gourma; H=Hausa; Ha=Hasaniya; M=Mooré; O=Oromigna; S=Somali; So=Soninke; T=Tamashek.

LOCAL	LATIN	
aaye (Eth T)	Diospyros mespiliformis	ebony
abarom (T)	Andropogon gayanus	Gamba grass
abish (Am)	Trigonella foenum-graecum	fenugreek
abu asabeil (A)	Steganotaenia araliacea	
adgi zana		
adjar (T)	Maerua crassifolia	
adress (Ha)	Commiphora africana	African myrrh
adri (Eth T)	Brassica carinata	Ethiopian mustard
	or B. integrifolia	
agadjini (H)	Boscia angustifolia	
ahirdjidjim (T)	Cassia italica	senna
akarkar (T)	Anogeissus leiocarpus	
alalo (O)	Trema guineensis	
	or Croton macrostachyus	
alcheso (Bo)	Cymbopogon sp.	oil grass
almet (Eth Té)		grass
amuzba		
an'anou (B)	Prosopis africana	
an'ansouire (B)		tree
anistayeti-andel		
anona (Bo)	Trichilia emetica	Cape Mahoghany
anza (H)	Boscia senegalensis	
aorawa (H)		
arak (A)	Salvadora persica	toothbrush tree
arcobcobai	Hyphaene thebaica	doum palm or gingerbread tree
arsar (Bo)	Gnidia stenophylloides	
awaicho (Bo)	Ricinus communis	castor oil plant
awlea (Eth T)	Olea europaea subsp. cuspidata	wild olive
baava (So)	Pennisetum pedicellatum	grass

babanous (A)	Dalbergia melanoxylon	African blackwood tree
babarbare		haricot bean
bage (So)		
balasa (D)	Commelina sp.	type of spiderwort
ballanji (Bo)		
bambei	Ipomoea batatar	sweet potato
bamia (A)	Abelmoschus esculenus	okra
banguedéré (M)		
barkoudi (M)	Annona senegalensis	wild custard-apple
barra (So)	Pennisetum pedicellatum	grass
barsim (A)	Medicago sativa	alfalfa
bazanga, el	Sorghum sp.	type of sorghum
belbeshre		weed
beri beri (A)	Sorghum bicolor	sorghum
bichure (Ha)		white millet
bik'a (Bo)	Pappea capensis or Combretum molle	
bilbilwo (H)		weed
bili (So)	Vetiveria nigritana	grass
bilil (S)	Acacia mellifera	
binne (So)	Sesamum indicum	sesame
biririhouta	Sorghum sp.	quick-growing sorghum
bisana	Croton macrostachys	
bor'rio (B)	Balanites aegyptiaca	desert date
botouro (B)		
bro'iwe (B)		tree
burate (Bo)		creeper
butiye (Bo)	Mitragyna stipulosa	African linden
cailcédrat (F)	Khaya senegalensis	African mahogany
camal gesh (A)		hay
chekomta (Eth T)	Ficus sp.	type of fig
cram cram (F)	Cenchrus biflorus	cram cram
dachi (H)	Commiphora africana	
dadache (Bo)	Acacia tortilis	
daero (Eth T)	Ficus sp.	type of fig
dagusha (Am)	Eleusine coracana	finger millet
dambalab, el (A)	Aristida mutabilis	type of triple-awn grass
dambare (So)		
dan heca		quick-growing millet
dâni (H)	Cenchrus biflorus	cram cram
dan tchima		quick-growing millet
dargaza (H)	Grewia bicolor	
dawa (H)	Sorghum bicolor	

dedecca (O)	*Acacia abyssinica*	umbrella thorn
deefe (So)		
deka (O)	*Grewia tembensis*	
delol (S)		
dere (So)	*Ficus umbellata*	type of fig
deye (So)		
digita	*Carissa edulis*	
	or *Syzygium guineense*	
dilo (H)	*Boscia senegalensis*	
dirtab (S)	*Canavalia ensiformis*	horse bean
dom (A)	*Hyphaene thebaica*	doum palm or gingerbread tree
dua (B)	M8	tree
dura (A)	*Sorghum bicolor*	sorghum
eligo (M)		
embuacho	*Rumex sp.*	
ensete (Am)	*Ensete ventricosum*	false banana
ergenssa (Bo)	*Premna resinosa*	
fa (So)	*Ziziphus mauritiana*	Indian jujube
fak turu (So)		
figuier (F)	*Ficus sp.*	type of fig
fonio (F)	*Digitaria exilis*	fonio
fonio sauvage (F)	*Panicum laetum*	wild fonio
fromager (F)	*Ceiba pentandra*	silk cotton tree
furza (Bo)	*Crotolaria rosenii*	
gaafe (So)	*Piliostigma reticulatum*	
galol (S)	*Acacia nilotica subsp. adstringens*	
gamba (H)	*Andropogon gayanus*	Gamba grass
garaaje (So)		
garga (G)	*Eleusine indica*	
gargir	*Eruca sativa*	rocket cress
garse (Bo)	*Dobera glabra*	
gasa		
gawo (H)	*Faidherbia albida*	apple-ring acacia
gese (So)	*Acacia senegal*	gum arabic tree
gesho (A)	*Rhamnus prinoides*	
gollos		
gombo (F)	*Abelmoschus esculenus*	okra
gundu gundu (H)		quick-growing millet
gurisa (Bo)	*Euphorbia depauperata*	
habeil (A)	*Combretum cordofanum*	
hagar (S)	*Commiphora sp.*	type of incense tree

hagarssu (Bo)	*Commiphora ogadensis* or *C. erythraea*	type of incense tree
hale(Bo)	*Acacia bussei*	
halfa (A)	*Desmostachya bipinnata*	bulrush
hamaricha (Bo)		tree creeper
hamessa (O)	*Commiphora sp.*	type of incense tree
hano (H)	*Boswellia dalzielii* or *Boswellia odorata*	frankincense tree
haraz (A)	*Faidherbia albida*	apple-ring acacia
hareze		weed
hargassa (Bo)	*Commiphora ogadensis* or *C. erythraea*	type of incense tree
haseba (Eth T)	*Combretum molle*	
hashab (A)	*Acacia senegal*	gum arabic tree
hasharat, el (A)		
hawri		
haya (H)	*Cyperus esculentus*	yellow nutsedge, tigernut
hidado (Bo)		
hido (Bo)	*Girardinia diversifolia*	
heglig (A)	*Balanites aegyptiaca*	desert date
hivanou (B)		
houanaou (B)	*Terminalia avicennioides*	
ifun		
ignine (Ha)	*Capparis decidua*	
ilmogori (O)	*Cardiospermum halicacabum*	balloon vine
imbis (Am)	*Allophylus abyssinicus*	
imigige (Ha)		
inchichi (S)		
intatie		
irgin (S)		
iria (B)		weed
jaaje (So)	*Graminae sp.*	grass
jebe (So)	*Lawsonia inermis*	henna
jomba (So)	*Vitex doniana*	
jongoone (So)		
jujubier (F)	*Ziziphus mauritiana* or *spina-christi*	Christ's thorn
kakito	*Medicago polymorpha*	type of clover
kalgo (H)	*Piliostigma reticulatum*	
kamsaongo (M)	*Ficus gnaphalocarpa*	type of fig
kancha (Eth T)		
kandiga (M)		
kangna (T)	*Acacia nilotica subsp. adstringens*	

kango (M)	*Balanites aegyptiaca*	desert date
kansah (S)	*Acacia etbaica*	
karasho (O)	*Commiphora boranensis*	type of incense tree
karité (F)	*Butyrospermum paradoxum*	shea butter tree
karkadeh (A)	*Hibiscus sabdariffa*	roselle
kassaoura (H)	*Acanthospermum hispidum*	
kbeibtadab (Ha)	*Euphorbia granularis*	
keglu-vando		
kelto	*Ximenia americana*	spiny plum
kénébgo		
kesie	*Lantana salvifolia*	
ketebene (So)		
kiassoua (H)	*Acanthospermum hispidum*	
kièguèndo (M)		grass
kihe		
kiide (So)	*Adansonia digitata*	baobab
kirikiri (H)	*Cynodon dactylon*	
kirné (H)	*Bridelia ferruginea*	
kiskinde (M)	*Boscia angustifolia*	African blackwood tree
	or *Dalbergia melanoxylon*	
kitr (A)	*Acacia mellifera*	
klaiba		
koanga (M)	*Borassus aethiopum*	African fan palm
k'obo (Eth T)	*Euphorbia sp.*	
k'obo (O)	*Ricinus communis*	castor oil plant
koigo (M)		
kongo (M)	*Borassus aethiopum*	African fan palm
kora (O)	*Acacia tortilis*	
kougaré (M)		
kouiga (M)	*Ficus thonningii*	
kouka (M)	*Khaya senegalensis*	African mahogany
koumoudoua (H)		weed
krusan	*Boscia senegalensis*	
kuanti		weed
kuñe (So)	*Faidherbia albida*	apple-ring acacia
kurumtia		weed
kuwa (Bo)		tree
laut (A)	*Acacia oerfota*	
leaw		
leet		
leham (Eth T)	*Syzygium guineense*	
lélogo (M)	*Leptadenia hastata*	
leyara (H)		grass

liby (S)	*Delonix alata*	
lubia (A)	*Vigna sinensis*	cowpea
mad'âtchi	*Khaya senegalensis*	African mahogany
makanisa (S)	*Dombeya goetzenii*	
makofa (Bo)	*Acetosa abyssinicus*	
mara (S)	*Acacia nilotica subsp. adstringens*	
mashela (Am)	*Sorghum vulgare*	greater millet or guinea corn
mat'agudesa (Bo)	*Hyparrhenia rufa*	jaragua grass
matous (B)		
mayo (S)	*Euclea schimperi*	
mesquite (Spanish)	*Prosopis chilensis*	
mileo	*Combretum aculeatum*	
mourai		
muatie		
muchuku		weed
mulukhia (A)	*Corchorus olitorius*	bush okra
nama (B)	*Cyperus sp.*	sedge
ndain (A)	*Bauhinia rufescens*	
ñecce (So)		millet
neem (Hindi)	*Azadirachta indica*	neem
néré (F)	*Parkia biglobosa*	locust bean
nihuge		
niwa (So)		
nobcé (M)	*Sclerocarya birrea*	type of plum tree
nobi (H)	*Cymbopogon schoenanthus*	camel grass
ñobugu (So)		petit mil
nonbo (H)		
nounaa (Ha)		wheat
obol (S)	*Tamarindus indica*	tamarind
oholley (Bo)		
o'o (B)	*Detarium microcarpum*	
oro'dodo (B)		weed
peleiga (M)	*Securidaca longipedunculata*	
pénkidiga (M)		
pimpirssi (M)		
pois de terre (F)	*Vigna subterranea*	Bambara ground nut
poumpoumssé (M)	*Calotropis procera*	sodom apple or Dead Sea apple
pousga (M)	*Tamarindus indica*	tamarind
pousse m'pougou (M)		
préferga (M)		
prunier (F)	*Sclerocarya birrea*	type of plum tree

rafu (Bo)	*Brassica integrifolia*	type of cabbage
	or *B. japonica*	
raisinier (F)	*Lannea microcarpa*	
raria (H)	*Chrysanthemum procumbens*	
rericha (Bo)		
rônier (F)	*Borassus aethiopum*	African fan palm
saake (So)		
saaraxotte (So)		grass
saasingull (So)	*Grewia bicolor*	
sabako (Bo)		
sabansa (Bo)	*Acacia mellifera*	
sabara (H)	*Guiera senegalensis*	
sabcé (M)	*Lannea acida*	
sabraya (Ha)		
sagla (Eth T)	*Ficus sycomorus*	sycamore fig
sallaha (Ha)		
sambe (Sò)	*Grewia bicolor*	
samreh (A)	*Acacia tortilis*	
savonnier (F)	*Sapindus saponaria*	wingleaf soapberry
sellam (A)	*Acacia ehrenbergiana*	
sericha (Bo)	*Albizzia sp.*	
serreh (A)	*Maerua crassifolia*	
sexenne (So)	*Balanites aegyptiaca*	desert date
seyal (A)	*Acacia tortilis subsp. raddiana*	
shibti (Eth T)	*Phytolacca dodecandra*	
shiferaw (Bo)	*Sesbania sesban*	sesban
shiga (F)	*Striga hermontheca*	witch weed
shitora		
shumbra	*Cicer aretinum*	chickpea
siada (A)	*Cyperus sp.*	grass
sidr (A)	*Ziziphus spina-christi*	Christ's thorn
siiga (M)	*Anogeissus leiocarpus*	
silikooré (M)	*Capparis corymbosa*	
silyingué (M)		
simsim (A)	*Sesamum indicum*	sesame
sirgirso (Bo)		
sodom apple	*Calotropis procera*	Dead Sea apple
sogsog (S)	*Acacia etbaica*	
sokkin gulle (So)		
soole (So)	*Schoenfeldia gracilis*	
soug'dri (M)		
sourtoutougou (M)		
striga	*Striga sp.*	weed

subakh	*Terminalia brownii*	
sukella (Bo)	*Delonix alata*	
sunut (A)	*Acacia nilotica subsp. nilotica*	
swhi (Eth Té)		
taanga (M)	*Butyrospermum paradoxum*	shea butter tree
tabar (So)	*Ipomoea sinensis*	type of twining plant
	subsp. blepharosepala	
tabr (A)	*Ipomoea cordofana*	
tadjart (T)	*(leaves of) Maerua crassifolia*	
takalite (Ha)		type of wheat
taleh (A)	*Acacia seyal*	whistling thorn
talh (Ha)	*Acacia tortilis*	
tambukh (Eth T)	*Croton macrostachys*	
tansalga (M)		
tanwa (H)		
taoura (H)	*Detarium microcarpum*	
taxaleeme (So)		grass
taya (M)	*Adansonia digitata*	baobab
taychêt		
tchiriri (H)	*Combretum nigricans*	
tebeldi (A)	*Adansonia digitata*	baobab
tebatay-andel		
tedba (Ha)		
t'ef	*Eragrostis tef*	tiny-grained staple cereal
tefe (So)	*Combretum glutinosum*	
terres azarack		
thahat (Eth Té)	*Acacia sp.*	
tichifitt (Ha)	*Combretum glutinosum*	
tijit (Ha)		
tim-timtinga (M)		
titiko (M)		grass
titimri		
tormos		legume
toticha		
tsabre (H)	*Cymbopogon giganteus*	type of oil grass
tuk'a (Bo)	*Helichrysum citrispinum*	
tumbe (So)	*Tamarindus indica*	tamarind
tumfafiya (H)	*Calotropis procera*	sodom apple or Dead Sea apple
tundub (A)	*Capparis decidua*	
turo (So)	*Ficus gnaphocarpa*	type of fig
ubacho (Bo)		
ulicha (Bo)		creeper
underab (A)	*Cordia sinensis*	

usder (Ha)		
usher (A)	*Calotropis procera*	sodom apple or Dead Sea apple
vi'chinmin (B)		weed
waidéga (M)	*Saba senegalensis*	
walchama (Bo)		
walda (Bo)		
wan'dé (M)		
wango (M)		parasitic weed
white pear	*Apodytes dimidiata*	
widèg'zaka (M)		
willimwiiga (M)	*Guiera senegalensis*	
wôgo (M)		
wolzare (M)		
worowolle (So)	*Striga sp.*	weed
woyira	*Canavalia ensiformis*	horse bean
xaame (So)		
xaarigille (So)		
xiile (So)	*Mitragyna inermis*	
xoofe (So)	*Dalbergia melanoxylon*	African blackwood tree
yaafe (So)	*Piliostigma reticulatum*	
yano (H)		
ye'o (B)	*Pterocarpus erinaceus*	African rosewood
yodga (M)		
yufa (So)		
zaaga (M)	*Faidherbia albida*	apple-ring acacia
zabiu (Ha)		
zamarke (H)	*Sesbania leptocarpa* or *Aeschynomene indica*	
zambné (M)		
zango		quick-growing millet
zengada	*sorghum sp.*	local variety of sorghum
zna (B)	*Striga hermontheca*	witch weed
zouré (H)	*Boscia salicifolia*	

INDEX

SE17 Sale/price of fish: C33 C40
MR34 N27 Skills: N27 Species of
fish: C13 C40 N27 (Water levels: see
Water)
Floods: S3 S15 SE9 SE17
Fodder: see Nutrition, Pasture
Folk beliefs/tales: B9 B11 MR2 N2 S18
SE2 (see also Proverbs)
Food: Aid: C13 E18 MR31 S80 (see also
Development/aid) Changes in food:
B8 B9 MR39 During times of
increased scarcity: B11 C1 N1 S80
SE5 (see also Famine) Preparation:
B5 E18 E24 M3 MR2 S43 SE2 SE9
making butter: M3 MR2 grinding
grain: N4 (see also Trees)
Fuelwood: B4 C13 E24 E68 E78 (see
also Trees)
Funerals: see Customs

Gender: Attitudes: men's towards
women: B11 B25 N17 Conflict: MR3
Complementarity: MR2 Division of
labour/responsibility: B4 B5 B9 M3
MR2 MR18 MR39 S43 S54 SE2
Grain: see Crops
Grasses: SE10 (see separate Botanical
Glossary)

Health: Childbirth: S80
Diseases/ common ailments: MR2
MR3 N41 new diseases: B11
Dispensaries/health centres: B4
MR37 Medicine: modern: MR2 MR3
SE2 traditional: E68 M8 MR2 MR3
MR34 N1 N3 N5 N27 S17 S37 S43
S52 S80 SE10 SE17
Houses: S72 S80
Hunters: C28 E81 N1 (see also
Chiefs/sheikhs, Magic)

Independence: SE5 SE10 SE13
Inheritance: B11 M8 M42 N1 N3 N17
Irrigation: B9 Pump: MR14 (see also
Farming)

Labourers: see Migration, Occupations,
Work
Lakes: see Water
Land: Clearance: E62 (see also

Deforestation) Division/allocation:
M10 MR31 Free land: MR14 Sale of:
N19 Scarcity of: N17 N41 Tenure
and tithes/rent: B11 MR3 SE13 (see
also Inheritance, Women)
Language: Metaphors/similes: S58
Names: C18 C37 MR2 MR39
Law: see State
Livestock: Animal preference: B11 B17
MR2 MR3 MR37 Camels: MR3 Care
of: MR18 Depletion of herds: MR3
S19 S25 Gestation periods: N3
Growth in herds: M8 M11
Identification of: N3 Interaction with
farming systems: E5 (see also Social
groups, Fertilizer: organic)
Investment in: B8 B11 B17 N5 N38
Price: B11 MR2 MR3 MR18 Ratio of
male/female in herd: MR2 N3 S19
Reconstitution of herds: MR2
Reproduction, control of: N3 Sale of
during drought: B11 E61 Size of
herd: C1 E74 MR37 Taming of:
MR18 Uses of: S15 Watering of:
MR18 (see also Diseases, Nutrition,
Pasture)

Magic: C40 Of blacksmiths: N5
Of fishing communities: C33 N27
Of marabouts: C3 MR2 MR34 N3
(see also Marabouts)
Malnutrition: N5 S3
Manure: see Fertiliser
Marabouts: Disciples: SE17 SE18
Mediators/decision makers: N3 (see
also Magic, Religion)
Market gardening: B9 B11 B17 MR3
MR31 MR37
Marriage: Arranged: MR2 N4 N5
Attitudes of women towards: MR2
Between cousins: N5 Bride-price: C2
C3 M3 M10 M11 S72 SE9 Co-wives:
N1 MR16 SE5 Dowry: N4
Polygamy: B11 E62 M10 N1 SE10
(see also Customs, Divorce/
separation)
Medicine: see Health
Migration: Lifestyle of migrants in

head of household: B5 S52 S63 head
of women's community association:
N4 widow: E68 M10 Work: E78
SE10 decrease in workload: MR34
N41 non-profitable/unpaid: C13
grinding grain: N4 (Profitable work:
see Occupations) (see also
Development/aid, Gender, Marriage)
Wood: see Trees, Fuelwood
Work:Administration: B9
  Blacksmiths: N5 Butchers: N33
  Coiffeur traditionnel: N3
  Fishermen: N27 S69 (see also
  Fishing) Midwives: MR2 N4 S37 S80
  (see also Health) Shepherds: B23
  Herbalists: E68 (see also
  Occupations)

Young people: Attitudes: old towards
  young: B11 B25 C33 M6 M8 M10
  M11 MR3 MR14 MR31 N17 young
  towards old: B8 B17 C33 C48 M5
  SE9
Yields: see Crops